INTERFACE FRICTIONS

INTERFACE

Sign, Storage, Transmission

A series edited by Jonathan Sterne and Lisa Gitelman

FRICTIONS

HOW DIGITAL DEBILITY RESHAPES OUR BODIES

Neta Alexander

Duke University Press   *Durham and London*   2025

© 2025 DUKE UNIVERSITY PRESS. All rights reserved
Project Editor: Bird Williams
Designed by Dave Rainey
Typeset in Portrait Text and Eurostile LT Std
by Westchester Publishing Services

Library of Congress Cataloging-in-Publication Data
Names: Alexander, Neta, author.
Title: Interface frictions : how digital debility reshapes our bodies / Neta Alexander.
Other titles: Sign, storage, transmission.
Description: Durham : Duke University Press, 2025. | Series: Sign, storage, transmission | Includes bibliographical references and index.
Identifiers: LCCN 2024053666 (print)
LCCN 2024053667 (ebook)
ISBN 9781478032168 (paperback)
ISBN 9781478028925 (hardcover)
ISBN 9781478061120 (ebook)
Subjects: LCSH: Mass media and people with disabilities. | Digital media—Social aspects. | Technology and people with disabilities. | User-centered system design. | People with disabilities. | Disability studies. | Accessible Web sites for people with disabilities. | Technology—aspects.
Classification: LCC P94.5.P46 A449 2025 (print)
LCC P94.5.P46 (ebook)
DDC 302.23087—dc23/eng/20250511
LC record available at https://lccn.loc.gov/2024053666
LC ebook record available at https://lccn.loc.gov/2024053667

Publication of this book has been aided by a grant from the Frederick W. Hilles Publication Fund of Yale University.

For Jonathan Sterne (1970–2025),

who taught me how to live in a body,

impaired

CONTENTS

Introduction
Disabled/Enabled ... 1

1   **Repetition, Reloaded**
On Refreshing, Latency, and
Frictional Aesthetics ... 25

2   **The Right to Speed Watch**
(or, When Netflix Discovered
Its Blind Users) ... 55

3   **Automating Trauma**
On Autoplay and the Unbingeable ... 85

4   **"Log In, Chill Out"**
"Horizontal Media," Night Modes,
and Sleep Apps ... 118

Coda
Digital Debility and the
Normalization of Fatigue ... 150

Acknowledgments ... 165
Notes ... 169
Bibliography ... 197
Index ... 213

INTRODUCTION
Disabled/Enabled

We start from the premise of difference.
—MARA MILLS AND JONATHAN STERNE, "DISMEDIATION"

Which bodies are enabled and which are disabled by specific technologies? How is the "normative" configured?
—LOCHLANN JAIN, "PROSTHETIC IMAGINATION"

Not Your "Average User"

While millions of Americans isolated themselves during the first year of the coronavirus pandemic, I found myself sheltering in place in a rural college town in central New York State. Bored and anxious after months of lockdown, I purchased a ticket for a collection of short films featured in the online edition of the 2021 ReelAbilites Film Festival, an annual program that showcases works by and about people with a wide range of disabilities. However, my attempt to stream the films failed repeatedly because of long buffering times and sudden disconnections. While frustrating, these moments of friction did not take me by surprise. The early months of the pandemic led to a global shift to remote work that, in turn, caused an unprecedented spike in bandwidth demand and a significant rise in latency for American internet users.[1] When I refreshed my browser in the hope of eliminating the buffering, the festival website kicked me out, forcing me to refill my login information and repeat the process of choosing a title to stream. After refreshing, trying a different browser, and restarting my router failed to solve these issues, I gave up and left my laptop on the table in my kitchen-made-office.

Once in bed, I could no longer ignore the lower back pain, headache, eye strain, and numbness in my right wrist and palm resulting from prolonged screen engagement. While these computer-induced health issues are increasingly common, I am more prone to them than other users as a result of a set of impairments.[2] I'm a "disabled cyborg," a pacemaker-equipped woman born with facial paralysis.[3] My congenital paralysis prevents me from fully closing my right eye and makes me more disposed to eye strain, dryness, and fatigue resulting from prolonged exposure to light-emitting screens. I also had Ewing's sarcoma, a rare cancer that left me with a platinum plate in my lower spine, increasing the risk for chronic back pain and forcing me to develop a set of postural changes so I can sustain multiple hours of computer use. Painfully aware of the negative effects of the always-connected life on my impaired body, I promised myself to limit my screen time the next day and immediately knew this was a promise I couldn't keep.

When I woke up in the middle of the night, I realized that the video player had automatically streamed the ReelAbilites films while I was asleep. Due to its built-in autoplay function and the limited time allotted to stream the films, I lost my ability to play them from the beginning. My sleep registered as engagement, frustratingly preventing me from watching these films while awake. At 3:00 a.m., my laptop's display was still calibrated to the warm end of the color spectrum, reminding me that its "night mode" feature, designed to filter out blue light, was automatically turned on. Both my laptop and the ReelAbilities platform kept functioning as if a human user was watching these films.

By that point, I had been teaching, lecturing, and socializing entirely online for months. As a cardiac patient, I felt a greater need to shelter myself than many. I wanted to escape my loneliness by immersing myself in the fictional worlds I found via the ReelAbilities catalog, but my desire was thwarted. This failed digital interaction made me painfully attuned to the ways in which specific design features—from the software error that made me unable to lower the video quality and thereby prevent buffering, to the built-in autoplay function that stopped me from accessing the films once they played—have produced an experience that was the very opposite of what I had been looking forward to. This was especially frustrating as ReelAbilites, which, like many other film festivals, was pushed to offer an online-only edition during the pandemic, prides itself in its investment in accessibility, offering features such as audio descriptions, captioning, and Zoom Q&As with ASL interpreters and live transcribers.[4] Still, instead of engaging with stories made by and for people with disabilities, I was left feeling alone and bruised by moments of friction in the interface and my inability to easily fix them.

This personal anecdote encapsulates various manifestations of pain: the psychological pain of isolation as well as the physical pain of a disabled body further debilitated by the abrupt shift to a life lived almost entirely online. These phenomena are neither new nor unique, yet they were pushed to the foreground by the pandemic. As Laine Nooney observed, we cannot tell the history of computation without attending to the ways in which personal electronics broke the human body and brought with it "a world of pain previously unknown to man."[5] But some bodies are more prone to computer-inflicted pain than others.

My unique embodiment and life experience, for example, created a messy ensemble of capacities, limitations, and needs. As a disabled and bilingual immigrant woman, I am not the average user of digital technologies. Since the rise of personal computers in the 1970s and 1980s, the "average user" of computational technology has been imagined and studied as a male, white, able-bodied, native speaker of English.[6] This fictional, "techno-chauvinist" idea mirrors the lack of diversity among web designers and software developers working across the tech industry.[7] Pushing against these trends, *Interface Frictions* focuses on non-average users, especially users with disabilities, to advance a new theory of the digital interface. The main question I seek to answer is how interface design creates contemporary conceptions of ability and disability. To do so, I study four ubiquitous design features and the respective mode of media consumption they are designed to produce: refresh and seamlessness, playback speed and speed watching, autoplay and binge-watching, and Night Shift (i.e., auto-dimming) and soporific media. These interface features are increasingly pervasive parts of daily life spent using the internet, yet they remain understudied, as scholars and users tend to ignore the ways design decisions have come to shape embodiment, temporality, contingency, and immersion.

The interfaces through which internet users interact with stories, information, and each other often perpetuate a hegemonic, able-bodied user position. As such, they create and encode inequalities of access to media and information, even when used for circulating films and television shows committed to inclusivity and social justice. Drawing on the work of disabled designers, filmmakers, artists, scholars, and activists, I historicize the four features I study by mapping the gap between their initial, stated goals and their short- and long-term effects once they became an industry standard. This is achieved by conducting interviews with software engineers and accessibility consultants, and by excavating design histories based on tech blogs, press releases, users' forums, and the Internet Archive. Drawing on these sources, I paint a detailed picture of how design features come to shape the lives of their users and rediscover the design alternatives they erased overnight. These roads not taken reveal how design decisions incrementally reconfigure ideas about the "normative" body.[8] From thumb-based gestures to autoplay and sleep apps, I explore how the omnipresent interfaces of our digital lives both offer relief from and potentially contribute to disabling conditions.

When we trace the origins of interface design features, non-average users emerge at every turn. Blind people developed sonic and tactile ways of communication that challenge the rise of *thumbification* through repetitive, thumb-based micro-movements of refreshing, swiping, or scrolling (chapter 1). Blind and Deaf users pioneered ways to compress time and control the playback speed of media, paving the way to speed listening and speed watching (chapter 2). Netflix subscribers who struggle with invisible disabilities like post-traumatic stress disorder (PTSD), depression, and suicidal ideation have successfully pushed the company to add the option to opt out of its autoplay feature (chapter 3). Digital users who struggle with insomnia, chronic fatigue, and other sleep disorders are central to understanding how light-emitting screens impact circadian rhythms (chapter 4). The human body is implicated in the ways we consume media, and thus the ways different users are watching, listening, and otherwise navigating cyberspace are crucial for any historicization of the digital user.

Interface Frictions moves beyond existing accounts of "usability" or "access" by bridging media studies, interface design, and critical disability studies.[9] This interdisciplinary approach is in debt to recent attempts to study media through the lens of disability. Advancing a theory of "dismediation," Mara Mills and Jonathan Sterne scrutinize how media produce disability not only through their ableist representations of non-normative bodies but also "through their very operations, their institutional existences, and their policy and juridical dimensions."[10] Instead of asking how we can make specific apps, interfaces, or media objects more inclusive for users with disabilities, a focus on dismediation emphasizes how these non-average users have tweaked, remade, and hacked existing technologies to better fit their needs. As such, it replaces technological determinism with a relational understanding of mediation-as-negotiation. Dismediation is also fruitful for my historical analysis, as it "starts from the premise of difference," pushing against the universalization of the spectator, user, or listener as male, white, and able-bodied, without ascribing value or hierarchy to one embodied position over another.[11]

Mills and Sterne, much like a growing group of media and science and technology scholars, reject what is commonly referred to in disability studies as the "individual" or "medical" model of disability, which frames it as a problem awaiting a solution by medical experts.[12] Instead, the "social model" of disability distinguishes between impairment, that is to say, any physical or mental condition differing from the norm, and disability, which is the set of barriers imposed on people with impairments that make it harder for them to navigate the world.[13] While limited mobility does not necessarily lead to, and is not necessarily experienced as, a form of disability, the lack of curb cuts or elevators might prevent wheelchair users from working or socializing outside their home.[14]

To use a less familiar example, my facial difference is an impairment that, under specific conditions, I might experience as a disability because of the growing ubiquity of biometric technologies that encode certain assumptions about the so-called normal human face. In a world in which facial recognition is increasingly used as a security method, from opening one's iPhone to skipping the lines for border control in most Western airports, my asymmetrical smile and the minor discrepancy between my eyes might prevent me from boarding a plane, using a smartphone, or accessing my bank account. This, however, does not result from my congenital difference; it is produced by the quantification and algorithmization of faces. Translating a set of features such as eyes, nose, and mouth into the probable distances between pixels transforms face recognition into a mathematical problem: "Eyes" are nothing but the distance between two or more darker pixels in an image. The algorithmic systems supporting this biometric technology, however, have been trained on datasets of mostly white, symmetrical human faces, making its widespread adoption potentially disabling for people with darker skin tones or, as in my case, facial paralyses.[15] This distinction between impairment and disability is key to understanding how prevalent norms about the shape, limitations, and needs of human bodies might create ableist physical and, as we shall see, virtual environments.

This example can also help us understand the potential limitations of the social model of disability and adopt instead the "political/relational model" introduced by Alison Kafer.[16] Critiquing the depoliticization of impairment and pain in both the medical and social models, Kafer reminds us that, much like disability, "impairment doesn't exist apart from social meaning and understandings."[17] Due to its focus on accommodation and design solutions, the social model also limits our ability to imagine radical futures in which both impairment and disability are understood as political, contextual, collective, and perpetually in flux. Training biometric technologies on more inclusive datasets, for example, might make it easier for people with facial differences or a dark skin to use them. Yet these technologies are likely to be employed to support and expand the police surveillance of marginalized communities, especially people of color.[18] What happens when assimilation contributes to, rather than dismantles, harmful and discriminatory systems? And is it possible to collectively imagine a future rejecting the dystopia promoted by for-profit tech companies and political fearmongers?

Instead of making capitalist institutions and ways of life more accessible to people with disabilities, both the political/relational model and the Disability Justice movement ask us to resist such ableist norms as the need for constant surveillance, measurement, and optimization of the human body.[19] Through a Disability Justice lens, access should not be treated as a "self-evident good" and, instead, should be interrogated to ask, Access to what and for whom?[20] Both models seek to move disability discourse from a single-issue framework to an intersectional analysis of systems of oppressions, in order to reimagine and rebuild more sustainable and community-based worlds.[21]

Advocates of the medical model might try to surgically fix my facial paralysis, while the social model can outlaw the use of biometric technologies trained on a non-diverse dataset of faces. The political/relational model of disability justice, on the other hand, can be used to question and challenge the underlying assumptions supporting a "security theater" that seeks to mathematically distinguish between "suspicious" and "non-suspicious" faces in order to imbue white, Western travelers with a (false) sense of safety while traveling.[22] In short, instead of asking how we can make biometric technologies more inclusive, we should ask, Who is using these technologies, and can they be employed in ways that do not replicate the sexist, racist, and ableist ideas that made their existence possible?[23]

These tensions between assimilation and resistance have made critical disability studies a growing, vibrant, and varied discipline. It is now practically impossible to offer an agreed-upon definition of the term *disability*, which attests to the challenges of any attempt to write a history of interface design from the perspective of users with disabilities. Yet, as I hope to make this work accessible to computer historians, media scholars, web designers, and others who have no previous knowledge of critical disability studies, a definition—rather than *the definition*—is necessary. Here I would like to follow in the footsteps of Elizabeth Ellcessor, who conceptualizes disability as a spectrum rather than a prescriptive, stable category of identity politics.[24] Drawing on her pioneering work on ableism and interface design in *Restricted Access* (2016), I will use the term "disability" to describe "any physical or mental condition that makes it difficult, if not impossible, to utilize default social, institutional, or physical structures without some form of accommodation."[25] The digital interface, I argue, is a techno-social structure designed to exclude some users while accommodating others.

By isolating moments of friction, rather than immersion, each chapter in this book unpacks the "ideal user position" that a design feature seeks to produce as well as the affective rupture from which we can better understand who is being excluded from using it.[26] My goal is threefold: First, to develop an interdisciplinary framework that explores the underlying assumptions and embedded fictions of some of the most pervasive design features found in internet interfaces. Second, to counter these fictions by revealing the frictions caused when diverse human bodies interact with interfaces whose logic and infrastructure remain strategically hidden. Third, to describe users with disabilities as figurative canaries in the coal mine, because their experiences in navigating interfaces not made to accommodate them can help us explore the unpredictable, counterintuitive, and uninterrogated effects of interface design.

Understanding these effects is especially urgent at the moment in which some of the most common design features become habitual and therefore invisible to end users. While users rarely pay attention to small changes in the interface, such as Netflix's decision to add a playback speed feature or to shorten its countdown before automatically playing a new episode, these design choices have an accumulative effect felt in their bodies. Taken together, the features I study habituate users to ignore their biological and emotional needs. Technologies touted as pleasurable, on-demand, democratizing, and empowering effectively promote an ascetic ideology by which the human body is either generalized as male, able, and white—or is ignored altogether. I use the term *ascetic* to conjure how digital technologies recast biological needs such as sleep, rest, movement, and nourishment as obstacles to screen engagement and enhanced productivity. Pushing against techno-utopian discourses of infinite growth and acceleration, critical disability studies return us to the lived, embodied, precarious, and singular experiences of bodyminds. These bodyminds have limited and fluctuating levels of energy, or "spoons," to use a disability studies concept I will explore in chapter 4, as opposed to bodiless minds that can be uploaded to the cloud and live happily ever after (or until the fossil fuels needed to sustain ubiquitous data centers make this planet uninhabitable, and new data farms are built on Mars).[27]

When users repeatedly ignore their bodies, they become more susceptible to *digital debility*—the slow and unrecognized ways in which digital technologies inflict harm on human bodies. To understand how digital debility has come to shape our lives regardless of our unique set of capacities and impairments, we need to study when and under which conditions ubiquitous technologies might produce physical pain, addiction, and lethargy.

A Theory of Digital Debility

While users shape technologies, technologies also shape their users. Desktop computers, laptops, tablets, electronic readers, and smartphones are all postural media conveying the world via a set of repetitive micro-movements used for human-machine interaction. Vision problems, wrist pain, "text neck," and a host of other health issues are all "the embodied human residue of natural interactions between light, glass, plastic, color, and other properties of the surrounding environment."[28] The negative effects of ubiquitous computing on the human body, however, are either ignored or flaunted by avid gamers and tech workers as a source of pride.[29] Yet what might happen if we took these incremental bodily modifications as a necessary condition of our growing dependency on screens and the limited postures and muscular movements they impose on their users? By offering a theory of digital debility, I challenge the binary distinction between disabled and able bodies. If the user suffers from pain directly produced by the daily encounter between their body and their devices, this oft-denied reality requires a theorization putting embodiment, capacity, and debilitation at its center.

Debility and disability should not be used interchangeably. I borrow the term "debility" from Julie Livingston, who introduced it to highlight "how fundamental social, moral, and biological dynamics are grounded in experience as people struggle to marshal care and rework meaning and lives within and around bodies that are somehow impaired or different."[30] Focusing on bodily impaired miners in Botswana, Livingston argues that not all impairments are recognized as a disability by either the impaired person, their employer, community, or state in which they reside. When working in a mine in which some impairments are not only common but expected, both employees and employers describe the temporary or permanent loss of capacities or mobility as normal. But who has the capacity to define normalcy and its boundaries?

Seeking to answer this important question by drawing on Livingston's research, Jasbir Puar further extends the category of debility to reveal the "violence of what constitutes 'a normal consequence.'"[31] Focusing on marginalized populations such as Botswana's miners (Livingston) or Palestinians living in the Occupied Territories (Puar), these theories disrupt the category of disability by asking who is able to employ it to access state support, communal legibility, institutional care, and other resources. For Puar, debility is a process that "foregrounds the slow wearing down of populations instead of the event of becoming disabled. While the latter concept creates and hinges on a narrative of before and after for individuals who will eventually be identified as disabled, the former comprehends those bodies that are sustained in a perpetual state of debilitation precisely through foreclosing the social, cultural, and political translation to disability."[32]

Livingston and Puar focus on the social, institutional, and geopolitical conditions that might lead to mass debilitation of marginalized communities. Their distinction between disability and debility, however, is also useful for reassessing the material conditions and daily rituals shaped by technological dependency. The interface, I argue, is part of a techno-social system of debilitation that is normalized, expected, and tolerated by the neoliberal cultural imaginaries of the internet as an emancipatory, consumer-based, and disembodied playground. While the features I study do not necessarily produce debilitation, I will show how they work in tandem to sustain a digital economy based on pain, compulsion, and fatigue. This analysis promotes a twofold understanding of digital debility: on the one hand, as a form of discrimination preventing some groups of marginalized users from accessing and navigating digital tools and, on the other hand, as a pervasive phenomenon among some of the most privileged groups in Western society: white-collar workers, tech workers, and the creative workforce. While I do not imply a similarity between these workers and the populations studied by Livingston and Puar, their focus on debilitation is a productive starting point from which to unpack how and why some impairments and injuries have come to be normalized.

Studying debility as an ongoing process can help us shed new light on the uneven distribution of computer pain throughout the chain of supply and demand. American white-collar workers are prone to different kinds of pain than underpaid workers in the Global South who are forced to labor in order to support the growing demand for hardware, microchips, and minerals required to build smartphones and computers. Still, these entangled circles of pain reinforce each other, as more extended and frequent dependency on technology necessitates the acceleration of both manufacturing and disassembling. Electronic waste, which exposes underpaid workers to acids and other toxins due to their dangerous proximity to disassembled hardware, can lead to disabilities such as chronic illnesses, birth defects, and infant mortality.[33] White-collar workers, on the other hand, are subjected to much more gradual, debilitating conditions caused by repetitive micro-movements and sedentary lifestyles.[34] Such comparisons can reveal what constitutes a "normal impairment" in different occupations, classes, and locations. The pain necessary to support the digital economy is experienced differently by content moderators tasked with watching

INTRODUCTION 9

graphic violence and torture videos in order to keep the internet safer for social media users and by Amazon warehouse workers reliant on cannabis oil "to numb anxiety and deaden the crushing workload."[35] The manufacturing, distribution, and usage of personal electronics are mired with pain, yet these multiple forms of discomfort, agony, and, in the worst cases, life-threatening labor conditions are seldom acknowledged by tech companies or end users. To study them in tandem through a framework of debilitation is therefore an important first step in mapping, politicizing, and resisting the ever-growing frequency of computer-based injuries.

Endlessly expanding the category of disability, as Aimi Hamraie warns, might lead to a "post-disability ideology" that risks denying the very real discrimination people with disabilities still face.[36] This is where the distinction between disability and debility is once again useful. While this book is invested in Hamraie's idea that "disability itself is a valuable way of being in the world," it wishes to uncover how technology can increasingly diminish bodily functions and capacities in ways mostly ignored by both users and scholars.[37] Rather than arguing that every internet user is either disabled or soon to be disabled, I explore the radically different embodied and cognitive experiences of users while attending to the incremental effects of technologies hailed as empowering, assistive, and liberating.

To this end, I offer three axes through which to study digital debility as inherent to the design, infrastructure, and economy on which the internet is based:

1. **Computer pain as "consensual impairment"**: As a direct result of the growing popularity of personal computers in the 1980s, vision problems and eyestrain became frequent symptoms of computer use while keyboard- and mouse-induced repetitive strain injury (RSI) "has attained the semi-official status of an 'epidemic' among computer users in Europe, Canada and the United States."[38] As demonstrated by Nooney, screen-induced pain is the result of the unnatural, repetitive, and sedentary bodily postures imposed by the personal computer: "Unlike television viewing, which is done at greater distance and lacks interaction, monitor use requires a short depth of field and *repetitive* eye motions."[39] The proliferation of smartphones and social media in the past two decades has made it increasingly impossible to balance computer use with the user's need for rest, exercise, and sleep. Despite the invention of ergonomic chairs, modular and motorized standing desks, and new physical therapy treatments for those suffering from lower back or neck pain resulting from extensive smartphone use, the shift to remote work during the pandemic

pushed to the extreme a decades-long trend of broken bodies tethered to glowing screens.[40] This is even the case when the very same technologies are touted as an easy, personalized way to treat and prevent bodily harm by using exercise apps and trackers, to connect with a medical expert via telehealth service, or to find others with rare conditions via online communities and support groups on social media. As a growing number of studies demonstrate, while these technologies can have proven benefits, they reinforce a technological dependency that makes opting out or limiting their use all but impossible.[41]

If some workers, such as content moderators, are required to spend hours in front of computer screens, how can we account for those who seemingly have more choice over their screen engagement? The prevailing willingness and eagerness of computer users can be partially explained as "consensual impairment."[42] In his study of noise and audile techniques, Sterne explores how people often subject themselves to painfully noisy environments, such as airplanes, public restrooms equipped with high-powered hand dryers, and live music venues, out of habit or simply to follow social and cultural norms. This kind of "audile scarification" is both normative and consensual, as it is "tied to spaces designed for people to inhabit."[43] For Sterne, it is "consent in the sense that people are going along with the scene rather than rebelling or exiting."[44] Despite the rising popularity of digital detox workshops and the "slow computing" movement, the vast majority of internet users have yet to try to live meaningfully off the grid or to rebel against surveillance capitalism.[45] By continuously using electronic devices, users partake in a system of consensual impairment through which their bodies are forced to sustain repetitive muscular strain. While it is possible to avoid music venues or construction sites, living without the internet is becoming increasingly impossible in an age of smart cities, digitization, and automation. This, as Sterne stresses, complicates our understanding of consent in relation to ubiquitous computing and its harmful bodily effects. Users do not choose to harm themselves; they are living under conditions of bodily impairment that they cannot opt out of.

For computer pain to become consensual, such injuries had to be normalized and tolerated for decades. The lack of public debate, warning labels, or successful regulatory efforts to hold designers and manufacturers accountable for debilitating injuries extends decades of erasure and disembodiment. Even when an impairment is identified, users are seldom compensated by the tech companies manufacturing the software and hardware that were likely to cause their injuries. This inability to translate debilitation into the legally binding category of disability can be traced back to hundreds of product liability suits against keyboard manufactures in the 1980s and the 1990s. Despite "a causal relationship between typing and RSI," these legal attempts remained mostly unsuccessful.[46] Studying these lawsuits, Lochlann Jain concluded that "the very category of what counted as an injury, of that which was culturally legible as unjust, compensable or avoidable is shown to be not only contentious, but literally illegible—medically, legally and socially—for much of the century."[47] This is a result, in part, of the "long 'incubation' period" of computer-related injuries and the difficulty of linking them to a specific cause or event, which prevented the injured from suing due to statutes of limitation.[48] That those who were most likely to suffer from RSI were female office workers tasked with typing reveals debilitation to be gendered and class-based. In court, women were asked to prove not only that the repetitive use of keyboards led to their debilitation but that "their bodies were 'deserving' of compensation."[49] A sexist culture sought to deny the dangers of pink-collar, highly gendered labor by casting the clerical and secretarial workforce as disembodied parts of the interface. Seen as an extension of their machines, women were told that their role is to optimize and automate the production and dissemination of data mostly produced by their male employers.[50]

While computer use has since been masculinized and reclaimed by geek culture and the tech industry, many of the issues explored by Jain still require our attention. Seen as consensual or even enthusiastic, the human-machine relationship cannot be easily translated into legal frameworks. Computer pain is still underrecognized or is discussed as avoidable, minimizing the very real muscular, cognitive, and bodily changes produced via daily reliance on monitors, touch screens, and personal electronics. Common RSI symptoms like "intense pain, prickling, stiffness, anesthesia and paralysis" are either belittled or attributed to misuse or overuse.[51] By normalizing the addictive design of personal electronics, tech companies have effectively laid the ground for the widespread acceptance of the consensual impairments correlated with their daily use.

Once again, focusing on people with disabilities can help us complicate these decades-old debates. Relying on digital tools like text-to-speech or Zoom for connection, education, and remote work, the experience of immunocompromised or homebound patients makes the study of computer pain more urgent.[52] People with disabilities are also more likely to depend on medical apps and telehealth services, forcing us to reconsider questions of privacy and consent while offering ways to mitigate the short- and long-term debilitating effects of lives lived mostly online. Attending to physical and emotional manifestations of computer pain, the following chapters build on a plethora of lived experiences to repoliticize and reembody the user, pushing against the violent erasure of the human body and its limitations.

2. **Technology as addiction**: That digital technologies, especially social media, are strategically built to maximize "time-on-device" is crucial for producing and sustaining consensual impairment.[53] As I study in chapter 1, the pull-to-refresh gesture exploits an intermittent reward model based on providing a release of dopamine at seemingly random intervals. The strategic unpredictability of this nascent feature habituates users to constantly refreshing their mobile phones by moving their thumb from top to bottom. This dopamine-seeking behavior supports the prevailing business model of "captology"—a set of design features built as "traps" that are aimed at captivating users and maximizing their screen time.[54] Features such as autoplay are also part of this trend because they automate both the video stream and the user's engagement with the interface (see chapter 3). The need to navigate online worlds via a series of micro-decisions and endless choices produces lethargic subjects who are more likely to become "captivated" by digital platforms.

Drawing on Natasha Dow Schüll's ethnographic work on casinos in Las Vegas, I read the human-machine interactions produced by the digital interface as creating a "machine zone" that "can suspend time, space, monetary value, social roles, and sometimes even one's very sense of existence."[55] Gamblers, Schüll demonstrates, are driven not by a desire to win but rather by an impulse to extend their experience of flow vis-à-vis a synergy with the slot machine. Much like refreshing, which is designed to continue one's session in face of disconnection, boredom, or anxiety, gambling offers a stultifying repetition that, in turn, help the gambler to "gain exit from the self."[56] Pushing against the gambling industry's suggestion that only those gamblers who are predisposed or mentally disordered might develop unhealthy behavioral patterns, Schüll is careful not to pathologize the so-called problem gambler. What she offers instead is to interrogate whether "the problems are in the product, the user, or their interaction."[57] Similar to Kafer's political/relational model of disability, which shifts our attention from the individual to their environment, Schüll studies addiction as the result of "repeated interactions" between humans and machines strategically designed to exploit cognitive, psychological, and biological vulnerabilities in order to maximize profit.[58] Designers are a key part of this process, as they "inscribe" machines with specific "scripts" that limit or direct the end user.[59]

The complexity and number of agents involved in the gambling industry—designers, gamblers, casino owners, regulators, and others—remind us that the metaphor of addiction cannot be easily expanded or employed. Tech addiction, which has so far not been translated into any medically recognized diagnosis, is especially problematic for several reasons. While numerous studies connect heavy computer and smartphone use to a host of mental health conditions, including depression, anxiety, and attention deficit disorder, the term "addiction" has been critiqued as misleading because of the many differences between substance abuse and internet use.[60] The *DSM-5*, the latest edition of the psychiatric community's authoritative diagnostic manual, includes a new potential diagnosis dedicated to "internet gaming disorder," yet the editors were reluctant to add an "internet addiction" diagnosis.[61] As summarized by Ido Hartogsohn and Amir Vudka, "while recreational drug use is an 'opt-in' technology, smartphone use is an 'opt-out' technology because it is inescapable and ubiquitous."[62] In the age of remote work, the boundary between healthy, necessary, and required use of electronics and addictive behavior is increasingly contested. To that extent, treatment of tech addiction is in line with many twelve-step programs that eschew the classic model of complete abstention from a substance, be it overeating, sex addiction, and so forth, yet still function as full-on addiction recovery programs.[63]

Instead of simply replicating the "the narcotic imaginary of media," which regards screen use as insidious and addictive, digital debility unpacks the similarities between design features like refresh or autoplay and gambling machines, with their reliance on unpredictable and random outcomes.[64] Building on Hartogsohn and Vudka, I wish to emphasize the importance of "set and setting" in determining whether a given interface feature is liberating or debilitating. In psychedelic drug research, the term is used to distinguish between variable effects of the same drug dosage on different users. These might include "the psychological, social, and cultural variables such as intention, expectation, social, or physical environment."[65] Bearing these distinctions in mind, I carefully consider set and setting when historicizing and analyzing the effects of digital design features.

This focus on user interface (UI) and user experience (UX) can help us move beyond the popular discourse that seeks to regulate or ban platforms such as TikTok or Instagram because they potentially contribute to "the mental health crisis" among American children and teens.[66] The surgeon general under President Biden, Vivek H. Murthy, called for requiring warning labels on social media platforms, stating that "social media is associated with significant mental health harms for adolescents."[67] Similar initiatives, including the legislative attempt to ban the autoplay feature and endless scrolling, which I study in chapter 3, can open up important conversations about the use of "dark patterns" and other captivating tools. At the same time, these public debates also tend to distract from the ways in which constant use of personal electronics—rather than the content being consumed—enforces a set of cognitive strains and postural limitations that might worsen physical and emotional conditions. What *Interface Frictions* opts to do is to investigate how specific design features inscribe behavioral patterns that make opting out less and less likely and how users with disabilities develop and employ alternative models of human-machine interactions.

3. **Technology as a source of exhaustion and fatigue**: Even when users are able to limit and control their daily engagement with screens, they are still likely to binge a show, go down a social media rabbit hole, play a carefully designed video game, or engage in other activities that limit or hinder sleep. Fatigue is therefore central to digital debility in two ways. First, as chapter 3 demonstrates, addictive features like autoplay push users to ignore their circadian rhythms and enable tech companies to declare sleep as their enemy.[68] Second, the soporific media industry monetizes the lack of sleep—as well as medical conditions like insomnia or sleep apnea—in order to bombard users with "sleep-inducing" technologies and products. As I explore in chapter 4, the paradox at the heart of this billion-dollar industry is that light-emitting screens and the overstimulation caused by electronic devices are proven to impede, rather than to regulate, sleep. The sleep apps and night modes promising to eliminate or at the very least to limit fatigue in fact teach users to take their smartphones to bed. As a result, many users can only fall asleep in the safety of an expensive, customized cocoon consisting of subscription-based apps, noise-canceling headphones, sleep trackers, and access to "sleep stories" and other soporific media. These tools both assume and require weary users who are willing to pay in order to improve the quality of their sleep.

Yet digitally induced fatigue extends beyond the question of how many hours one is able to rest. For Tung-Hui Hu, "digital lethargy" is the result of the ongoing physical and emotional exhaustion produced by the sharp and unpredictable transitions between fastness and slowness, hyperactivity and paralysis, that have come to characterize digital capitalism.[69] While computational logic is associated with predictability, Hu explores the ways in which "one acts, and perhaps nothing happens, or perhaps something happens."[70] This oft-denied lack of causality is isolating to the point of eradicating any real possibility of collective action. For Hu, the digital is not a paradigm shift from earlier modes of labor; instead, it reminds us that for many, especially people of color, stasis is a way of life, as they are still forced to ceaselessly navigate a world that, at best, is not made for them and, at worst, is hostile to their existence. If consensual impairment is crucial to understanding why people choose to engage in harmful activities, Hu centers "endurance" as the pivotal temporality of digital capitalism, claiming that the trauma of a racist, sexist, and capitalist system is in fact amplified by digital tools that normalize constant connectivity, optimization, and productivity. Both theories posit a subject whose body incrementally loses capacities through the use of ubiquitous technologies.

PHYSICAL PAIN, ADDICTION, and fatigue are not exclusive manifestations of digital debility. They draw on other, more familiar adverse effects of digital technologies, such as algorithmic bias; the use of "prototypical whiteness" in biometrics, AI, and machine learning; and the automation of racism, sexism and ableism—all urgent subjects explored by others.[71] The growing literature on algorithmic bias demonstrates how machine-learning algorithms are used to perpetuated discriminatory hiring norms, criminal sentencing, and loans and credit allocations, all of which are most likely to harm people of color and other minorities.[72]

Attending to both digital features and the algorithmic systems they are designed to conceal, *Interface Frictions* explores the role of latency (chapter 1), compression (chapter 2), automation (chapter 3), and light (chapter 4) in producing digital debility. While challenging the assumptions that are central to media theory around spectatorship, media postures, or the attention economy, each chapter concludes with an alternative imagining of digitality rooted in artworks, "crip" studies, and disability media. My hope is that these roads not taken will allow the reader to envision other paths for media use and design that could undo some of its present harms. A theory of digital debility demonstrates how technologies cripple their users, yet my engagement with "crip interfaces" invite us to hack, tweak, and reinvent our personal devices.

Cripping the Interface

Before we explore crip interfaces, we must first define both terms, especially as "crip" is a term rarely used by web designers. Throughout the twentieth century, "crip" was used as a shorthand for the derogatory "cripple." In the past two decades, however, it has been reclaimed by disability activists and scholars to connote taking pride in disability activism and worldmaking.[73] When used as a verb, "cripping" is a "critical strategy borrowed from queer studies."[74] Both queering and cripping share "resistance to cultural homogenization," as they advocate for dismantling the binary between normal and abnormal.[75] Concepts such as "bodymind" seek to bring attention to the impossibility of separating the two, rejecting the binary distinctions between mind and matter, rationality and emotion, so-called able and disabled bodies, and even health and sickness.[76] But while the various verb forms of "crip" are frequently used in critical disability studies, this analytical framework has yet to gain a foothold in computation histories and science and technology studies.

The holistic view of bodymind, however, is especially productive because techno-utopias of decorporealization have powerfully shaped the cultural imaginary surrounding the internet, while serving to deny the extent of digital debility caused by constant connectivity. From the 1990s paeans to the information superhighway as "the great equalizer for the handicapped and home bound" to the growing popularity of transhumanism, the tech industry (and the sci-fi novelists who inspired it) have toyed with fantasies of bodiless existence for decades.[77] Tracing how the desire to conquer nature and rid oneself of one's body has evolved into a billion-dollar longevity industry is beyond the scope of this book. Yet I wish to sustain a focus on these fantasies of disembodiment insofar they illuminate why both users and science and technology scholars have treated disabilities as an afterthought or a regulatory demand. The ideal internet user, as Ellcessor contends, "perpetuates the individualism and romanticism of digital media cultures as well as a neoliberal emphasis on the self as constructed through constrained consumer choices."[78] Ableist design standards assume an ideal or preferred user position such as an average-sized man who navigates the internet while sitting in a chair and using a mouse and/or keyboard. A user, however, might also be a low-vision, bedridden woman navigating the web via a screen reader and speech-to-text software while trying to distract herself from her chronic pain. To imagine such a user can draw attention to the fragility and unknowability of the human body in ways that undermine much of the post-human logic of our current techno-worlds.

Much like the human body, the interface is a process rather than a static object. As Alexander Galloway suggested, the interface is not a seamless, neutral mediator of software; it is the "generative friction" in the "zone of contact."[79] At the heart of Galloway's theory is the idea of the interface as an "effect," a technique of mediation or interaction, and as such it is used to distinguish between different layers or materials. I draw on his analysis to expand the idea of the interface beyond the graphic user interface (GUI) or the MacBook screen to include "nonoptical interfaces (keyboard, mouse, controller, sensor); data in memory and data on disk; executable algorithms; networking technologies and protocols; and the list continues."[80] Still, the media theorists Galloway is in dialogue with, from Marshall McLuhan to Lev Manovich, tend to assume that able-bodiedness is a preliminary requirement for full participation in techno-social worlds.[81] Rejecting this assumption, as well as the use of "prosthesis" or "amputation" as metaphors for media use, I promote a multisensorial, disability-informed theory of human-machine interaction.[82] To do so, I shift the focus from the technical stack—as explored through moments of translation between software and hardware—to the unique embodied experience of the user. What might happen when we make the impaired user the focal point through which to study how interface design reshapes the user's body? What can a postural and embodied sensitivity reveal about the media use of different, ever-changing bodyminds?

Interfaces are constantly in flux, shaping their users and reorienting them toward specific behaviors and communities. I intentionally use the term "user"—rather than "spectator" or "viewer"—throughout this book despite my focus on emerging spectatorial modes such as speed watching and binge-watching. This choice resists the ableist, Western obsession with the visual by cultivating a multisensorial sensitivity through which to study human-machine interactions as muscular, sonic, tactile, and embodied. I read the playback speed feature, for example, as central to the ability of blind Netflix subscribers to navigate and engage with films and television shows by listening to audio descriptions at higher speeds than intended by their creators. Here, watching is, in fact, listening, making the term "user" more inclusive, as my historical analysis brings together various motivations for gaining control over the speed of media consumption. This term also enables me to bring features associated with streaming technologies such as playback speed and autoplay together with features like refresh and night mode, eliding the distinction between spectatorship and other computer-mediated activities such as writing, waiting, scrolling, swiping, playing, and even sleeping.

Finally, the broad category of usership allows me to trace the effects of these features across multiple loci, from laptop screens to mobile phones. Since users constantly shift between handheld and monitor-based devices, often using more than one device at the same time and switching between vertical and horizontal screens, both media historians and science and technology scholars should follow users as they aim to shed light on habitual new media. To that extent, I read sleep apps as content-agnostic postural media. These apps, I argue, are widely popular not because they recruit A-list Hollywood stars to whisper "sleep stories" into the ears of their premium subscribers, but rather thanks to their ability to nudge users into changing their bodily position from sitting to lying down. Employing dark colors and minimalist design, these apps extend the use of personal electronics into the bedroom (and, more often than not, the bed itself). Here, the drowsy user might start with navigating a visual interface, but if the "sleep story" is successful, they will soon close their eyes and transform into a listener. This slip between visual and sonic modes of engagement, alertness, and drowsiness is central to my analysis of digital usership.

The "user" is also a historical construct born in tandem with the GUI. In the pre-GUI era of personal computing, hobbyists were able to interact, experiment, and explore the code and its limitations by typing text into the command-line interface. The shift from the pre-mouse command line to the GUI birthed the user as we know it "by creating a user/programmer dichotomy."[83] The programmer writes the proprietary code sustaining the black box design—which, as developed and popularized by Steve Jobs' Apple, seeks to eliminate edges, seams, and screws, while making it difficult or impossible for hobbyists to fix the hardware or tweak the software—while users are invited to interact with a bright-colored "desktop" consisting of clickable folders imitating the logic and workflow of their offices. The GUI led to the rise of interaction design, a field whose canonical works tellingly include Don Norman's *Invisible Computer* (1998), as it draws on ideas of seamlessness and invisibility I explore and critique in chapter 1.[84] Touting intuitive, minimalist, and user-friendly design, interaction design promises that "the best interface is no interface."[85] The interface is thus a means to an end, a tool designed to recede into the background so that the user can become as fast and efficient as possible.

Yet even the most user-friendly interfaces replicate hidden assumptions about who this user might be. Take the hand pointer, which was developed by Susan Kare in the 1980s for the Macintosh computer and consists of a white hand with five fingers. According to Michele White, this prevalent graphic symbol "conceptually recognizes and establishes whiteness and able-bodiedness as the norm" because it is "designed to assert that the white material body is present" everywhere in the computational interface, positioning the imaginary white user as able to click and control every button or feature.[86] Several decades later, white hand pointers continue to be the default, yet they can sometimes be changed by employing Apple's and Windows' "accessibility" system preferences, associating "other color options with disability."[87] This slip between racism and ableism, as we shall see throughout the book, is not anecdotal. As critical disability scholars repeatedly argue, ableism cannot be isolated from other systems of oppression, including sexism, white supremacy, capitalism, and settler colonialism, because they "are categorically and phenomenologically entwined."[88] As a new generation of computer historians reveals the forgotten contributions to computer science of women, queer, and transgender programmers from various racial and ethnic backgrounds, an intersectional approach is key to illuminating why these groundbreaking ideas were often rejected, ignored, or stolen from their originators.[89] An intersectional critique of the GUI, for example, can draw attention to the ways in which the shift from the black background of the command-line to the allure of Jobs's "wasteful whiteness" was ideological, racist, and ableist, positing both whiteness and vision as the implicit attributes of computer users.[90]

The GUI is also a productive example of how design decisions can exclude some users with disabilities while empowering others. The first commercial GUI, Apple's Lisa, was marketed as an "accessible" interface designed to "lessen the burden of knowledge required to complete a task."[91] In practice, however, it excluded blind users because it was incompatible with screen readers or voice synthesizers. As a result, the new, hard-won "electronic independence" achieved by blind users of early personal computers was put on hold for several years.[92] At the same time, the GUI was celebrated by users with learning disabilities. Users who found it difficult to read or write were suddenly able to navigate a visual system by clicking instead of typing. As described by Mike Matvy, an American psychologist with a learning disability, "it is as if MAC were designed specifically with my needs in mind."[93] Replacing a text-based interface with a clickable one radically changed the way different users interacted with their computers, empowering people with dyslexia while preventing people with low vision or blindness from applying for a wide range of computer-supported jobs.

The accessibility issues created by the point-and-click design of Jobs's GUI were eventually solved by retrofitting and adding new software to make the interface compatible with screen readers.[94] This delay, however, attests to how designers of new technologies neglect to consider a variety of users, forcing them into a waiting or a standby mode until new tools are developed. By the time a technology becomes more accessible, newer technologies flood the market, and disabled users might feel that they are perpetually desynchronized with their normative counterparts. Such delays conjure people with disabilities as slower and therefore occupying a less technologically developed world than able-bodied users.

The ableist notion that the disabled user is the one who might be left behind, rather than speed ahead, ignores the long and rich history of disability hacktivism and "crip technoscience."[95] In their 2020 manifesto, Aimi Hamraie and Kelly Fritsch define crip technoscience as a method and a field of research "acknowledging that many of the technologies that have enabled disabled people to gain access to the social world have been produced through military-industrial research and development, imperial and colonial relations, and ecological destruction, all of which contribute to the uneven debilitation of human and non-human life."[96] To mitigate these tensions between enhanced accessibility and the destructive logic of what Bill Gates hailed as "friction-less capitalism," crip technoscience calls us to "conjure frictional practices of access production, acknowledging that science and technology can be used to both produce and dismantle injustice."[97] By cripping the interface, I explain how disabled users might speed ahead against expectations *or* create more friction on purpose and slow the system down—depending on the context.

This is not to claim that every mode of media consumption and user interface must be equally accessible to every single user—a goal that is both unattainable and, as John Lee Clark reminds us, not always desirable—but rather to open up the political question of sensory and "access entitlement" and to call media scholars to further study differing habits of decoding.[98] Crip sensitivities also move beyond hand-machine interaction, to highlight a wide range of ways in which people with disabilities might interact with computers, from head and mouth sticks to speech-to-text technologies.[99] Personal computers, game controllers, and other electronic devices use only a small fraction of the human sensorium, a point I will return to in chapter 1.[100]

Able-bodied users, I argue, adapt to the extraordinary demands of an ableist world by engaging in crip spectatorial activities pioneered and made possible by people with disabilities, from speed watching to light calibration tools such as night mode. To that extent, *Interface Frictions* advances a theory of crip interfaces that pushes users to reflect on their dependency on their screens. The case studies I explore, from the experimental video game *Seventy-Eight* to the video art work CRIP TIME (2018) and media made by and for bedridden people, bring together narrated accounts of users with disabilities, autoethnography, and critical theory. These experiments in frictional aesthetics provide playful alternatives to the design scripts embedded in refreshing, speed watching, binge-watching, or expecting a computer to lull its user to sleep.

What might happen if we unpack the history of some of the most ubiquitous design features from the point of view of multiple different users, closely accounting for their ever-changing embodied experience? How can users and makers who are blind, deaf, insomniac, depressed, or chronically ill illuminate the multiple embodiments and lived experiences often excluded from design scripts? And how can we account for those features that, despite being marketed as assistive and empowering, are experienced as ableist and debilitating by some users?

Chapter Breakdown

Interface Frictions is structured around four chapters, each of which explores a spectatorial mode and a common friction, from anxiety to fatigue (see table 1.1). Starting with elderly users' failed attempts to refresh vaccine distribution websites during the pandemic, chapter 1 offers a history and theory of refreshing. What kind of media literacy and muscle memory are invoked by this repetitive daily gesture? Moving from the invention of the thumb-based pull-to-refresh feature on mobile phones to auto-refreshing software preventing blind users from effectively using their screen readers, I trace the refresh back to radar technologies and the military-industrial complex. The chapter concludes by surveying alternative design solutions that arise from frictional aesthetics, asking how crip interfaces can enable users to directly engage with the software, rather than desperately refreshing their devices?

If "seamful design" calls designers and users to strategically increase friction, speed watching can be read as its mirror image: a productivity tool described by users as a means of time hacking that can help them become digital "super-users."[101] The recent public debate surrounding Netflix's attempt to add a playback speed feature to its streaming platform, however, stresses the potential frictions between different modalities of media consumption. World-renowned filmmakers pushed Netflix to shelve this idea, claiming their films were not meant to be watched twice as fast as they intended. Yet, citing "requests from our deaf and blind subscribers," Netflix decided in August 2020 to introduce this feature despite the initial backlash from filmmakers. Chapter 2 explores what led to this decision and what the marketing discourse surrounding it can teach us about how corporations monetize accessibility by engaging in "cripwashing." Pushing against the ableist myth of the "super-user," I build on the work of Mills and Sterne to argue that speed watching was anticipated by blind students who hacked their phonographs in order to play early talking books at a faster rate. Speed watching should be read as a mode of survival enabling different users to advance a wide range of goals: media accessibility, the thrill of speed, or avoiding boredom.

Much like playback speed, the autoplay feature radically shifted the way users engage with online content. Embedded into streaming platforms in the early 2010s, it not only popularized binge-watching by automatically playing another title, but also reformatted narrative and aesthetic conventions of serialized content. Chapter 3 explores how the recommendation algorithms and ever-shrinking countdown clocks have reshaped media consumption over the past decade. The chapter offers a historical analysis of autoplay based on tech blogs,

	SPECTATORIAL MODE	DESIGN FEATURE	DOMINANT FRICTION
CHAPTER 1	Buffering	Refresh	Perpetual anxiety + addiction
CHAPTER 2	Speed watching	Playback speed	Eye strain + cognitive overload
CHAPTER 3	Binge-watching	Autoplay	Potential emotional triggers + fatigue
CHAPTER 4	Soporific media	Night Shift	Fatigue + addiction

TABLE I.1 Chapter Breakdown

press coverage, and an interview I conducted with Robert Sweeney, one of the software engineers who created and implemented autoplay for Netflix. Sweeney's account reveals the frequent gap between the stated goals of design features and their unintended consequences. While the autoplay feature was introduced in part to improve A/B testing for Netflix's recommendation system, it quickly became the most successful feature in the company's history, pushing it to change its key performance indicator from "retention" to "hours watched."

One unplanned effect of autoplay, I argue, is the automatization of trauma. This was the result of Netflix's controversial decision to autoplay previews on its home page, reluctantly exposing users to disturbing content that can trigger anxiety and hinder sleep. I draw on Nicolette Little's theorization of "platform violence" to analyze how this default feature proved harmful to subscribers suffering from PTSD, as it confronts them with stories about rapists, serial killers, hate crimes, and domestic abuse.[102] Following numerous complaints and an online petition, Netflix eventually introduced the option to disable autoplay, showing that users can actively reshape interface design. By historicizing autoplay on Netflix and beyond, we can understand how design features are shaped by regulatory, algorithmic, and social forces. How did autoplay become one of the most prominent business models in the digital ecosystem? Why is it crucial for the success of streaming platforms, despite exposing users to potentially harmful content? And how can alternative features and "trauma-informed design" help us reimagine algorithmically shaped media consumption?[103]

Autoplay works in tandem with Apple's Night Shift and other tools designed to filter blue light from screens after sunset to encourage users to take their personal electronics to bed. Studying the soporific media industry, chapter 4 begins by contrasting Apple's claims that its Night Shift feature "may help you get a better night's sleep" with the recent literature on "sleep hygiene." Night Shift, as well as various similar features marketed by Apple's competitors, is part of an emerging ecosystem of sleep-supporting media, which includes a plethora of design features, sleep apps, and sleep trackers. Night Shift and the popular sleep app Calm, I argue, privileges a subject who cannot disconnect from their technology. Rejecting this techno-solutionism, this chapter offers a theory of digitally induced exhaustion.

Focusing on Calm's popular "sleep stories," I argue that sleep apps are content-agnostic because their promise lies in the postural transitions they produce, rather than in their ever-expanding media libraries. By inviting their users to switch from sedentary engagement with their devices to lying down, these postural media create a sense of intimacy, safety, and attachment. At the same time, these subscription-based apps individualize the problem of sleep by denying the inherent nature of digital lethargy. What I call *crip horizontal media*, on the other hand, offers an alternative to the tech-based model of sleep-inducing apps and devices. By studying three crip interventions made by bed-ridden artists—a painting by Frida Kahlo, a video essay by Hannah Bullock, and a collection of pandemic shorts by Dayna McLeod—I explore sleep as part of a collective and communal ethics of care.

The four design features and spectatorial modes explored in *Interface Frictions* introduce an interdisciplinary theory of the digital interface and its somatic temporalities of waiting, compression, endurance, and drowsiness. As different as these states seem to be, they all produce and sustain an unrecognized friction between the interface and its real-life user. Due to the growing ubiquity of remote work and video-conferencing platforms, we are now accustomed to watching each other through plastic and glass screens. Zoom and other video-conferencing platforms, which I explore in the conclusion, can be read both as crippling interfaces—turning the home into an office, promoting a sedentary lifestyle, deepening the digital divide—and as crip interfaces allowing people with disabilities to engage with the world in unprecedented ways. It is those nuances and contradictions that populate every page of this book.

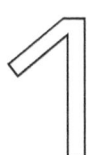

REPETITION, RELOADED

On Refreshing, Latency, and Frictional Aesthetics

The internet is "a medium for friction-less capitalism."
—BILL GATES

The promise of feminist technoscience lies in challenging hegemonic narratives about technology as always enframing or deterministic, and in imagining the transformative possibilities for crip hacking, coding, and making as frictional access practices.
—AIMI HAMRAIE AND KELLY FRITSCH, "CRIP TECHNOSCIENCE MANIFESTO"

In February 2021, while millions sheltered in place because of the COVID-19 pandemic, websites designed to provide Americans with access to the much-awaited vaccines instead subjected users to endless bugs, errors, and breakdowns.[1] Senior citizens, one of the first groups eligible for a vaccine, particularly struggled to book appointments, as many of them were unaccustomed to filling out forms online or to hacks such as using multiple devices in order to increase one's chance of success. Philip Orlando, a sixty-five-year-old from Reading, Massachusetts, told a local news website he had tried—and failed—to book an appointment about two hundred times in twenty-four hours.[2] Similar account of users desperately refreshing appointment websites prompted *The Atlantic*'s Anne Applebaum to compare America's vaccine distribution to "Soviet-style queues for cabbage."[3] While the federal government gave a contractor $44 million to develop a national vaccine scheduling system, it turned out to be so poorly designed that all but nine states opted out before even trying to adopt it, even though it was offered to them for free.[4] Despite the fact that these websites were specifically designed for elderly users, their failures exposed the extent to which ageism and ableism inform even those platforms targeting the most precarious populations. This already-forgotten historical moment recasts unreliable digital infrastructures and faulty interface design as matters of life and death, rather than mere technical annoyances.

There are many ways to explain the jumpy start of America's vaccine distribution websites. The most obvious explanation is the gap between supply and demand. Orlando, for example, was competing with almost a million eligible Massachusetts residents to book one of just sixty thousand available time slots. Other contributing factors included the structural limitations of the complicated and time-consuming process of federal contracting and the decision not to use a cloud computing service that scales up server power to meet demand, which led to repeated crashes.[5] While COVID-19 presented the United States and the world with a new viral threat, these interface and infrastructure design flaws were not unique. When the Obama administration enthusiastically launched the website HealthCare.gov on October 1, 2013, as part of its implementation of the newly approved Affordable Care Act, only six Americans were able to sign up for health insurance on the first day, despite the nearly $1 billion spent on designing the website.[6]

While the refresh is seldom studied in the context of public health (if it is studied at all), what these examples teach us is that latency arises at various points in the technical stack and that refreshing can happen at various junctions, from the data server to the interface. The interface, however, is where those various compounding latencies become visible for the end user, who is then faced with frustration, anger, and, in some cases, the anxiety and fear of missing one's chance to receive a potentially life-saving vaccine. As I explore below, these difficult feelings are made worse by the fact that the refresh produces unpredictable results. Although refreshing pushed Orlando and other senior citizens to the beginning of an invisible queue, in the case of the German online appointment system, the same technique could hack the system by opening up new time slots when used via a different interface. That the same feature can generate contradictory outcomes, depending on design decisions unknown to users, is one of the many tensions explored in this chapter.

By isolating moments of digital latency, this chapter unpacks the many uses and misuses of refreshing: from public health to social media, and from a clickable button and a bodily gesture to a hacking technique. Moving across different types of interfaces, including computer screens, smartphones, and game consoles, I explore the refresh as a sublimation of difficult feelings such as helplessness, frustration, boredom, and anxiety. While most users won't break their MacBooks or throw their phone through the window, they might have intense emotional, cognitive, and affective reactions to these moments of friction.

While latency and breakdown are not unique to digital systems, refreshing is different from restarting a computer or a gaming console. Simply put, the refresh is an act or function of updating the display on a screen by asking the data server to load the newest version of a web page. On a Windows-based computer, pressing the F5 function key or Ctrl+R refreshes a web page on all popular browsers (e.g., Chrome, Edge, Firefox, and Internet Explorer), while Mac users can press Command+R to achieve the same effect. In most browsers, there's also a refresh icon, ↻, an arrow that forms a circle. To these we should add the pull-to-refresh gesture on mobile phones, the history and significance of which will be explored later.

As it serves multiple functions and goals, the refresh is nearly synonymous with internet use. *Frustration-motivated refreshing* or *diagnostic refreshing* seeks to restore continuity by trying to fix a moment of buffering or a glitch, shortening the loading and waiting time; *boredom-motivated refreshing* asks the server to reload data that will hopefully be more interesting and exciting than what the user currently sees; *identity-proof refreshing* is designed to signal to an algorithmic system that the user is a human rather than an AI or a bot, and as such it is often used as a security feature;[7] and *refresh-as-a-hack*, as I study below, recasts refreshing as a shortcut, for example, to finding newly available tickets to buy or securing a scarce resource such as a visa appointment or a limited Black Friday deal. This latter category, despite its subversive potential, has also been co-opted by corporations that invite users to refresh in order to "unlock" better search results (see fig. 1.1). This gamification and monetization of the refresh transforms a feature associated with negative feelings into a source of agency and savviness.

With its promise to enact change, eliminate unwanted content from the screen, or accelerate the speed of information, refreshing empowers users as they navigate their online lives. Yet it also elicits difficult feelings of "againness" and *stuckness*, temporal categories I will explore later.[8] Refreshing, I argue, is crucial for a digital economy based on the promise of seamlessness and instant reward that are, in fact, gambits designed to maximize users' screen time and extract their data. As such, it is key to the rise of "persuasive technology," defined by B. J. Fogg as "any interactive computing system designed to change

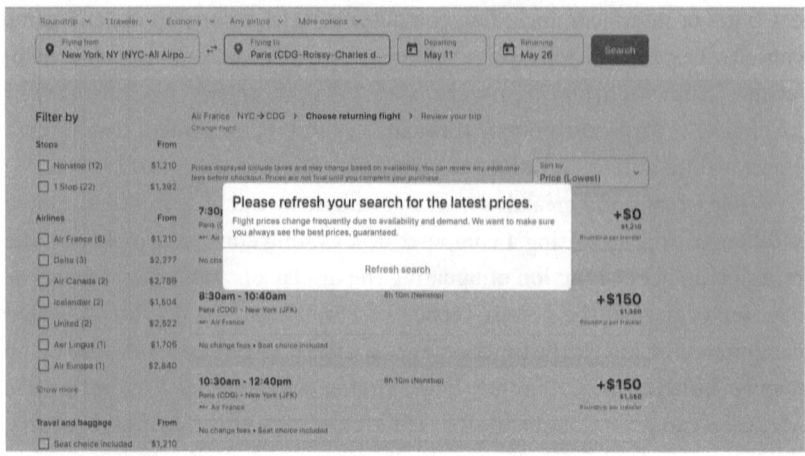

FIG. 1.1 A screenshot of Expedia's "refresh search" message, promising users that, by refreshing, they are guaranteed to see "the best prices." (Source: Expedia)

people's attitudes or behaviors."[9] Offering a historical account of the refresh, this chapter unpacks these tensions between empowerment, persuasion, and captivation.[10]

Refresh answers a difficult question: *Why is the internet so boring?* With access to all of human knowledge, the early web germinated utopian visions promising not only the democratization of information and resources, but also the eradication of boredom.[11] As the pandemic made painfully clear, however, one can spend an entire day online, clicking the mouse or the keyboard or moving one's thumb across a glass screen, expecting something meaningful to happen, and still be confronted with a stupefying sense of tedium. This tedium cannot be distinguished from the limited embodiments afforded by digital and mobile interactions. As Jaron Lanier noted, "individuals live in this constant sort of fetal position" and "are seated in a soft chair looking at a world through a glass square, be it the windshield of the car or the screen of a television or computer."[12] Echoing Michele White's description of the folded body of computer users, these observations paint a troubling picture of how computers gradually break the user's body—albeit in varying speeds, intensity, and levels of harm.[13]

Drawing on the framework of digital debility explored in the introduction, I historicize the refresh through its three axes: *physical pain* manifested as carpal tunnel syndrome, eyestrain resulting from excessive screen use, and other health issues; *addiction* resulting from fully adopting the reward-based behavioral mechanism developed by the gambling industry by strategically deploying randomness and unpredictably; and *digital lethargy* taking the form of "busy idleness" that oscillates between hyperactivity and paralysis.[14] Drawing on the experiences of users with disabilities, I also study the refresh as potentially excluding because of the pull-to-refresh's focus on repetitive, micro-movement of the thumb and auto-refreshing techniques incompatible with screen readers.

The framework of digital debility and the analysis of the refresh as discriminatory push us to imagine new ways to navigate "digital dams"—various disruptions and noises resulting from technological, legal, industrial, economic, or political structures and limitations.[15] The artworks and design tools I explore offer multiple creative ways to turn friction and repetition into loci of reflection, rest, or, in some cases, protest. Uncovering seams at the level of both software and hardware, this multiplicity of interactions germinates new theorizations of refreshing, scrolling, and swiping—those repetitive, micromuscular movements that have come to define the user experience.

The Myth of Seamlessness

Because refreshing is a prevalent reaction to the precariousness of digital infrastructures, it signals a set of cultural and technological expectations. Waiting is a relative term; it can mean something different based on shifting geographical and economical contexts. In parts of the world where grids fail regularly, users wait for media quite distinctly, or they use analog media alongside or instead of digital devices.[16] And while buffering is a routine and much-expected phenomenon in countries or places without high-speed internet, the economy of latency and refreshing demands a different reading when encountered within the broader discourse of civic involvement and users' agency in highly connected Western countries, where the ability to endure buffering has consistently diminished and "internet rage" abounds.[17]

As Jason Farman and other media scholars have demonstrated, Americans are growing ever more impatient with the need to wait for online data, a fact that holds far-reaching implications in an attention economy profiting from maximizing screen time.[18] Even barely noticeable delays of half a second can dramatically effect site traffic, as Google and Amazon found out early.[19] For Farman, the tension between the jargon of techno-utopianism and the daily experience of users results in a paradox: "Though the mythologies of the digital age continue to argue that we are eliminating waiting from daily life, we are actually putting it right at the center of how we connect with one another."[20] In this analysis, "time is a medium that communicates," and waiting is the message.[21] Refreshing, as we shall see, sends contradictory messages as it reveals a tension between activity and passivity, a desire to leave the platform and a wish to stay longer.

Frustration, internet rage, and what I elsewhere called "perpetual anxiety" have become increasingly prevalent in popular culture.[22] Perpetual anxiety can take the form of connectivity anxiety, battery-life anxiety, or, with the emergence of connected homes and the Internet of Things, an entirely new set of anxieties "about the ways media devices might be looking back at us."[23] Our growing attachment to high-speed internet birthed an entire industry of loading symbols, from Apple's "rainbow wheel of death" to Yelp's Hammy the dancing hamster (which I will return to later). That an iconic loading icon is colloquially known as the spinning wheel of death attests to a cultural imaginary that links the user's potential death of boredom with the computer's "death" because it is stuck.

These prominent anxieties are now used to sell apps and products promising a better, faster connection. In a 2021 commercial for the "hybrid broadband" service of the UK-based internet provider BT, frustrated users turn increasingly violent when faced with buffering.[24] As a case study of how tech companies recast latency as the ultimate villain, while using its threat to sell premium services, the BT commercial merits a close reading.

The opening shot slowly reveals a dark-haired, white woman repeatedly clicking her mouse while a video titled "funny scenes" is buffering on her bright computer monitor. After a few seconds of desperate pleas, she stands up, smashes her router, and throws the monitor into an aquarium near the living room wall. A startled fish jumps out of the aquarium seconds before it shatters in an explosion that leaves a huge hole in the apartment wall. Once the hole is exposed, other neighbors in the building, including a dark-skinned man and a white man who lives in an attic, are seen attacking their routers and electronics in similar fits of aggression. The ninety-second commercial ends when a male narrator asks, "Why suffer broadband rage?" and concludes, "BT hybrid broadband is unbreakable."[25]

While Dylan Mulvin understands this commercial as banking on the growing popularity of "rage rooms," commercial spaces where consumers pay to break old electronic devices and home appliances as a form of stress release, I understand it vis-à-vis the desire to project pain from the human body onto the black box that causes it.[26] In this reading, the source of rage is associated with digital rather than analog media. The diverse group of seemingly able-bodied actors cast by BT to portray the "average" user all make facial expressions that reveal a torturous relationship with their screens and routers. Instead of the joyful destruction of defunct VCRs promised by rage rooms, or the elaborate revenge fantasy of punishing a malfunctioning printer presented in the 1999 comedy film *Office Space*, no relief awaits those miserable souls who endlessly mumble "reconnect the router" in their dark, cramped apartments.[27] Instead

FIG. 1.2 A still image showing a woman growing taller and hitting the ceiling as a result of "broadband rage" in BT's "Unbreakable Internet" commercial. (Source: YouTube)

of recentering one's body, the promised catharsis can only come from switching internet providers.

This commercial propagates the idea that a momentary network delay can be solved by upgrading to premium services with enigmatic, magical names like "hybrid broadband." Yet it also reveals a deeper truth about how digital technologies reshape their users. In the first scene, the desperate woman becomes so upset with her router that, much like Marvel's Hulk, she rapidly grows bigger and taller. The digital disconnection is depicted here as remaking the human body to the point that her domestic space can no longer contain her new, monstrous self (see fig. 1.2). The commercial aims to produce a comic effect, yet it exposes how the digital space is not only a playground where our avatars roam possible worlds while our biological bodies, with their imperfections, pains, and needs, can be easily ignored. Our dependency on the digital, BT implies, also facilitates a set of interactions that might have direct, harmful effects on the human body and its environment. With its parade of broken bodies, this commercial offers a visual depiction of digital debility ironically promising to neutralize these injurious effects by reinforcing the attachment to an even-faster network.

This commercial, as well as endless commercials promoting faster internet speeds by switching to 5G networks, attests to tech companies' monetization of waiting time.[28] As Sean Cubitt contends, "the purpose of control over information is to delay transmission. We think we pay more for premium service delivery of news and entertainments; in fact, the money pays for timely arrival, and its absence ensures a deliberately delayed and often downgraded delivery."[29] In the digital upgrade culture, users are habituated to constantly wait for the next product, service, or infrastructure promising to solve the problems caused by their current technological tools.

While BT and other internet providers demonize buffering in order to sell their "unbreakable" internet, streaming platforms similarly shift the responsibility for seamless connection to users by designing and promoting free, user-friendly "speed tests" websites. In the past decade, YouTube and Netflix heavily invested in the "platformisation of the Internet," offering speed tests designed to put pressure on internet service providers (ISPs) around the world.[30] The participatory and empowering interface design of these speed tests' websites, as studied by Evan Elkins, is used to accelerate the companies' expansion into new markets while habituating users to "a global society whose ideal, normative conditions are *connected* and *fast*."[31] As free tools helping consumers to check their internet speeds and, if needed, switch to a faster ISP, these speed tests promote the idea that fast, reliable connectivity is a necessity and "a human right," while treating users "as individuals who can make informed choices about their service providers in an ideal (and often illusory) marketplace of competing ISPs."[32] As I explore in chapter 3, the autoplay feature connects this ideology of seamlessness with prolonged engagement, formulating spectatorship and media consumption as endurance tests for both infrastructures and human bodies.

While some streaming platforms fetishize speed by adopting a humanitarian discourse, other tech companies incorporate "false latency" and waiting into their business model.[33] Facebook, for example, deliberately slowed down a "security check" feature to convince users that it is thorough and therefore trustworthy. Cell and internet providers throttle the connection once a user hits their data limit, making slowness a constant threat used to ensure timely payments and upgrades to "premium" data packages. Despite its growing ubiquity in the digital economy, false latency is a business model that is rarely discussed by policy makers, media scholars, or internet users.

A prominent business model, false latency reminds us that the digital economy, despite its obsession with acceleration and scaling, is built on repetitive, strategic shifts between slowness and fastness, friction and flow. If, as the next chapter demonstrates, critical disability studies can help us replace the false binary of slow/fast with that of calibration, the framework of digital debility developed throughout this book reframes latency and refreshing as more than deterrents to a fetishized digital seamlessness; they produce, but can also mitigate, forms of pain users experience en masse yet rarely talk about.

Within the ubiquitous world of seamless design, however, latency is still theorized and understood as a problem awaiting a solution. As software is often seen by users as "black magic," a moment of buffering is recast as an encounter with a demon—a malicious entity that takes over our body and mind when we least expect it.[34] Refreshing is often, although not always, a hopeful abracadabra reaction to the frustrating encounters with digital dams. It is a cognitive and bodily habit denying the extent to which digital, algorithmic, and compression technologies are all inherently imbued with latency, bugs, and glitches. Even when acknowledged, buffering and other digital dams are trivialized or downplayed by both users and media scholars. To counter this tendency, I trace the refresh back to radar technologies and other tools that weaponized latency. Historicizing the refresh, the next section moves us away from the promise of seamlessness by revealing how this feature might contribute to ableist interactions between humans and their technologies.

BUTTON, GESTURE, HACK:
A HISTORY OF THE REFRESH

Like the internet itself, the refresh button is a product of the military-industrial complex.[35] Early computer screens and graphic interfaces "emerged from the problem of integrating real-time human feedback into computerized radar systems developed by the US military in the early decades of the Cold War."[36] Radar technologies refreshed their screens every 2.62 seconds to deliver "a moment-by-moment graphic display of the changing air situation."[37] This military strategy had long-term implications for human-machine interactions. As summarized by Bernard Dionysius Geoghegan, "[early computer and internet pioneer] Douglas Engelbart credited his experience as a radar operator with inspiring the host of interactive and graphical technologies adopted in personal computing of the 1970s and 1980s. For Engelbart, radar offered a model of a virtual datascape capable of rendering any information in lively animated graphical and haptic forms."[38] Both capacities, the animated graphics and the haptic affordances of computer interaction, have come to define the history of the refresh as a button and, later, a bodily gesture enabling a smartphone user to pull down their finger in order to reload an app or a web page.

This literal weaponization of the refresh button both informs and differs from its current function in the digital ecosystem.[39] In radar technology, latency is lethal. In algorithmic trading, which is increasingly prevalent, "low-latency traders" depend on ultra-low latency networks where every microsecond counts.[40] Tracing the refresh back to radar technologies therefore alerts us to the decreasing duration of lag time. A history of "the moment" in digital infrastructure and human experience reveals how, in the 1970s, a "moment" was nearly three seconds long. It also reframes the lag time on government websites for public health as part of decades-old legacy of potentially fatal computational latency, from missing an enemy aircraft to missing a COVID-19 vaccine appointment.

These high-stakes examples echo the etymology of "latent" not only as "dormant, underdeveloped," but also as "a disease that is present but not yet producing symptoms or clinical signs."[41] This definition brings together latency and *undetectabilty*. Radar was invented to detect that which the naked human eye cannot see. In medical discourse, on the other hand, undetectability is used to describe an HIV patient who, as a result of pharmaceutical treatment, "has lowered the load of the HIV virus to levels that are insignificant statistically and that render it non-contagious."[42] Within these frameworks, latency is not just an annoyance forcing the user to wait; it redefines the user's relationship with their body, technology, and others. For media scholar Kristin Veel, these notions of uncertainty and lack of control originating from the medical discourse very much inform computational latency. Instead of uncertainty emerging from one's body—am I sick even if I have no symptoms?—these anxieties are now tied to such digital parameters as "the medium (wired or wireless), the size of the packet, the gateway nodes (such as routers) that examine and possibly change what is sent, and (in the case of internet latency) the server's occupation with other transmission requests."[43] The result is uncertainty or perpetual anxiety, experienced by users whose lives and livelihoods rely on digital black boxes. Connecting latency to health, we should also consider how viruses, cookies, and other injectables, as well as the firewalls, virtual private networks (VPNs), and other techniques for fighting them can create extreme latency, which only adds to the anxiety as users wonder whether the latency is normal or a sign of impending illness manifested as spyware.[44]

To that extent, the refresh is a *pharmakon*. It simultaneously decreases the tension of uncertainty by translating it into a bodily movement and reminds users that they are destined to "update to remain the same."[45] A useful tool to diagnose, reload, and interact with software, refresh also contributes to digital debility in ways that remain mostly unexamined. As it entails repetitive microtemporalities and muscular movements, refreshing is crucial for an attention economy in which programmers and avid computer users describe "long lasting and intense pain" in their index fingers, thumbs, and other fingers used for mouse and touch-screen navigation.[46] Analyzing narratives of pain and addiction on online forums for computer technology workers such as Slashdot and Ars Technica, White concludes that "for some individuals, a certain amount of pain and bodily damage is an acceptable trade-off in order to continue using a computer," while "others make distinctions between intermittent and unbearable pain that will permanently prevent programming, gaming, and money making."[47] This reflects the distinction between debility, as an ongoing, gradual process, and disability, as the loss of capacities due to injury, accident, congenital condition, or sickness. It also returns us to latency as undetectability, in that these fervent computer users only notice the injurious effects of their sedentary, "folded over" lifestyle when it is too late to treat them.[48]

That the refresh supports and sustains a loop of dependency and physical harm is denied by most users due to its pleasurably addictive design. While its promise to detect something new and exciting is rarely fulfilled, it nevertheless imbues the user with a sense of anticipation, agency, and control. This is not unique to digital technologies. Describing his infatuation with the colorful "load" bars flashing on analog gaming consoles, Kristoffer Orum muses: "Today I remember my hopes for the computer games much more vividly than I remember what the actual games where like. It was a fledging interest in the possibility that the world might contain something other than the mainstream monoculture of the suburbs."[49] Other media and gaming scholars joined Orum in fetishizing the ultraslow modem connections of pre-broadband computer networks, with their unbearable noises and aesthetics of delay and slowness.[50] Theirs is a nostalgic appreciation of the ebbs and flows of the early internet that paints a picture radically different from the tormented users in the BT commercial or the online forums studied by White. In these accounts, the load, the wait, and the patience they entail inform a more hopeful relationship with technology, opening a space for the user's imagination and for a daily ritual the mere existence of which is more exciting than the content of the virtual encounter.

These early accounts of joyful waiting have long been replaced with the anxiousness of the pull-to-refresh gesture on mobile phones. Today, the pull-to-refresh is one of the most pervasive gestures of mobile users, alongside scrolling and swiping. Despite the growing popularity of no-hands interfaces based on audio input or the use of other body organs such as the foot, head, or tongue, the thumb has come to be associated with touch screens and mobile devices.[51]

While the refresh function was originally achieved by pressing a key or clicking a mouse, American software developer Loren Brichter introduced the pull-to-refresh function on mobile apps in 2010. Brichter first embedded this function into the Twitter app Tweetie. Initially, he placed a refresh button at the top of the Tweet list because users typically expected new tweets to appear there, but as the refresh button utilized valuable real estate that Brichter wanted to use for other features, he decided to make a "leap from a button to a gesture."[52]

A second and final iteration of the pull-to-refresh added visual feedback when refreshing, so that users could better understand the new gesture. This design also included a text alerting users that if the top of the page is pulled beyond a threshold and subsequently released, a refresh would occur. Brichter's innovation was patented by Twitter in 2013 and subsequently adopted by Facebook and a plethora of other apps.[53] "Stretching" the screen, users were empowered to feel as if they were stretching space-time, forever filling their days with new, global streams of data.

When designers build human-machine interactions around hands and fingers, they are following a long history of "buttonization."[54] In her historical analysis of push buttons, Rachel Plotnick theorizes the buttonization of emotions as a digital process by which "one can express a feeling much as they might choose a snack from a vending machine."[55] Still, despite the importance of the human hand in digital systems and the recent rise of haptic media studies, labor historians and media scholars tend to ignore hand-machine relationships.[56] Tracing push buttons to the nineteenth century, Plotnick connects digital interfaces such as the touchpad and the mouse to the desire to command humans and machines from afar while hiding the complex, messy, and unreliable electrical systems needed to sustain these communications.

Shifting from a button to a gesture is more than a technical change, as they invoke different cultural and historical contexts. In the case of push buttons, their early use most commonly involved calling servants or employees to do the pusher's bidding. "In this regard," Plotnick explains, "button pushing acted as a form of summons or demand to conjure one's wishes into being. Button pushers often confronted the complexities of making individuals appear and disappear at a whim."[57] While refreshing a social media feed could be read as enacting a desire to make individuals disappear (for example, when a user refreshes her Instagram feed as soon as she encounters a photo of her ex-girlfriend), it holds its own affordances. If Plotnick reads the digital "finger" as replicating the electrical current binary of on/off, the pull-to-refresh gesture negotiates technology in search of both continuity *and* disruption. It spells out, "I wish to stay on this platform while seeing something different." This tension mirrors the ambivalence we often feel about our technologies: We want to continue using them while blocking out their potentially harmful, disturbing, or boring elements. The handheld device helps users repress or ignore these conflicting desires as it perfectly fits the palm of the hand, providing the illusion of full and complete control to those whose palms, fingers, and wrists align with normative ideas of the human body.

Not all hands, however, are the same. The "thumbification" of the refresh had far-reaching implications for disabled users, as it created a new norm of human-machine interaction. This focus on the human finger excluded a wide range of ways that people with disabilities interact with computers: "capacitive head and mouth sticks, switch access (via eyes, tongues, and other body parts), and 'sip and puff' (assistive technology used to send signals using air pressure through a straw, by inhaling—sipping—and exhaling, or 'puffing')."[58] The popularity of the pull-to-refresh across multiple apps and platforms ignores these embodiments while also making some apps less compatible with screen readers and therefore less accessible.[59] As such, this history of the refresh demonstrates how disabling interfaces might replicate ableist assumptions even when this was not intended by their designers.

This ableist design script also dominates commercials and instructional guides for technological products. Apple's promotional ads, for example, have mostly featured white, able-bodied computer and smartphone users.[60] Launched in 2007, review models of the original iPhone were provided only to four American male journalists, who then published mixed reviews complaining about the "skinny little virtual keys on screen" and the need to alternate between keyboards in order to insert numbers and punctuation.[61] Rejecting these early complaints, Steve Jobs proclaimed that the iPhone was "the best pointing device in the world" and went on to declare that "we're born with ten of them, our fingers."[62] In White's reading, "through such notions, Jobs and the designers of the phone produce a script that asserts what constitutes a body and how the body functions."[63] This design script effectively excluded not only users who were born with fewer than ten fingers or with no fingers at all, but also people with arthritis or Parkinson's, as well as those whose long fingernails prevented them from using the touch-based keyboard.[64] Based on tactile encounters between the body's electric current and the "capacitive screen," smartphones are also less responsive to "the calloused-hand carpenter and the sodden-fingered dishwasher," as well as those whose fingertips are burned or scarred.[65] In short, these devices fictionalize a user based on assumptions about the user's gender, occupation, and bodily capabilities.

Much like Apple, the gaming industry often assumes an able-bodied user. In reconceptualizing the design of their console controller for the release of the Xbox One, Microsoft spent over $100 million on development and testing to ensure that "the final design would mesh seamlessly with the so-called 'golden hands'—Microsoft's internal shorthand for a class of 'core' game players who were the primary audience for the redesign."[66] In targeting "hardcore gamers" in the bourgeoning e-sports industry, David Parisi argues, "the design of the Xbox One controller expressed a fantasy of its desired subject."[67] It is a fantasy that excluded those users whose bodily, sensory, and cognitive functioning differs from the highly demanding and strategically addictive standard of video game design. The adoption of "golden hands" also served to naturalize and normalize the idea that gamers should engage in rigorous, repetitive training regimes in order to be able to play for hours or even days without taking a break, often in order to monetize their dexterity and endurance.

Criticizing the limited embodiments afforded by common game controllers, Miguel Sicart proposes a set of questions and provocations: "What if we rejigger the tactile elements in these controllers? What if caressing becomes a way of giving input, one that is followed by feedback from the rumble motors? What if squeezing the analog triggers was actually an analog way of providing input, a matter of careful degrees of sensation? What if shaking, balancing, vibrating were ways of touching the controller?"[68] Such "queer game controllers," Sicart hopes, could "turn that body into a source of pleasure."[69] By opening up a multiplicity of bodily interactions, they might move users away from thumbification into a more playful state of going in and out of flow. That companies like Apple and Microsoft have been creating voice-based and camera-based controllers suggests that multisensorial interfaces are becoming more popular. Such modifications for those who have trouble with finger gestures, however, are still being sold separately and tend to be expensive.

Despite the growing popularity of voice-based technologies, the pull-to-refresh is a useful reminder that thumbification is here to stay. While excluding some users who are incapable of performing this bodily movement, the "leap" from button to gesture has also contributed to digital debility by ingraining the refresh into digital natives' muscular memory. Even if the idea of "amusing ourselves to death" has long roots in media studies, dating back to Neil Postman's seminal critique of television, the intensity and speed introduced by the pull-to-refresh have pushed it *ad absurdum*, forever producing and consuming content, auto-refreshing ourselves and others.[70] The ubiquity of this feature narrows the ways in which one can in fact be "refreshed," returning the user to a problematic "normal" that constitutes constant media engagement. That radical refreshment might look like digital disconnection is forever ignored and denied by these addictive design tools.

As such, the refresh is the cornerstone of the "liveness" and "realtime-ness" that Wendy Hui Kyong Chun and Tara McPherson define as central to the logic of the digital ecosystem.[71] Much like the invention of "breaking news" cemented television as a live medium, the internet offers a similar promise of staying informed via never-ending updates. Refreshing the pain of others, to paraphrase Susan Sontag, can easily turn dead civilians, natural disasters, and brutal images of war into new streams of dopamine-releasing images and information. This tension between shock and pleasure is further supported by other design features such as a bright red "LIVE" icon at the top of many news articles and a clickable "See more updates" accompanying headlines about developing catastrophes.

I was reminded of Sontag's seminal work on the moral complexity of war photography when refreshing the *New York Times*' reporting on the death toll of a devastating earthquake in Turkey and Syria on February 6, 2023. As I refreshed the home page on my Android app, the number of dead jumped from 7,700 to 8,100 within one pull-to-refresh gesture (see fig. 1.3). This moment collapses the pleasure of feeling more informed than the yet-to-refresh others with the shock of coming to terms with the catastrophic results of the natural disaster. The home-page design, with its use of red and black on a white background, created a feeling of both emergency and agency, as I constantly refreshed the mounting number of casualties from the safe distance of my home, where the very same electrical and digital infrastructures ruined by the earthquake delivered live footage of a humanitarian crisis unfolding on my beloved, handheld device.

Rejecting the supposed correlation between exposure to war photography and moral action proposed by Virginia Woolf, Sontag warned that photos of destruction and loss might produce contradictory, unpredictable results as they serve to strengthen rooted narratives held by those who examine them.[72] This results from a lack of context or the loss of indexicality in the age of mass media, when even the most horrific photographs can be quickly dismissed as "staged for the camera" and a "fabrication."[73] Published in 2003, Sontag's *Regarding the Pain of Others* is an early warning not to confuse evidence with persuasion, justice, or pacifism. In the age of AI-generated images, texts, audio, and video, these concerns gain a new sense of urgency, as nothing circulating on the internet can be seen as clear-cut evidence.[74] Then and now, "photographs of an atrocity may give rise to opposing responses. A call for peace. A cry for revenge."[75]

Sontag's analysis was written before the internet took its current form, and it does not account for the extent to which addictive design features hinder the ability to meaningfully engage with images and stories. Rereading Sontag in the age of constant connectivity, Sean Cubbit asks whether "the network diagram places us, or could place us, under any similar ethical or political obligation" to that studied by Woolf in relation to photography.[76] The "network condition of circulation," Cubbit contends, removes the ethical demand in ways that both replicate and differ from analog media.[77] Refreshing merges dopamine release with curiosity, boredom, and the desire to stay informed, making catastrophic headlines disturbingly gratifying. Unlike the newspaper reader envisioned by Sontag or a television viewer glued to breaking news, the internet

FIG. 1.3 A screenshot of the *New York Times* app reporting on a deadly earthquake on February 6, 2023, and featuring the word "LIVE" in red on the top left corner, alongside a red time stamp stating when the article was last updated. (Source: *New York Times*)

user is invited to fully control the speed and frequency of updates vis-à-vis the micro-movement of their thumb. This reinforces a sense of bodily agency and control just as catastrophic headlines remind us of the precarity of the human body and the systems supporting it.

Not every user, however, is able to refresh when exposed to painful and graphic imagery. Associating internet use with trauma, recent studies of the content moderation industry reveal the destructive effects of daily exposure to graphic content, especially when the worker is not allowed to refresh their screen as they are paid to watch, tag, and remove content deemed unsafe or triggering for social media and streaming platforms.[78] Rejecting the model of trauma as a singular, one-time event, Amit Pinchevski analyzes lawsuits in which former content moderators sued companies like YouTube and Facebook for compensations due to work-related PTSD. In these cases, "recurrence does not mean watching the same images, but the same types of images (child abuse, political violence, etc.) across multiple contents, whose incremental impact might result in a 'traumatic affect,' an uncontrollable intensity taking over the subject."[79] Two of the moderators who decided to press charges went as far as describing their post-traumatic symptoms as "an internal video screen" replaying the distressing images inside their heads in a nightmarish form of auto-refresh. As described by Pinchevski, "It is as though the technical logic of replay migrates to the mind, where it becomes internalized and keeps replaying, repeating the recurrence of distressing images. Both trauma event and posttraumatic reexperiencing are repetitive. Trauma emerges here not as resulting from the unimaginable suddenly taking place, but from the unimaginable *repeatedly taking place*, indeed routinized, through ceaseless audiovisual reproduction."[80]

As canaries in the coal mine, traumatized content moderators remind us that repeated exposure to online content can cause severe physical and psychological damage. In this retelling, refreshing is a privilege not everyone gets to enjoy, as these underpaid contractors, many of whom live and work in the Global South, are not allowed to refresh when they encounter graphic content, as unnerving as it may be. This example, while extreme, also teaches us that difference does not preclude repetition's numbing effect. Even when scrolling through varied stimuli and formats, the effect can be incremental boredom, alienation, and, in the case of graphic content, pain and trauma.

The enforced repeated exposure of content moderators is a reminder of how marginalized workers are often the first to bear the brunt of new computational technologies. While computation historians and scholars tend to focus on white-collar programmers and CEOs, "computing technology was pushed upon the clerical and administrative labor" traditionally composed of underpaid women, many of whom were women of color.[81] As Shoshana Zuboff and Laine Nooney demonstrated, the advent of computer monitors for the use of the 1980s workforce negatively impacted the health of women tasked with switching from paper-based to monitor-based data entry.[82] These reluctant early adapters of computers, who replaced walking, writing, talking, socializing, and shifting positions with repeatedly typing the same keys while staring at a light-emitting monitor, reported eyestrain, stiff and sore wrists, increased stress, and lack of motivation.[83] Computer pain, Nooney concludes, is everywhere, yet it has never been evenly distributed, felt, or recognized.

Bearing these longer histories of computational labor in mind, I argue that what is unique about refreshing is not just its promise of liveness, but the tension between this promise and the reality of *stuckness*. It is this temporality, rather than those studied by Chun and McPherson, that is central to the production of digital debility. To that extent, interface design functions as a visual metaphor, as it allows users to pull the screen down to refresh until their thumbs get stuck at the bottom of the mobile screen. Despite its promise of dopamine release, the "stretchiness" of refreshing has a limit resembling hitting a wall. With daily, obsessive use, these micro-movements of the thumb—from top to bottom (refreshing and scrolling), or from side to side (swiping)—might result in carpal tunnel syndrome or other forms of "intense pain" that gamers and programmers routinely describe.

It is here that critical disability studies offers a more nuanced approach to hand-machine interaction. The notion of stuckness cannot be distinguished from the repetitive, sometimes obsessive nature of either clicking or pulling to refresh. Accessible approaches to reading and typing, however, incorporate multiple fingers and, in some cases, multiple body parts. Braille, for example, requires "pre-Braille training" that teaches children and adults finger sensitization and finger strengthening by using such exercises as molding clay, touching soft and hard surfaces, and using a special booklet to identify different fabrics. To that extent, reading or typing Braille is more akin to playing a piano than using a single body part.[84]

A more recent innovation, a language called Protactile, pushes this idea further by recasting the entire body as key for communication. As described by DeafBlind poet and writer John Lee Clark, Protactile was developed by DeafBlind people as a tactile language breaking "many taboos related to touch, including touching one another's bodies instead of just moving our hands in the air. A grammar soon developed to coordinate all that contact."[85] This includes "fumbling around" new spaces; using hands, legs, knees, shoulders, and other body parts to communicate based on an agreed-upon system of movements and gestures; and training American Sign Language (ASL) interpreters and non-DeafBlind people in how to use the new language. Protactile, while still in its early stages, reminds us that communication could mean "bodies in contact" and a multisensorial experience. This is a model different from the thumbification of every human-machine interaction.

These different approaches to literacy and play recast human-machine interaction as multisensorial, providing us with an alternative logic to that of thumbification. The notions of stuckness and boredom are less likely to occur in an environment designed for multiple modes of embodiment. Despite tech companies' promise of endless choice, ubiquitous design features might in fact narrow the range of possibilities of how we interact with our machines and, by extension, with each other.

FROM "HAMMY" TO HACKING

Today, websites and apps auto-refresh in frequencies and at speeds that make manual refreshing redundant. As early as 2013, Brichter himself announced that "vertical swipe interactions" should evolve to perform other actions, thus giving birth to a new style of app interactions: "The fact that people still call it 'pull-to-refresh' bothers me—using it just for refreshing is limiting and makes it obsolete. . . . I like the idea of pull-to-do-action."[86] Yet the persistence of the pull-to-refresh exemplifies the addictive potential of interface design. In the age of auto-refreshing, Shannon Mattern argues, using the pull-to-refresh has come to resemble the "door close" button in the elevator or the "push to cross" button at a crosswalk: "both are there primarily to offer a semblance of user control," while also attesting to an always-diminishing endurance for waiting and lag time.[87] The refresh holds the user's attention long enough to make sure they stay logged in, rather than switching to a different platform or turning off their device. In this it is similar to the buffering icon, whose evolution from a static image of an hourglass to the colorful, animated graphics known as "throbbers" tells the story of an industry heavily invested in denying its own limitations.[88]

Keeping with this trend, the design of the pull-to-refresh has become much more playful than that of elevator or traffic buttons. In his analysis of the business strategies through which apps like Seamless and Yelp "listen in on our adult lives, then speak to us like children," Jesse Barron describes his infantilizing encounter with Yelp's mobile app: "Yelp's identity is anchored by its pull-to-refresh icon, a little hamster in a rocket ship. This hamster has a name. It's Hammy. While you are refreshing a page of search results, Hammy does a side-to-side dance, and then the rocket blasts off toward the top of the screen. . . . Who is the person who enjoys this? Yelp is for adults with disposable income and a high degree of mobility, two things that usually—should—preclude friendships with stuffed animals."[89]

That Brichter's gesture birthed an animated hamster is one of the many quickly forgotten origin stories of digital standardization. The decision to turn this bodily movement into a game—offering users an immediate reward in the form of a dancing, lovable rodent—is read by Barron as part of a broader adaption of "cute design" by tech companies.[90] Indeed, in a *Forbes* article by Yelp UI designer Yoni De Beule, he explains that "when we found our iPhone settings page to be seriously lacking in the fun department, we decided to roll up our sleeves and fix it. We were quickly drawn to the idea of adding a hidden element to the bottom of the settings page. A user would have to pull up to reveal the easter egg."[91] After much deliberation, including pitching a dog and a "ninja panda" as the Yelp mascot, the company decided to integrate Hammy into its reloading animation and error message pages.[92]

Thanks to its whimsical dance, Hammy distracts users from Yelp's contested monopoly over small businesses, while making daily chores like feeding oneself or choosing a restaurant feel more like a game.[93] As employee of the month in "the fun department," it makes users less likely to contemplate how their refreshing feeds into a business model where "Yelp, like Google, makes money by collecting consumer data and reselling it to advertisers."[94]

The pull-to-refresh has gamified a plethora of digital interactions, from spying on our friends to checking stock prices. In recent years, popular apps added yet another way to make refreshing more playful and satisfying. In 2022, for example, the Twitter app started making a new sound. When users pulled down to refresh their timeline, notifications, or direct messages (DMs), they heard a robotic chirp that sounds like a futuristic bird or frog. While this noise was painted by the tech press as "polarizing," *The Verge* reported that "some people have been mesmerized by it."[95] This grouping of a muscular movement with a sonic stimulus replicates children's toys that make a sound when pressed, further implicating users into the culture of refreshing.

Watching Hammy dance is playful and pleasurable, as it draws on a familiar game dynamic where, according to Juan Llamas Rodriguez, "the instantaneous reaction of the system to the player's input ideologically functions to sell interactivity as agency."[96] To that end, the Yelp user resembles a gamer who "imagines themselves as having a right to be in the virtual world, a right to choices and a right to prosper in it."[97] The gaming analogy can also help us understand the refresh as replacing ludic features—levels, lives, enemies, and so on—with what is essentially "the fundamental dynamics of arcade games . . .

doing a series of actions with the goal of being able to continue doing these actions for as long as possible."[98] Instead of flapping a bird's wings to keep it flying or shooting rows of aliens, refreshing enables users-turned-gamers to continue their online engagement until their bodies can no longer support the postural, cognitive, and muscular demands of screen use.

Yet the refresh is also different from a video game; it is designed to conceal an unwanted action (the buffer loading data) by visually and sonically distracting the user. It magically appears at the very moment of a loss of agency to sustain the illusion of choice and control over the black box. As such, the refresh is a particularly fruitful case study because it challenges the distinction between active and passive users. When repeatedly refreshing, users are both passive, letting a reflex or muscle memory take over rather than actively turning away from their malfunctioned or boring interfaces, and active, reclaiming their agency by asking for something other than the content appearing on their screen. This feature not only recasts adult users as children, but also implicates them in digital forms of "busy idleness," where the user oscillates between two poles, "lagging or racing ahead of the subject."[99] In the case of refreshing, this oscillation can also manifest as frantically switching between multiple devices, checking one's laptop while waiting for one's phone to refresh, or vice versa. Even when successfully reloading new data, the refresh produces a subject forever desynchronized, either too slow or too fast to align themself with others and the networked machine.

The sense of empowerment provided by the refresh is fleeting and elusive, as the user operates within a limited system designed by others and drawing on playful animations, cute mascots, and multiple sound effects. Even those able-bodied users who have digital literacy, full control of their hands, and rapid muscular reactions cannot always predict whether a refresh will function *as a shortcut or as a restart*. Keeping this inherent unpredictability in mind, I would like to end this historical overview of the refresh by reading it as *a hacking technique* designed to compensate for the limitations of the computational-bureaucratic complex. While some state-sponsored websites exclude users such as Philip Orlando from accessing essential health services, others help people navigate and survive within opaque systems of borders, regulations, and citizenship. While examples are abundant, I will focus on the German appointment system during the COVID pandemic as a recent case study of refresh-as-hack.

When living in Berlin, one is required to go to a *Bürgeramt* to apply for a driver's license, register an address, get a tax ID number, and a plethora of other bureaucratic torments. To do so, one needs to book an appointment on a government website. An online calendar shows open times in blue and filled times in red. However, at the height of the pandemic in 2022, it became almost impossible to find available appointments. Ideally, the calendar should auto-refresh whenever new time slots are added or previously filled ones are canceled. In practice, this rarely happened. Refreshing every couple of minutes, one might get extremely lucky, but most of the time every appointment is shown in red.

This is especially frustrating for noncitizens trying to apply for a visa or a residence permit. As a popular expat website explains: "Most of the time, there are no appointments available. This is not a bug. Keep the calendar page open, and refresh it every 5–10 minutes. If you wait too long, you must re-enter your information every time. New appointments become available *at random times*."[100] This sense of navigating a system based on uncertainty, randomness, and opacity is key to the production of digital debility and a sense of perpetual anxiety. Much like buffering, a disturbance whose length is unknown, the digitization of essential services has recast an already cumbersome system as a human-less maze where one is expected to go through a long process of trial and error in order to (hopefully) come up with the optimal way to hack it. This strategic use of refresh, which is not unique to German websites, has become a popular hack and an open secret among expats in Berlin, with dozens of tips and messages discussing "best refresh techniques" on groups such as Berlin Scholars.

This is a telling anecdote, as it offers a new plot twist in the short history of the refresh. Instead of a design feature meant to "nudge" the server to reload in case of latency, the refresh becomes a hack helping users to find a shortcut within a system designed to make them wait. Whether a button, a gesture, or a hack, the refresh provides a sense of empowerment and agency, which then contributes to its addictive potential. It is part of the gamification of digital systems. This reading, however, assumes a digitally savvy user who is willing and able to create a game out of poorly designed systems. Much as elderly users of vaccine distribution websites are less likely than younger users to successfully navigate a flawed and hastily designed registration system, immigrants and those not fluent in German are less likely to game the *Bürgeramt* system than native speakers.

When the idea of empowerment proves empty and the user is faced with a computational-governmental complex that, by definition, sees citizens as data, we can predict a debilitating psychological experience based on the failure of the refresh function. In these moments, refreshing again and again can worsen the frustration or, depending on the opaque algorithms, eliminate it altogether. This exploration of repeated bodily movements and daily rituals is a useful reminder of the various tensions informing the digital ecosystem—the very same tensions frictional aesthetics aims to expose and explore.

AGAINST FLOW: FROM SEAMFUL DESIGN TO FRICTIONAL AESTHETICS

Frictional tools can bring playfulness, resistance, and reflection into a culture built on the myth of seamlessness. They also reframe access as a creative tool, rather than a regulatory confinement, a growing trend within the New Disability Arts movement to be further explored in the next chapter.[101] Drawing on Aimi Hamraie and Kelly Fritsch's "Crip Technoscience Manifesto," I wish to offer a set of frictional aesthetics and new lexicons of waiting-as-hacking.[102] At their best, these tools can put seamlessness itself to the test by challenging the hidden assumptions and goals of a seamless approach to design.

If the original goal of seamless design was to offer "invisible tools" that allow the user to "focus on the task, not the tool," seamful design opts instead to create "beautiful seams," drawing attention to both hardware and software.[103] These seams, if successful, can help users "perceive and appropriate them for their own use," while taking into account a multiplicity of ways to use a product.[104] Seamful design advocates are also invested in how human-machine interaction is shaped not only by software and hardware but also by social interactions between users and their changing needs throughout the day.[105] In the case of mobile phones' signal strength, for example, seamless design would not include a visible indication of the network to which the phone is connected, so as to make the interface as clean and decluttered as possible. Eliminating this information from the mobile home page, cell handover remains deeply embedded in the infrastructure, but in a way that "to the user . . . is handled seamlessly."[106] Seamful design, by contrast, invites users to check for sources of connection, so they could, for example, locate and move to better cell tower. Such design not only provides users with enhanced ways to improve reception and the quality of their phone calls; it actively makes the invisible, supposedly seamless process of cell handover legible by visualizing the very moments of friction: switching from one tower to another. With seamful design, users gain a better understanding of the inner workings of the multiple layers of the technical stack, becoming less likely to adopt the mysticism of immateriality.[107]

But how can designers tweak an interface to counter the harmful effects of obsessive refreshing? Consider a recent tool launched as part of Google's Digital Well-being Experiments, a website inviting programmers and design studios to upload open source features and browser extensions facilitating "a better balance with technology."[108] While the website is supported by Google, a company whose ad-based business model profits from constant surveillance and prolonged engagement with digital content, the experiments are designed

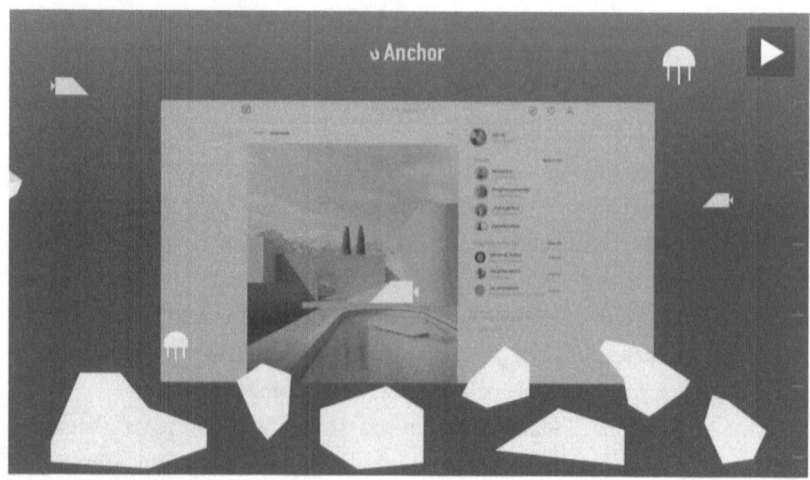

FIG. 1.4 A screenshot of Anchor, a Chrome extension that adds a dark blue filter, marine creatures, and rocks to the bottom of social media feeds. (Source: "Anchor"—Chrome Web Store)

by independent studios, and the code is available on GitHub, allowing users to customize them to fit their needs.

In one digital well-being experiment, a group of designers launched a Chrome extension called "Anchor," which seeks to provide a playful alternative to refreshing one's social media feed. Instead of endlessly scrolling in search of new, dopamine-inducing information, it visualizes infinite scrolling as a deep-sea dive, complete with whales, fish, and other aquatic creatures (see fig. 1.4). As described by its creators, Anchor "plays on this feeling of sinking. The further down you scroll, the deeper you dive—and you can watch as your screen slowly turns a dark blue, a little fish swims across your screen, and finally, you hit a (literal) rock bottom."[109] With the code available on GitHub, the designers encourage users to come up with their own "scrolling experiments," visualizing the way constant scrolling and refreshing might suffocate, rather than recharge, the user.

Using simple graphics, Anchor calls attention to the technical stack at play in every app or website using endless scrolling, demonstrating how seamful design can be used to slow down consumption and develop a more reflexive and intentional relationship with one's personal electronics. By forcing the user to ask, "Do I really want to continue scrolling?," it breaks the habit of refreshing and swiping and supplements it with the pleasure of "finishability"—an affordance of analog media I will further explore in my analysis of autoplay in chapter 3.[110]

Still, seamful design should not be confused with frictional aesthetics. While the former can be traced back to web designers hoping to create better, more useful products and help companies brand themselves through trendy ideas like "digital well-being," the latter was developed by disability scholars and activists who use design to attack the ableist, racist, and sexist entanglements supporting surveillance capitalism.[111] The digital detox experiments commissioned by Google once again shift responsibility to the user, while failing to consider the broader techno-social system in which the user operates.

But if seamful design is a source of profit for tech companies, how might frictional aesthetics and crip technoscience offer an alternative to the prevalent logic of flow and refreshing? Queer and disabled game designers who deploy boredom or frustration offer radical answers. Studying this recent trend, queer game designer Jess Rowan Marcotte shares their personal discovery of frictional narratives and the crip time they embrace: "Before it was even a conscious part of my game design practice, I have been making games that take what is invisible and make it visible again, often making the invisible hypervisible. Leveraging awkwardness, discomfort, imbalance and other queerable concepts is one of my core design approaches, creating indeterminacy and unsettledness. In my games, I create spaces for critical reflection and conversations . . . privileging questions over answers, clarity over stealth, disruption over comfort, and reflection over immersion."[112]

In a 2017 conference talk, Marcotte called designers to strategically employ friction and frustration to "take people out of the flow state."[113] This approach is deeply committed to questions of embodiment, affect, and temporality explored by both queer and disabled scholars. This can entail creating games that are slow, boring, or confusing in order to go beyond common approaches to controller-based embodiment: "Let them remember that they have bodies, and encourage them to think about that embodiment. Let them interact with something other than plastic."[114] Here the aim is not to create the ideal conditions for a state of flow in which the player can fully disconnect from their environment and corporeal needs; instead, designers like Marcotte invent gaming environments in which the player is invited to become more attuned to their fatigue, frustration, anxiety, or sadness.

This provocation pushes against the prominent design scripts of seamlessness and flow dating back to the early days of commercial internet. In 1996, Donna L. Hoffman and Thomas P. Novak employed the concept of flow to analyze computer networks. For them, flow is defined as "the state occurring during network navigation which is 1) characterized by a seamless sequence of responses facilitated by machine interactivity, 2) intrinsically enjoyable, 3) accompanied by a loss of self-consciousness, and 4) self-reinforcing."¹¹⁵ This definition has since been criticized by game designers and science and technology scholars. Brian Schrank, for example, replaces the notion of enjoyability with that of subjugation: "Games or cultures that foster flow allow people to be perfectly subjugated within their systems. When a system is designed with optimal flow, people forget that they are being subjugated: their doubts and distractions are kept to a minimum, and all human labor is positively absorbed into the system."¹¹⁶ This returns us to the gamification of the refresh as a way to maintain the illusion of flow even as the system breaks down. Game-like refresh icons like Yelp's Hammy distract users from the more problematic aspects of the app, providing them with a sense of agency and interactivity.

Drawing on Schrank's critique, Marcotte set out to build a game that forces the user to sit with their frustration and carefully reflect on the socioeconomic forces that produce it, rather than obsessively refreshing the pain away. One of those forces, Marcotte proposes, is gender-based discrimination. In 2014, Marcotte collaborated with Allison Cole and Myriam Obin to create a platform game called *Seventy-Eight*, its title a reference to the difference in pay between men and women. At the time, for every dollar a man made, a woman could expect to make seventy-eight cents (not accounting for intersectional identities). As Marcotte describes it:

> In this game, you play a woman who can't seem to please the system. Made in a weekend at the GAMERella game jam, the game features audio recordings of gendered insults that we asked other jammers to record, based on what they might expect to hear aimed at a woman who was considered to be underperforming, a woman who was considered to be performing at a normal level, and a woman who was thought to be overperforming. The appropriate audio plays when the character is at the bottom of the screen (underperforming), the center (performing adequately), and at the top of the screen (overperforming). The character is damaged if they are either too much to the bottom of the screen or too high up.¹¹⁷

This game could be read as part of the educational gaming industry and its trendier and more interactive equivalent, "virtuous VR," that is, virtual reality games and artworks designed to put the user in the shoes of a marginalized subject such as a refugee or a blind person.¹¹⁸ As Lisa Nakamura and other media scholars demonstrated, these high-profile works provide a seamless, 360-degree graphics that often fetishize and detract from the difficult stories they wish to tell.¹¹⁹ The simple design of *Seventy-Eight*, on the other hand, serves to amplify the user's frustration and boredom without offering them the option to refresh as a reprieve. Moreover, what makes *Seventy-Eight* important within the context of seamlessness and stuckness is the designer's unusual choice to program glitches and bugs into the user interface: "In programming this game, I created phantom key presses and invisible changes to the platforms that would cause the avatar to jump or walk without player input."[120] For Marcotte, these choices were meant to make the game "feel systemically unfair, but they read so subtly that they felt like glitches or mistakes."[121] Invoking longer histories of "glitch feminism" and early net art, Marcotte's game uses the interface to reveal deeper glitches inside both the technological stack and a sexist work culture in Silicon Valley and beyond—glitches that cannot be fixed with a simple refresh.[122]

Bringing together aesthetics and activism, *Seventy-Eight* employs glitches and randomness to deliberately disrupt the user's flow, in order to "represent the invisible forces of systemic oppression that might trip people up in the workplace."[123] For Marcotte, this game is a failure in terms of user engagement and pleasure. However, with its attempt to induce paranoia rather than the "loss of self-consciousness," such games invite players to sit with their difficult feelings. The game strategically employs positive reinforcement and built-in systemic failure to expose the inner workings of these very same strategies in late capitalism. Due to inherent and prevalent sexism, it is female-identifying people who often get stuck despite working harder than others.

Conclusion: Cripping the Refresh

In the spirit of the crip technoscience manifesto, I would like to end this exploration of refreshing with a series of provocations, aiming at imagining alternative feedback loops that can limit, rather than support, the impact of digital debilitation. How can we reimagine repetition as opening up a space for knowledge, healing, and grieving? How can disabled artists challenge the temporalities of stuckness and trauma?

What if, for example, we replace refreshing with transitioning? This more gradual form of change has been recently explored by writer Amber Rose Johnson and multidisciplinary artist Carolyn Lazard. In their 2021 collaboration, *Notes from the Panorama*, they invoke disability justice and Black disability politics by employing repetition as a means of renewed embodiment after long months of pandemic-imposed isolation.[124] Much like other video artworks by Lazard, who lives and works with chronic illness, this work attends to the body and to the care labor needed to sustain it. Produced for the Black Embodiments Studio during the second year of the pandemic, this seven-minute video art piece is comprised of a sequence of historical photographs and archival footage of Black people playing and resting, with open captions that serve as "a score for touch, slowness, and meditation" specifically for Black and Brown viewers.[125] This work draws on Lazard's style of captions that functions as "scores"—open-ended scripts inviting audience members to activate the work, their bodies, and each other. As performance scores, these captions instruct or otherwise engage with audiences, requesting their participation in the artmaking process.

In *Notes from the Panorama*, the captions are read aloud at a slow pace by Johnson and Lazard, one at a time or in unison, accompanied by meditative music. The work begins with the following statement: "Increasingly, many of us are shifting out of a season of separation / and into a season of intensified social intimacy—/ touching, / entering, / holding, / sharing." The soft tone in which this score is being read aloud conveys a sense of grief rather than enthusiasm, a grave realization that those who lost their lives to COVID will no longer be able to enjoy any of these embodied sensations. As the captions remind us, "for some of us this shift is still anticipated / for some of us, there is no shift." To engage in daily activities such as resting, socializing, or touching oneself is to survive, and BIPOC people are less likely than other groups in the United State to survive COVID.[126] Johnson and Lazard explain that their collaboration is intended to "slow time and support embodied awareness during major transitions in the pandemic, which has only intensified the need for rest in Black and Brown communities."[127]

Throughout the short video, the creators use the word "repetition" or "repeatedly" multiple times. They invite the viewer not to refresh but rather to engage in pleasurable forms of reawakening one's body through gentle muscular movements, not unlike the pull-to-refresh gesture. In Mara Mills' reading of this work, "Statements such as 'Consider the memories of touch that your body holds' and 'Touch the underside of something in your environment . . . sense its texture through repetition' are interspersed with instructions for tapping in the mode of EFT (Emotional Freedom Technique) or acupressure."[128] Emphasizing the variations between human bodies and experiences, the viewers are asked to repeatedly tap their eyebrows or to ask a loved one or a care worker to do so for them (see fig. 1.5). Unlike refreshing, with its anxious anticipation for increased stimuli, the question proposed by Johnson and Lazard is: What does my body want? The open-endedness of this question offers an alternative to the casino-inspired conditioning of digital media. The slow pace of the reading and the use of archival images produce an aesthetic of reflection and vulnerability, celebrating the bodies of those who survived while remembering the bodies who were lost to racism, ableism, and sickness. What *Notes*

FIG. 1.5 A still image from *Notes from the Panorama* depicting two Black girls lying on the grass in a fenced backyard. Courtesy of Amber Rose Johnson and Carolyn Lazard.

from the Panorama reminds us is that transitioning from one desire to another is a timely, delicate process that might induce as much pain as joy.

Inspired by this meditation on the unequal toll of the pandemic, could we invite disabled artists and web designers to come up with new loading regimens, perhaps those that make use of multisensorial, haptic, and sonic technologies rather than audioless visual GIFs? What might a library of crip-loading symbols and refreshing gestures look like? A hand testing a router for reflexes could be one answer. A map exploring the colonial atrocities supporting global information streams could be another one.[129] And a gentle vibration could take us in an entirely different direction.

The artworks and design solutions explored above imply that there are multiple creative ways to turn friction into a space for reflection, rest, rejection, and protest. Drawing on the framework of digital debility, this chapter historicized the refresh through its three categories—physical pain, addiction, and digital lethargy. With this acknowledgment of the constant tension between empowerment and debility we can start to imagine new ways to navigate digital dams.

The refresh conjures a user who is simultaneously active and passive, pushed to consume the pain of others through a thumb-based micro-movement.

Despite Britcher's modest intention to clear out valuable screen space by turning a clickable button into a bodily gesture, his pull-to-refresh had outsized effects. The story of refreshing as a military technology, security feature, diagnostic tool, desperate plea to the computational deities, and business model is one worth telling even if this feature might eventually be replaced by voice-activated, augmented, or otherwise "invisible" interfaces. As it touches on the very forces and affects that make the internet both exhilarating and boring, refreshing is a function and a process deeply embedded in our relationship with our machines.

Much like the refresh, the playback speed feature reshapes how users engage with digital media. Ranging from early audiobooks to Netflix's 2020 attempt to introduce a playback speed into its interface, the next chapter argues that speed listening and speed watching are crip temporalities that are not always used for enhanced productivity. Conceptualizing speed watching as a crip method of calibration and pacing, I reveal how disability activism was crucial for developing a more open-ended and customized media experience. Here the interface can advance the logic of digital debility by perpetuating habits of sensory overload and content cramming, pushing speed watchers to try to squeeze more content into their busy days. But it can also enable new modalities of art making and appreciation, exposing the tensions at the heart of the digital ecosystem.

THE RIGHT TO SPEED WATCH

(or, When Netflix Discovered Its Blind Users)

To slow down is to die.
—TIM BLACKMORE, "SPEED DEATH OF THE EYE"

Crip time is uncertain time.
—MARÍA ELENA CEPEDA, "THRICE UNSEEN"

Monetizing Accessibility

In October 2019, Netflix started testing a feature on a small group of Android phone users that allowed them to change the playback speed of film and television shows. This made it possible to watch films like James Cameron's *Titanic* (1997) in a succinct ninety-seven minutes, instead of a sprawling three hours and fourteen minutes, without missing the plot twists, special effects, and dialogue. By compressing time, it was the viewer, rather than the protagonist Jack Dawson, played by Leonardo DiCaprio, who felt like "the king of the world."

Netflix was not inventing the wheel. Similar features have been incorporated into podcasts, apps, media players, and streaming platforms such as Vimeo and YouTube for over a decade. Yet, despite this ubiquity, Netflix was pushed to terminate its experiment with speed watching following a public outcry from Hollywood filmmakers and actors, among them Judd Apatow, Peyton Reed, and Aaron Paul. Apatow, the self-proclaimed leader of the resistance, panned Netflix in a tweet amassing thousands of retweets and over 30,000 likes: "No Netflix, don't make me have to call every director and show creator on Earth to fight you on this. Save me the time. I will win but it will take a ton of time. Don't fuck with our timing. We give you nice things. Leave them as they were intended to be seen."[1] There is a certain irony in claiming that giving viewers more control over their time would result in Apatow wasting his own precious time. Whose time matters here? Is the timing and pacing of a film sacrosanct? More fundamentally, has Hollywood ever really had control over the "nice things" it produces?

Apatow argues that filmmakers present their films in a fashion consistent with their artistic vision and that the timing of a film is part of that vision. Yet his fury denies the extent to which films have always been compressed, extended, or creatively re-edited to maximize profit for distributors. In the early days of moviegoing, projectionists and theater managers had full control over the speed of films. Being a projectionist was once a life-threatening profession for this very reason, as the highly flammable nitrate film had to move slowly, but not too slowly, past the burning heat of an arc lamp. On May 9, 1908, the trade publication *Moving Picture World* warned, "There is no hard and fast rule that can be laid down governing speed. . . . It is as likely as not that the speed should be changed several times in different portions of the same film."[2] Today, the common practices of altering movies to make them more appropriate for in-flight entertainment and of releasing theatrical cuts alongside director's cuts—something Apatow himself has done with several of his films—are yet more reminders that commercial films are compromises between filmmakers, producers, and distributors.[3]

"Time-shifting" devices such as the remote control, DVR, and VCR have reassigned control from distributors to viewers since the 1970s by allowing them to record their favorite shows for future viewing and to pause, fast-forward, and rewind them.[4] Ever since Sony Betamax promised viewers they could "watch whatever whenever" in the mid-1970s and the Supreme Court recognized recording television shows for belated playback as fair use in 1984, audiences have developed what Lucas Hilderbrand calls "access entitlement."[5] As Netflix itself asserted on the company's blog, playback speed is "a feature that has long been available on DVD players—and has been frequently requested by our members. For example, people looking to rewatch their favorite scene or wanting to go slower because it's a foreign language title."[6] Still, in order to appease the high-profile Hollywood brigade, Netflix emphasized it was only testing the playback feature on smartphones and tablets, devices normally used during the daily commute, when subscribers might not have the time to watch a full-length feature film.

Despite these explanations, as well as the fact that Netflix subscribers could already easily speed watch by using a browser add-on, the pushback led the company to shelve the new feature for almost a year. Later, when it was finally re-embedded into the platform's web interface and mobile app in August 2020, Netflix chose to market the playback feature in part as an attempt to serve users who are hard of hearing or visually impaired. In an interview with National Public Radio, Everette Bacon, a board member of the National Federation of the Blind, applauded Netflix for improving accessibility for blind and deaf subscribers by enabling them to control the speed of audio descriptions and subtitles:

> Blind individuals—many of us use a screen reading technology on our computers and our phones, and we have learned and adapted over time to speed that up on a regular basis. We've also been listening to audio books for years. . . . And we've always been able to speed up that process. And so allowing us to do the same thing on a show like a documentary or some type of other content, it really helps a whole lot when you're trying to consume such great content in mass quantity.[7]

That Bacon alluded to audiobooks in his discussion of Netflix will not surprise those familiar with the history of disability activism and aural speed-reading. Long before audiobooks became a billion-dollar industry, talking books were created for blind readers. However, these recordings were deemed too ornamental and slow-paced by some of the people they were meant to serve. In their historical study of schools for the blind in the 1940s, Mara Mills and Jonathan Sterne recount the stories of students who hacked phonographs in order to listen to their homework at a faster pace.[8] Negotiating between the mechanical apparatus, the desired listening speed, and the changing pitch of the speaker (often known as the "chipmunk effect"), blind students "wrapped tape around the motor shaft to increase its circumference and thus drive the turntable faster."[9] "Blind speed-reading," Mills and Sterne remind us, "required the opposite assumption about what listeners would want: an easy sonic font—a flatter vocal affect—that did not call attention to itself and that allowed the auditor to skim, to easily find chapter and section headings, and to move through the text at different rates."[10] Efficiency and control, for these blind readers, were more important than the expressiveness of voice and music.

What aural speed-reading teaches us is that the desire to speed through a show or a film cannot simply be theorized as a productivity hack and should not be dismissed as sloppiness or laziness that lacks respect for artistic ambitions.

Instead, in this chapter, I build on various accounts of people with disabilities to study speed watching as an equalizer, a technique enabling different users to gain access to a vast amount of material and to choose whether they would like to skim or closely engage with it. Alongside time hacking, manipulation, and compression, which are essential for any theory of media consumption, I reframe speed watching around *scaffolding*, *calibration*, and *pacing*, three temporal categories I borrow from critical disability studies.

Attending to the promise of enhanced user control, this chapter builds on existing theories of speed and comprehension to argue that speed watching opens up new ways to interact with media as well as new motivations to do so.[11] That digital media can be used to manipulate time has been of interest to film and media scholars for decades. Famously, Friedrich Kittler argued that digitally enabled temporal manipulation is what distinguishes digital from analog media, for example, the computer from the phonograph and cinema.[12] While George Méliès and Thomas Edison toyed with slow motion, speeding-up, and time reversals in their early silent films, digitization birthed "an era of unlimited possibilities of intervention," with sensory output "beyond all human threshold."[13] The ability to rearrange a stream of temporal data, or what Kittler called "time axis manipulation," lies at the very heart of computation.

His 1990 essay "Real Time Analysis, Real Axis Manipulation," while published decades before the popularization of playback speed features on digital platforms, is useful in setting the stage for any discussion of speed watching, as it reminds us that both analog and digital media require signal delays or acceleration (as is the case, for example, in color televisions or in film projectors), and are therefore always already subjected to manipulation.[14] This short meditation on temporality and media imbues acceleration with a sense of beauty, pleasure, and playfulness. And so, when Kittler describes how Edison turned a phonograph to play music at "significantly higher speeds," he concludes that "frequency shifts endow even the most mediocre trumpet with brilliance; dull adagios can be accelerated to prestos."[15] As we shall see, this celebratory tone is strikingly different from the moral panic characterizing much of the press coverage of the playback speed feature, which draws on purist ideas of art appreciation.

Like Kittler's analysis, scholarship on temporal manipulation of images—especially the recent work on "slow cinema" and "intensified continuity"—tends to focus on production rather than consumption.[16] Drawing on these theories of shooting and editing, how can we explore the affective and libidinal economy authorizing users to compress, slow down, or accelerate a film in ways that were never intended or imagined by its makers? And what are the paradoxes, motivations, and specters that inform speed watching and its set of possibilities?

To answer these questions, my analysis brings together theories of efficiency and time management with histories of accessibility and universal design. I read Netflix's decision to rebrand a controversial interface feature as an "accessibility feature" as an attempt at "cripwashing," a term I borrow from Melania Moscoso Perez.[17] While Netflix's initial imagined user was an able-bodied, sophisticated consumer of global media eager to rewatch a favorite show or view films in a foreign language, the company initiated a public relations partnership with the American Council of the Blind only after it received pushback from Hollywood filmmakers. By so doing, it reimagined the ideal speed watcher as deaf or visually impaired, strategically using the growing awareness around accessibility and disability rights as a shield against further criticism.

How can we negotiate the histories of care, empowerment, and community building embedded in aural speed-reading with the marketing jargon of a tech giant aiming to maximize screen time and increase its stock price? Is the imagined speed watcher an able-bodied subject striving to hack time or a person with a disability trained in flexible modes of media consumption? Highlighting these tensions, this chapter offers a historical journey through the changing landscape of both disability activism and time management. As these two fields are rarely studied in tandem, save for ableist attempts to position the disabled subject as slow, lazy, or needy, it is particularly pressing to recognize that the early listeners of audiobooks were *faster*, rather than slower, than sighted users.[18] Turning this hierarchy on its head opens an exciting new terrain of "crip time" that, as described by Alison Kafer and other disability scholars, offers an alternative to the "productivity, capacity, self-sufficiency and achievement" touted by late capitalism.[19] With its emphasis on sensory endurance and enhanced productivity, it is tempting to study speed watching through the framework of digital debility. As a tool for compression and rewiring one's brain, it directly supports a culture of digitally induced fatigue and addiction. Moving beyond the slow/fast and the disabled/able-bodied binaries, however, I will draw on recent theories of crip temporalities as "new rhythms, new practices of time, new sociotemporal imaginaries" to show that speed watching holds multiple, even contradictory, meanings.[20]

WHO IS THE SPEED WATCHER?

Speed watching is often described in tech blogs and the trade press as a means for creating a digital Übermensch.[21] In a 2015 article in *Forbes* entitled "Why I Watch TV Shows and Video at Twice the Speed," for example, a contributor named Jan Rezab described this technique as a form of "time-hacking" and explained that "for most of us, time—or lack thereof—seems to be an issue. As an entrepreneur, founder, CEO, and parent, I'm always on the lookout for great ways to squeeze more time out of the day."[22] After speed watching television shows and full-length features at double their intended playback speed for two years, Rezab insisted that his new habit does not reduce his ability to fully comprehend, remember, and enjoy digital content. In fact, he is now an even more efficient viewer-entrepreneur-founder-parent-CEO.

The fact that Rezab opens a short essay on media consumption by confessing his need to "squeeze more time out of the day" testifies to the prevalent understanding of speed watching as a solution to the problem of wasted time advanced at the expense of art appreciation. That, indeed, was the dominant tone of the media coverage of Netflix's initial attempt to introduce the playback speed feature. One telling headline on the *ABC Arts* website reads: "Netflix's speed watching trial joins a long history of content cramming, but may be bad for artists and viewers."[23] Similar headlines that declared speed watching "as stupid as it sounds" cast it as a clash between users and creators, in which both groups are destined to end up with an aesthetically compromised experience.[24] This is in line with earlier press coverage framing the boundless desire for optimization and acceleration as a threat to the unity of the mise-en-scène, dialogue, and soundtrack. In 2016, for example, the *New York Times* explained that speed watching might "save hours over the season of a series," yet it "undermines the rhythm of a production and can dilute some creative elements."[25]

This moral panic recalls much longer debates around art appreciation, authorial intention, and the ideal conditions for media engagement. Lamenting the death of cinema and cinephilia, Susan Sontag famously declared that to be "kidnapped" by the movies "was to be overwhelmed by the physical presence of the image. The experience of 'going to the movies' was part of it. To see a great film only on television isn't to have really seen that film."[26] Sontag asserts that an uncompromised aesthetic experience exists, but only in the movie theater.

Film theorist Julian Hanich also associates domestic spectatorship with a deficient attention that limits viewers' abilities to immerse themselves in a narrative. Underlining the irony of this theoretical shift, Hanich contends that "the cinema, once praised or derided as a place of distraction by film theorists and cultural critics, is now valued by many as a sanctuary of focused attention and concentration."[27] Hanich locates cinematic pleasure in a "joint deep attention" invoked by being surrounded by strangers in a dark movie house. Under these supposedly ideal conditions, a sense of "heightened tranquility" produces a "pensive spectator" whose attention is entirely focused on the fictional world unfolding in a predetermined pace on the big screen.[28] For Hanich, the unique characteristics of the cinematic dispositive are "non-mundane space, the impossibility of manipulating the film, and the silence of the auditorium"—the very things that speed watching, with its emphasis on customized, individual consumption, threatens to annihilate.[29]

Manipulating a film to one's liking makes for a "an individualized, even narcissistic" mode of spectatorship.[30] According to Laura Mulvey, this might produce "possessive spectators," who "commit an act of violence against the cohesion of a story, the aesthetic integrity that holds it together, and the vision of its creator."[31] For both Mulvey and Hanich, giving up the desire for enhanced control endows moviegoers with "the freedom from having to act," a ready-made solution to decision fatigue and digital lethargy that can only be fully enacted once viewers surrenders themselves to the apparatus.[32]

In cinema and beyond, compression techniques have long been understood as a trade-off between speed and comprehension. Outside the movie theater, the century-old phenomenon of speed-reading links time management to both work and leisure. The debates around speed-reading, while taking us on a short detour, can shed light on speed watching as they consist of similar arguments around efficiency, self-improvement, and retention.

Speed-reading manuals gained popularity during the 1920s and 1930s and led to a redesign of Western typography for increased efficiency.[33] Drawing on early work on optical physiology, speed-reading advocates like Edmund Huey pioneered neurological methods for an "organized, methodized form of skimming, of consuming larger and larger units in a single glance" as early as 1899.[34] The original discourses around speed-reading as a necessary skill to manage information overload were crucial for the idea that one can train oneself to read faster and faster. The promise to unlock the brain's potential proved crucial to a new era of information overload, which Kenneth Cmiel and John Durham Peters date back to the early twentieth century and its "copious culture" of museums, collections, and print publications and the popularization of knowledge production and dissemination.[35] Bombarded by facts, avid readers and early media consumers adopted "the culture of happy summary" and its promise of "crystallized denser truths" vis-à-vis abridgment techniques like *Reader's Digest* Condensed Books, statistical sampling, Gestalt psychology, and other tools designed to get "the nub of the matter" in the "fast-moving world" of the 1920s and 1930s.[36]

Summaries and statistics, however, can often feel like a compromise between saving time and savoring the aesthetic or linguistic achievements of the artwork. Speed-reading, on the other hand, monetizes the promise to consume an entire book in half the time. Long before speed-reading apps became ubiquitous, such methods were popularized by American educator Evelyn Wood during the 1970s and 1980s. Developing a technique called "dynamic reading," Wood created and marketed a system said to increase a reader's average reading rate of 250 to 300 words per minute by a factor of three to ten times or more, while preserving and even improving comprehension.[37] Wood, who prided herself in her ability to read 2,700 words per minute, drew attention to the ability to save time by "reading down the page rather than left to right, reading groups of words or complete thoughts rather than single words, avoiding involuntary rereading of material and applying their efficiency to varied material."[38] Speed-reading techniques have since been simplified and widely adopted thanks to the rise of digital technologies and mobile apps.

In fact, early theories of online reading tended to confuse it with speed-reading. In 1999, for example, James Sosnoski introduced the concept of "hyperreading" as "screen-based, computer-assisted reading" and compared it with skimming and "fragmenting."[39] In her 2010 overview of "hyperreading" theory, N. Katherine Hayles asserts that literacy scholars tend to theorize online reading much like Woody Allen describes his alleged experience of taking a speed-reading course: "I was able to read *War and Peace* in twenty minutes. It involves Russia."[40] Pushing against this dismissiveness, Hayles reminds us that reading techniques such as scanning and skimming predated the internet and are essential for archival research and scholarship involving a great deal of material. In digital environments, she concludes, "hyperreading has become a necessity. It enables a reader to quickly construct landscapes of associated research fields and subfields; it shows ranges of possibilities; it identifies texts and passages most relevant to a given query; and it easily juxtaposes many different texts and passages."[41] Nevertheless, even Hayles cannot avoid contrasting "hyperreading" with "close reading," a mode of sustained focus and attention. Within this prevalent binary, either one can skim a text without fully engaging with it or one can take the time to read closely and therefore retain much more information.

More disturbingly, online hyperreading is supposedly debilitating because it rewires the brain in ways that make readers more prone to distraction and less capable of performing close reading.[42] This concern, popularized by Nicholas Carr's *The Shallows: What the Internet Is Doing to Our Brain* (2010), reinforced the notion that speed versus comprehension is a zero-sum game.[43] Studies exploring the relationship between acceleration and literacy gained a new sense of urgency following the advent of speed-reading apps like Spreader or Spritz, which lure potential (sighted) readers by promising them the ability to "inhale content" once they "regain the efficiencies associated with not moving your eyes to read."[44] With interfaces that present single words at the center of the screen at a pace determined by the user, the apps vow to suppress the need for saccades, the twitches back and forth that our eyes perform across a line of text. While the productivity-focused marketing jargon of speed-reading apps targets sighted, overworked people like Rezab, similar techniques have proven beneficial for accommodating reading disorders such as alexia and aphasia, attesting to the therapeutic potential of a no-page reading mechanism.[45]

Speed-reading apps redirect the science of "optimal viewing positions" to compensate for the loss of physical engagement of visual or subvocal systems.[46] Studying the popularity of these apps, Nathan Jones and Sam Skinner propose a set of questions that can help us unpack the similarities and differences between speed-reading and speed watching: "How does rhythm enter into the semiotic regime now that a text engulfs us, rather than an ocular drift, back and forth across a body of text? Furthermore, with speed-readers, do we enter the text, in a mode approaching a trance state? Is this a realm in which the distractions of self-reflection and self-awareness are occluded, or appear only as spectral undefined borders? Could this bodiless and selfless reader be the foundations for a new literary subject?"[47]

By replacing this new literary subject with a new digital user, these queries could be applied to speed watching. Yet speed-reading differs from speed watching in that it lacks a sonic component. For non-sighted users, speed watching is experienced as speed listening. As such, it can challenge existing studies that measure the speed threshold needed for reading comprehension.[48] Both techniques, however, are informed by an assumption that media engagement can and should be accelerated, encouraging a linear form of data extraction in which the rewinding or rewatching of scenes is less likely to occur because of the pace of engagement.

Despite over a century of experimentation with reading's threshold of legibility, speed watching has been left mostly unexamined. One of the rare loci in which it was explored is in museum education. In her study of the film program of New York's Metropolitan Museum of Art in the early twentieth century, Haidee Wasson examines how museums attempted to manage viewers' time and attention in order to develop a slower "museological gaze."[49] As part of the growing popularity of time motion studies in the 1920s and 1930s, a report entitled *The Behavior of the Museum Visitor* concluded that "the average museum-goer looked at every piece of art for about three seconds."[50] Alarmed by these findings, the Met commissioned films that "offered a particular viewing speed as well as a unique scale by which to see the museum and its objects differently."[51] The aim was to teach visitors "how to look," and the means was regulating the speed of consumption. Behind the project was the supposition that an inability to reflect on art is a result of "an undisciplined eye."[52] This could be changed by producing films that focused on each item for ten seconds on average, enabling museumgoers to give their legs some rest while training their minds to slow down their hectic pace. The goal was ambitious: "such techniques of visual display served to effectively address not simply a more *attentive* museum-goer but a more *retentive* one, that is, a museumgoer who ostensibly learns more."[53] An antithesis to speed watching, these early attempts to induce slow watching proved key to museum education.

Ironically, museum educators striving to slow down art appreciation and contemporary speed watchers hoping to hack time share a similar fantasy of disciplining the human mind. Both groups react to notions of infinite acceleration and the pursuit of efficiency, and they share the belief that cognitive capacities can be rewritten or improved upon, exploiting the plasticity of the human brain. This is in line with the rise of "cognitive capitalism" aimed at extracting surplus value from hidden cognitive processes instead of muscle or machine power.[54] The eye is recast as a motor that can be slowed down or sped up as needed, and the fragmentation of the eye and the mind from the rest of the body effectively serves to deny the physical pain and muscular strain caused by daily use of screens and electronics.

Instead of acknowledging the plethora of ways in which technology can inflict harm on human bodies, the emergence of compressed spectatorial experiences created by speed watching is often seen by both tech reporters and avid speed watchers as yet another manifestation of infinite acceleration. It is therefore central to a cultural climate in which "to slow down is to die," as Tim Blackmore concludes in his study of special effects in Hollywood.[55] This results in the first of several paradoxes: While speed watching endows the viewer with the notion of omnipotence and agency, it serves a capitalist logic of constant productivity, the prolongation of the workday, and the inability to distinguish labor from leisure—the very same ideologies supporting digital debility. As one worried journalist rhetorically asked when reporting on their disappointing and disorienting speed-watching experience, "If keeping up with your favorite show is this much of a chore, are you sure you even like it in the first place?"[56]

Yet the history of the playback speed feature, which has so far been ignored by media scholars, suggests a more complicated narrative of a digital feature first disseminated by users and amateur coders and, a decade later, popularized by companies like YouTube, Vimeo, Pornhub, and, more recently, Netflix, Zoom, and WhatsApp. To that extent, Netflix is a latecomer, and its study can shed new light on the conflicts that recur throughout the history of speed manipulation. Attempting to provide the first-ever historical account of the playback speed feature, the next section demonstrates how the lack of standardization led to discrepancies between audio and video consumption, as well as to various pleasures associated with accelerated spectatorship.

A COMPRESSED HISTORY OF THE PLAYBACK SPEED FEATURE

While technologies enabling the user to control the speed of listening, reading, and gaming have long and varied histories, digital speed watching based on frame skipping was first introduced in the early 2000s. Initially, it required downloading video programming software like AviSynth or using plug-ins like MySpeed for YouTube. These early tools for manipulating the playback speed without changing the audio pitch are described in various tech blogs from the time.[57] In the past two decades, independent web developers released numerous browser add-ons and extensions that enable users to speed watch most video players without having to code. The Playback Speed Controller, for example, allowed Netflix users to speed watch films and shows years before the company embedded the feature into its platform.[58] However, speed watching only gained popularity once YouTube and other streaming websites incorporated it into their settings and when add-ons such as Chrome's Playback Rate enabled users to change the playback and audio speed while browsing the internet.[59] This offered a compacted experience suited to consumers who often watch films on devices with a battery life of several hours or less or who "snack" on a television show while commuting to work.[60]

Unlike fast-forwarding a VHS cassette or skipping a segment on a DVD, digital speed watching affords the ability to follow both audio and video outputs. In analog systems, transmitting the frames at a faster-than-normal rate generates the fast-forward effect. There is an inevitable loss of audio and frame synchronization, and the viewer's ability to follow the fast-forwarded sequence remains extremely limited. With a digital encoder, on the other hand, only a subset of frames is included in the accelerated digital stream, yet, despite this system of compression and frame skipping, the result is still intelligible.[61]

These technical differences produce a distinctive epistemological experience. The choice to fast-forward or skip to the next chapter is often a compromise between the viewer's schedule and the length of the work. Since fast-forwarding a VHS results in a blurry and imperceptible image, the viewers are not able to know what, exactly, they are missing, and this knowledge gap puts them in a limbo of watching and not-watching. Speed watching offers a different affective and epistemological experience. It enables the user to consume a story and its action scenes, romantic encounters, and surprising plot twists while maintaining its unity, linear progression, and climax, resulting in the illusion that *nothing went missing*. As the audio pitch remains very much the same, this tool is particularly useful for blind users who listen to dialogue, sound effects, and soundtracks, as well as to audio descriptions.

As Netflix rightly noted, the playback speed feature has become all-pervasive. Streaming websites like YouTube, media players like VLC or Windows Media Player, podcast apps like Spotify, text messaging apps like WhatsApp, and assistive technologies such as screen readers now offer a feature that enables users to adjust the playback speed of video or audio content, from a crawling 0.25× to a blistering 3×. This feature, however, has yet to be standardized. As of 2023, YouTube's settings offer eight speeds, from 0.25× to 2×, while Netflix offers only five speeds (0.5×, 0.75×, normal, 1.25×, and 1.5×) (table 2.1).

Zoom enables viewers to watch its recordings by choosing one of four speeds: normal, 1.25×, 1.5×, and 2×. That the leading video conferencing platform only enables users to speed up content, rather than slow it down, attests to the hidden assumptions embedded in such design features.[62] Having transformed the domestic space into an office during the COVID-19 pandemic, Zoom is a productivity tool reshaping our media consumption habits in a way that aligns with Rezab's self-identification as a time-hacker. At the same time, online training platforms such as Vector Solutions, which offers colleges and universities workshops such as "Preventing Harassment and Discrimination" in order to comply with New York State regulations, for example, do not enable their users to change the speed of the video player to make sure they won't speed through the ninety-minute overview of potentially disturbing or illegal manifestations of sexist, ableist, and racist bias in the workplace.[63]

That Pornhub, by contrast, offers four viewing speeds—0.5×, normal, 1.5×, and 2×—indicates the libidinal and erotic potential associated with enhanced viewer control. Seeking bodily pleasure, the speed watcher is invited to watch porn whenever and however they are so inclined, perfectly aligning the on-screen sexual act with their own libido. This interface-supported pleasure connects the growing popularity of speed watching with the historical allure of the cinematic image. Building on the work of psychoanalyst Michael Balint and his study of "philobats," or thrill-seekers, film theorist Peter Wollen argues that chases, races, and other rapidly cut action scenes are "auto-erotic," since they provide viewers with the thrill of excitement and danger and offer them "unfamiliar situations.... far removed from the zones of safety and normality."[64] This echoes an early analysis by Hugo Münsterberg, according to which the "unnatural rapidity" of the photoplay in comparison to both real life and

SERVICE	MINIMUM SPEED	MAXIMUM SPEED	NUMBER OF SPEED OPTIONS
Netflix	0.5x	1.5x	5
YouTube	0.25x	2x	8
Pornhub	0.5x	2x	4
Zoom	1x ("Normal")	2x	4
Pocket Casts (podcast app)	0.5x	3x	26
Spotify (podcasts only)	0.4x	3.5x	10

TABLE 2.1 The lack of standardization in playback speed features across platforms, circa 2023.

the staged productions of the theater is able to "heighten the feeling of vitality in the spectator."[65]

As opposed to early cinema, digital speed watching affords an optimization of agency and control, rather than the allure of spectacle both celebrated and derided by Münsterberg. The agentive pleasure derived from a notion of time-hacking compensates for the loss of the hand-eye relationship essential for earlier forms of analog media. Consider how the emergence of novels as a literary form birthed a new kind of reading embodiment, as the speed of reading was dictated by the speed of page turning, and how analog acceleration (putting the film reel through the projector faster) initially synchronized the body of the projectionist with the speed of the moving image. As digital technologies desynchronize users and their bodies by way of digital debility, techniques like refreshing or speed watching can be read as a way to regain control over one's schedule, comfort, and needs.

Another important difference between cinema's intensified continuity and digital speed watching is that the latter is framed within a culture of multitasking and time-hacking. This is especially true for podcast apps such as Spotify and PocketCasts, where users can use a "trim silence" feature and, unlike Pornhub's or Zoom's meager four options, listen to content at speeds ranging from 0.5× to 3.5×. These differences between audio and media players are not incidental, and they support the idea that users accustomed to speed listening are more likely to enjoy speed watching.

Returning to Netflix, the company's playback speed feature differs from that of other platforms in two significant ways: As of 2023, it limits the maximum playback speed to 1.5× (slower than YouTube's 2× or podcast apps' 3×), and, after a user finishes speed watching a work, it reverts back to "normal" as a default setting. The latter stands in contrast to YouTube, which automatically plays all videos at the same speed unless the user actively changes it at the beginning of a new video. These self-imposed limitations potentially mitigate the tension between content creators and viewers by letting filmmakers retain some control over the maximum playback speed and preventing users from unintentionally (or even unconsciously) slowing down or speeding up content. They attest to the hidden power struggles informing design decisions.

These design features shape a media landscape in which audio consumption, possibly aided by "assistive technologies," adheres to different standards than video.[66] That the standardization of playback speed has yet to be established provides media scholars with a rare opportunity to closely study a "social process by which humans come to take things for granted."[67] If, as Dylan Mulvin attests, "standardization is a process of forgetting," then pointing out those differences at an early moment in their development is a crucial reminder of the invisible ways design decisions can deeply shape our lives.[68] Standards "shape the capacities that people have to build their own worlds," but a yet-to-be-standardized mode of media consumption also leaves room for playfulness, resistance, and hacking techniques resembling those developed by blind students manually speeding up their phonographs.[69]

Since its introduction in the summer of 2020, Netflix's playback speed feature has been most likely to serve two groups of users: able-bodied time-hackers and subscribers with hearing or sight impairments. Of course, blind or deaf users are also subjected to the logic and demands of capitalism and can see themselves as time-hackers just as much as Rezab. While the time hacker and the disabled user might be one and the same, the differences between these *imagined* speed watchers feed a cultural imaginary that enables different users to approach media according to their ever-changing bodily, cognitive, and emotional needs. Attending to the tension between time management and "crip time," the next section demonstrates how different these potential worlds might be.

ON SCAFFOLDING AND CALIBRATION

Returning to Hanich's vision of the movie theater as a silent, meditative space, film scholars often assume a universal, able-bodied moviegoing experience. Much of film theory ignores how, historically, people of color and other minority groups were told "not to stare," recasting looking as disturbing or threatening to other, especially white, people and endangering their ability to safely immerse themselves in a public viewing ritual among strangers.[70] The investment in a joint deep attention also denies the rich sensory experiences of differently abled people, which can include voluntary and involuntary sounds, body movements, tics, and the need for tactical sensory stimulus in order to sit through a two-hour film. Even for moviegoers who identify as able-bodied, the movie theater is seldom a quiet place. Due to the concession stand business model, they are subjected to popcorn crunching, drink gulping, conversations, and restroom breaks. Neither a dreamscape nor a library, the cinema more closely resembles a cacophonic audioscape where strangers come together to watch a film at high volume.

Despite the unattainability of a pure cinematic experience, the distinction between the wholeness of film and the "polluted" televisual text has been used to contest accessibility features such as closed-captions and audio descriptions.[71] In her analysis of the ableism of documentary listening, Pooja Rangan unpacks the ways in which accessibility features have been recast by film scholars as "a degradation of the 'original' cinematic text" that risked drowning able-bodied users in verbose subtitles or fatigue-inducing sensory impressions.[72] According to Rangan, this "long cinematic tradition of austerity thinking meant to define and control the desirable conditions under which (able-bodied) viewers interact with films."[73] The myth of a pure or whole cinematic text threatened by the needs of spectators with disabilities replicates the ableist "loss-of-wholeness" thesis of disability, according to which impairment, injury, or sensorial difference necessarily lead to a lesser, inferior experience in a body that has lost its presumed stability and coherence.[74] The assumption of a universal able-bodiedness often results in compromised, compressed techniques of access, for example, the withholding of important information, such as nudity or race, from audio descriptions, in an attempt to provide purportedly neutral, unbiased replicas of visual input.[75]

When filmmakers and journalists ask spectators not to change the playback speed in order to maintain the integrity of works of art, they are applying ableist, or at least purist, ideas of spectatorship. The debate around speed watching gives voice to previous tensions around the assumed wholeness of both the work of art and the body and mind of the user. As we will see later in this chapter, films made by disabled artists can help us challenge such assumptions.

In the context of speed watching, the notion of dis-/ability as a spectrum is especially productive, as the recurrent use of ubiquitous computing might lead to gradual debilitation, manifested as wrist pain, weakened eyesight, back pain, migraines, and other health issues. As explored in the introduction, technologically induced pain is common, pervasive, and ignored by both media scholars and users.[76] To recenter the human body in computer history, as Laine Nooney demonstrates, science and technology scholars should focus on supposedly "unhistoric," intimate moments of habit creation and the unintended use of personal electronics.[77]

How can we write a history of the playback speed feature while closely attending to both the ways screens might damage the user's body and the forgotten histories of blind users teaching themselves to listen to audiobooks faster? How can the very same design feature, much like the refresh function, enable *and* disable? Two moments in the lives of people with disabilities calling for more flexible ways of media consumption can help us begin to tell a very different story about speed watching.

The first moment took place in 1944, when an American boy named Harvey Lauer was a middle school student at the Wisconsin School for the Blind. As recounted by Mills and Sterne, Lauer's teacher assigned several chapters of a talking book, *Ivanhoe*, as a supplement to their braille textbook. Overwhelmed by the workload, Lauer and several of his classmates were "scheming about ways to speed through the night's reading."[78] When their teacher refused to lend them an older phonograph player, the speed of which could be tweaked, they "hacked" the classroom record player instead. Years later, when Lauer was active in the National Federation of the Blind, he learned that "these sorts of hacks had been taking place at state institutions across the United States, where blind students everywhere longed for the return of variable speed turntables to control the rate of their reading."[79]

By telling Lauer's story, Mills and Sterne uncover the ways in which such an unhistoric moment of an adolescent insight intersects with longer histories of time compression and expansion in audio recording. In the early 1970s, Lauer was one of the test subjects for the Varispeech, a so-called time compression device that converted recorded sound into a stored signal, which could then be sampled at a rate determined by the user "without any change in pitch or loss of intelligibility."[80] Despite the short-lived success of Varispeech, it proved pivotal in turning blind readers into both test subjects and consumers for commercial time-stretching machines.

These histories remind us that aural speed listening can be pushed to the extreme more efficiently than speed watching. While even the most experienced speed watcher cannot fully comprehend a film sped up four or five times, many people who are born blind can train themselves to easily understand speech accelerated far beyond the maximum rate intelligible to sighted people. One study found the absolute limit of comprehension for sighted people is ten syllables per second, while some blind people can comprehend speech sped up to twenty-five syllables per second.[81] This, however, should not be confused with the "super-crip" stereotype attributing remarkable organic or congenital "listening powers" to blind people; instead, non-sighted people develop a different relationship to sonic cues as they navigate an ableist world.[82] As Mills and Slater write, "blind ways of listening are learned through schooling, improvisation, and community protocols for using sound to infer and hack environments built for vision."[83] Thanks to a lifelong process of learning, practicing, and training, blind people become more accustomed to interpret and construe rapid streams of sonic information.

Much like Lauer, who adopted speed listening at a young age, deaf philosopher Teresa Blankmeyer Burke's frustration with school led her to train herself in speed-reading as early as she could. In a short essay published in 2016, Burke narrates our second unhistoric moment of habit formation:

> I'm a speedy reader; always have been. (It's a family trait that goes back at least five generations.) I have used speed-reading as a disability accommodation strategy since I was a kid in elementary school before I had the label to put on it. At the beginning of the school year, I would read through all of my textbooks during the first week or so, then would use that information as *scaffolding* for retrieving more information. At that time, in the pre-internet days, this meant checking out library books on those subjects. Read faster, read more, was how this hard of hearing kid stayed on top of things.[84]

What Burke describes is not a technological hack à la Lauer, but rather a bureaucratic and logistical one: the ability to read through a year's worth of homework in two months, thanks to her mother's job as a librarian. Her choice of the verb "scaffolding" helps us to further develop crip theories of learning and retention. In psychology, scaffolding is a metaphor for how we attain knowledge, one opposed to the view of the brain as a bin (which implies a limitation of space and lack of structure).[85] Some prefer scaffolding as a concept because it shows our brains aren't limited in what they can know. Knowledge needs only a foundation, a scaffold, to build on. Scaffolding therefore opens a more flexible, ever-changing understanding of knowledge formation that supports multiple modes of media consumption. For Burke, this process took the shape of acceleration and compression, preparing for the school year as soon as it began.

Despite the many differences between them, Burke's and Lauer's investments in enhancing speed and comprehension unfold a different set of motivations than Rezab's. For many deaf and blind students, speed-reading affords a flexibility otherwise omitted from an ableist curriculum.[86] This echoes Maria Elena Cepeda's notion that "crip time is uncertain time," as it obeys an episodic nature that abruptly shifts between remission and paralysis.[87] Not knowing "what's coming around the corner," people with disabilities are forced to hack time in ways both similar to but different from overworked, able-bodied subjects. More often than not, media scholars employ the framework of crip time to commend the potential benefits of slowing down or leaving the rat race behind. What can be more useful, however, is "to consider the benefits—or even the necessity, for some—of cripping [time] by calibrating speed and intensity, slowness and rest."[88] These accounts recast the human eye not as a motor but as part of a bodymind with multiple, albeit oft-denied, limitations.

Reframing speed watching around "scaffolding" (Burke) and "calibration" (Cepeda) can complicate the prevalent notion of time hacking. In this retelling, the need for speed is not a result of cognitive capitalism and the demands it places on human bodies. Rather, it is a coping mechanism in a world in which people with disabilities are forced to dedicate immeasurable energy and time to secure the basic accommodations they need. Returning to Burke, she described having to write close to two hundred emails in order to locate and vet a local interpreter for an academic lecture she was asked to give: "It isn't being deaf that's the issue, it is all the time that it takes!"[89]

Even when limited, the ability to speed watch ASL or videos with closed captions opens up new worlds of equality and pleasure. Yet, following Burke, it is important to note that the very features hyped by Netflix and other tech companies as accessibility tools often imply new demands on the time of disabled users. Whenever an interface changes, existing technologies such as screen readers and voice recognition software need to be recalibrated and perhaps replaced in order to remain compatible. As disability scholars Ellen Samuels and Elizabeth Freeman explain, "every time new course software is adopted or an email system is updated, many disabled users must spend additional tedious hours figuring out how to use it with their adaptive tech, if the new platforms are even usable (often they are not, despite legal requirements in the United States)."[90] This, once again, highlights the tension between acceleration and latency in a cultural and technological ecosystem of upgrades and planned obsolescence.

While deeply needed, the shift to self-customizable media players also forces users with disabilities into a surveillance ecosystem in which their behavior is constantly tracked by tech companies like Netflix, Google, or Apple, extending ableist historical lineages of utilizing such users as test subjects without paying them or acknowledging their contribution to the final product.[91] A recent study of wearable hearing technologies, for example, found that applications specifically designed for use outside of health care facilities rely on "users who send data and information on their individual hearing experiences, needs, and wishes to audiologists, doctors, hearing aids producers, and third parties."[92] Unlike hearing people, who can choose between multiple platforms and apps or (at least theoretically) decide to limit their use of technology, deaf and hard-of-hearing people often face a medical-industrial complex pushing them to deploy new hearing technologies.[93] In those cases, opting out from surveillance is more challenging or even impossible.[94]

The additional demand on one's time is also made worse by the notions of "perpetual temporal debt" and "temporal poverty" prevalent among people with mental and physical disabilities.[95] Designer and disability activist Alex Haagard, who has a chronic illness that leads to constant exhaustion and fatigue, writes: "I've come to realize that even when the barriers of physical space are rendered nonexistent, and when digital space is configured as accessibly as possible, with captioning and bathroom breaks and a cameras-optional policy, as long as a space is fixed in time, it remains fundamentally inaccessible to me."[96] Haagard draws our attention to how design features such as the short-lived Twitter's "Fleets"—which allowed users to create time-limited posts that disappear after twenty-four hours—often not only are incompatible with screen readers at the time of launch, but also ignore "the fundamental inaccessibility of a feature that is designed to disappear after a single day."[97] Once again, this temporal poverty results not from the supposed slowness of a body considered disabled, but rather from the need to negotiate offline and online worlds built on ableist notions of imagined users. So blind users might in fact be capable of faster listening than sighted people, but the need to update their assistive technologies and changing their screen readers to be compatible with new features is time-consuming, unpaid, and unrecognized. This is all the more onerous for chronically ill people accustomed to pacing as a way of life, shifting between periods of hyperproductivity and flare-ups necessitating rest.

The world Haagard describes is that of "chrononormativity," or the ableist conception of life stages as linear and oriented toward productivity. Coined by Freeman in 2010, the concept of chrononormativity critiques the temporal systems that, governing "invisibly," determine whether one is a productive citizen or a costly burden on those who are yet to be disabled.[98] Chrononormativity is based on a series of ableist assumptions, such as one's ability to avoid or ignore fatigue, work eight or more hours a day, and employ full muscular and cognitive control throughout the work hours. It denies and ignores the demands involved in negotiating life as a person with disabilities in an ableist world. Instead of calibration and pacing, chrononormativity applies such medical categories as prognosis, remission, recurrence, chronicity, and terminality. It produces and sustains an illusion of causality and certainty that disability activists, writers, and scholars have long challenged.

Much like Burke and Haagard, American artist Joseph Grigely, who became deaf at the age of ten, is invested in making these invisible demands more legible. To achieve this, he maintains an extensive archive of his conversations and requests for accommodation, organizing them into installations of varying sizes. Spanning several decades and over two thousand notes, letters, and emails, his body of work explores what he calls "access math," which, in his case, amounts to an average of six hours per week.[99] Assuming a forty-hour work week, Grigely estimates more than six working years of his life "have been spent in unpaid and largely unacknowledged activism ... and it doesn't include the time I was too depressed or angry to be very useful or productive as a human being."[100] Due to access math, disabled people are often required to be more productive, overworked, and faster than those who are not required to dedicate time to medical checkups, securing accommodations, navigating the disabling inferno known as the US health insurance system, or locating a pharmacy where they can purchase prescription drugs.[101]

While Grigely's work doesn't directly engage with speed watching, it highlights the constant temporal negotiations imposed on people with disabilities. It also resists the ableist view associating disability with slowness and instead makes manifest the unpaid labor of care that people with disabilities often take upon themselves. It is this exhausting and infuriating context that makes the need for scaffolding and calibration a lifelong necessity. Much like Burke's successful attempt to scaffold her syllabus by speed-reading her homework in advance, speed watching ASL or closed-captioned videos can give deaf viewers the option either to align themselves more closely with ableist time structures or to calibrate their energy according to their ever-changing needs.

Users like Lauer, Burke, or Grigely, however, are often ignored by tech companies. In line with the newspaper articles that associate speed watching with the desire to increase productivity, Netflix executives initially imagined speed watchers somewhat like the sighted, hearing Rezab, rather than a blind or deaf user. As summarized by *Forbes*' Matt Klein, the company's initial motivation had very little to do with disability rights: "How do you increase viewership metrics quarter-over-quarter, year-over-year? Approaching the equation by attempting to increase subscribers is myopic. Saturation is tough. You also can't increase the time frame for people to watch Netflix, there are only so many hours in the day. But what you can do, and what Netflix has done, is shrink the content to fit more of it within subscribers' existing time frames. Same timespan each night, but more content watched, all without growing subscription numbers. Brilliant. For the stock."[102]

Universal design helps us understand how features initially designed for people with disabilities often end up serving a more generalized population of users. This was the case when an assistive technology company starts marketing its products as workplace ergonomics or when closed-captioning, which took years of Deaf activism to realize for broadcast, became "a staple of fitness clubs, airport waiting rooms, and a handy tool for language learners."[103] As these examples demonstrate, disability and activism have shaped mainstream media technologies. In 2023, *Atlantic*'s Devin Gordon reported that "everyone watches TV with the subtitles on," a trend he attributed to the popularity of text-based videos on TikTok, the global success of "foreign language" films like Bong Joon Ho's *Parasite* (2020), and the rise of television shows like *Industry* (HBO, 2022) where a diverse cast with multiple accents rapidly fire technical jargon.[104]

Closed captions, however, were not always embraced by streaming companies. In fact, Netflix's decision to market the playback speed feature in terms of accessibility is particularly suspicious when contrasted with its 2010 attempt to dismiss a lawsuit filed by the National Association of the Deaf (NAD). Three years after the company launched its streaming service, the lawsuit argued that the Americans with Disabilities Act (ADA) applies to Netflix and other online businesses.[105] Dismissing this claim, Netflix argued in court that it should be excluded from the ADA as it "applies only to physical places and therefore could not apply to website-only businesses."[106] The District Court of Massachusetts ultimately sided with NAD, and as a result Netflix and other streaming platforms were required to provide closed-captioning to ensure equal access to the deaf and hard-of-hearing communities.

The lawsuit was a milestone in disability activism. Shortly after Netflix lost its legal battle in 2012, the Disability Rights Education and Defense Fund's directing attorney, Arlene Mayerson, stated: "The court has ensured that the ADA stays relevant as much of our society moves from Main Street to the

Internet. Netflix's argument that the neighborhood video store is covered by the ADA, but it, with its over 20 million subscribers, is not, was soundly rejected by the Court."[107]

Almost a decade later, the very same conglomerate that fought to dismiss a lawsuit representing over fifty million deaf and hard-of-hearing Americans strategically approached the National Association of the Blind to roll out its playback speed feature. By collaborating with disabled users, Netflix reversed a standing trend: Instead of marketing an accessibility feature to a mainstream audience, a feature designed for the "average," sighted user has been reintroduced as an accessibility feature for blind and deaf people. Aimed at maximizing profit, this act of cripwashing proved effective at silencing the critique coming from Hollywood and erasing the longer history of Netflix's resistance to the ADA.

If, as Mills argues, "disability capital" is historically the product of using disabled people such as Lauer as test subjects for new technologies, more recently it has been transformed into an "assistive pretext, whereby disability serves as a precursor and pretense—a justification for research funding, or the test market for a technology that is ultimately directed elsewhere."[108] A growing number of studies show that web designers assume users "to be white, male, abled, English-speaking, middle-class U.S. citizens, unless specified otherwise."[109] Yet users who occupy the "otherwise" category are often pushed to the foreground when companies like Apple, Google, or Netflix opt to promote controversial design innovations.

It isn't just that Netflix subscribers—whatever their dis-/ability status might be—owe a historical debt to deaf Americans who took the company to court and to those blind students who hacked their record players almost a century ago. An ongoing lineage of disability activism deepens our understanding of media consumption and interface design as ever-changing negotiations between uncertain, unpredictable bodies and those who create stories and works of art.

ON *CRIP TIME* (2018) AND COLLECTIVE ACCESS

Scaffolding, time hacking, data extraction—speed watching is a means serving many ends. The power to accelerate, while a survival tool for some users, offers others an empowering sense of agency. This technique can serve the logic of cognitive capitalism and digital debility, which force themselves on disabled and able bodies alike. But the tensions I highlight also reveal speed watching's subversive potential. If the previous section centered differently abled media consumers, this final section widens the focus to include disabled filmmakers and video artists. This will show how the negotiation of playback speed can be incorporated into an aesthetic form, while also moving us away from an individualized model of both production and consumption. Instead of an imagined conflict between a single, "genius" filmmaker and an impatient consumer, the works explored below embrace a more collective approach to access.

Experimental and avant-grade filmmakers such as Michael Snow, Pipilotti Rist, and collaborators Rebecca Baron and Douglas Goodwin have long toyed with the plasticity of moving images by accelerating the playback speed *ad absurdum*.[110] As I have explained elsewhere, these joyful experiments included the use of superimposition to condense Snow's seminal *Wavelength* (1967) into *WVLNT: Wavelength for Those Who Don't Have the Time* (2003), a fifteen-minute hallucination that brings together acceleration and saturation.[111] Baron and Goodwin's *Lossless* series (2008), five short films exploring the materiality of the digital and its source code, is another example of the creative potential of playback speed. Instead of a low-resolution copy of the original, Baron and Goodwin appropriate canonical films such as Maya Deren's *Meshes of the Afternoon* (1943) in a way that makes them "gainful" rather than "lossless": "through various techniques of digital disruption—compression, file-sharing, the removal of essential digital information—they reveal the gain of a 'new' media, full of material forms ripe for aesthetic sleuthing."[112] Much like *WVLNT*, the result has a mesmerizing, surprising allure.

In *Lossless #5*, for example, a water ballet crafted by the famed Busby Berkeley is compressed into an organic mitosis (see fig. 2.1). The ghostly three-minute work achieves what Berkley strove for: converting human bodies into an integrated circuit of endless movement. The bird's-eye view and the soft focus generate an image of an organism coming to life in a way that simultaneously distorts and distills the original film's achievement of complete and seamless synchronization.

It is this seamlessness that speed watching promises to maintain. Rather than a clunky DVD, a snowy VHS tape, or a flammable filmstrip passing through a projector, speed watching skips frames to assure the viewer that one can hack time without paying a price; it recasts reduction as intensification. This sense of "gainfulness" is crucial for an understanding of compression techniques through the lens of critical disability studies. By compressing canonical films, Baron and Goodwin remind us that the same footage and soundtrack could be used to reveal an entirely different authorial intent. Their short works connect speed watching to remix culture and its logic of appropriation and playfulness. Instead of fetishizing a (false) notion of the pure viewing experience, these

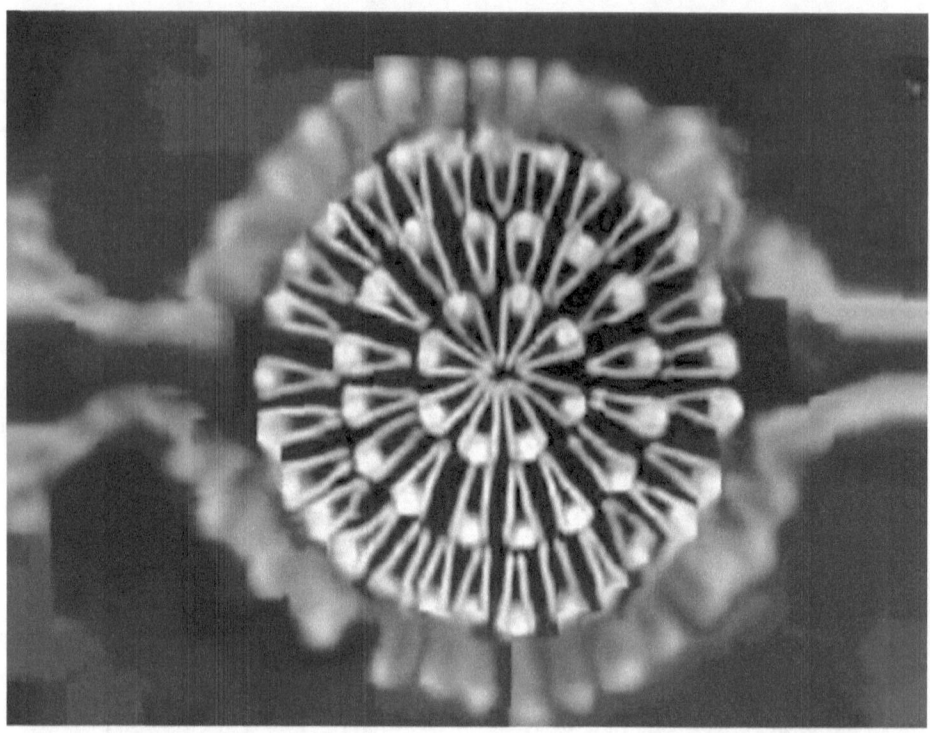

FIG. 2.1 A still image from *Lossless #5*, depicting a bird's-eye view of dozens of synchronized swimmers in mid-act. The swimmers are organized in three circles, surrounded by a blurry halo. Courtesy of Rebecca Baron and Douglas Goodwin.

artists rejoice in the multiplicity of interpretations, shapes, and temporalities afforded by moving images.

This critique of a stable authorial intent that must be preserved vis-à-vis highly specific viewing rituals is further developed in Caroline Lazard's CRIP TIME (2018), which brings scaffolding and calibration into our history of speed. As such, the reading I offer below is in dialogue with Rangan's reading of Jordan Lord's *Shared Resources* (2021).[113] If, in Rangan's account, Lord was able to introduce "baked-in access" into a personal documentary centering on his family by creatively using accessibility features such as open captions and burned-in audio description, Lazard strategically employs durational techniques such as the long shot and fragmentation in CRIP TIME. In both cases, these filmmakers challenge storytelling conventions in ways that celebrate repetition, latency, and ambiguity.

Lazard, an American artist who is chronically ill, works across a range of media including photography, performance, sculpture, video art, and the written word. Lazard is a founding member of Canaries, a collective of women-identified, femme-presenting, and gender-nonconforming artists living with autoimmune conditions and other chronic illnesses, which has exhibited projects and screenings since 2015. The group's name references "canaries in the coal mine," a shorthand for those whose sensitivities are early indicators of adverse conditions in the environment.[114] In a 2022 interview, Lazard described this collective mode of production as a way to negotiate the perils of chronic illness: "As a group of chronically ill people, each of us was moving through these cycles of wellness and unwellness.... Oftentimes, when one person didn't feel well enough to work, another person would be able to. It was about maintaining this *hydraulic system of labour* that comes from collectivity."[115]

This "hydraulic system" ties the calibration associated with crip temporality to cooperative ideas of rest, healing, and community building. Lazard's decade-long collaborations—including their recent *Notes from the Panorama* (2022), which I studied in chapter 1—can help us think of pacing as a *communal*, rather than an individual, survival technique.[116] In Lazard's example, one person can slow down while another speeds up in order to ensure continuity when faced with pain, fatigue, and uncertainty. This mode of creation echoes ideas of "access intimacy" explored by Rangan, Mia Mingus, and Leah Lakshmi Piepzna.[117] What these disability scholars offer is an understanding of access "for the sake of love, community, and connection," where it is no longer an individual responsibility or regulatory demand, but rather an opportunity to create "moments when we are pleasantly surprised and feel seen."[118] Theirs is a collective call to reframe the alleged conflict between authorial intent and the conditions under which people with varying experiences and embodiments interact with works of art. While Lazard's works have been exhibited in world-renowned museums and galleries, they are also made available through Vimeo and on the artist's personal website, inviting viewers to interact with the works on their own terms. Within the New Disability Arts movement, this is part of a "disability minimalism" inviting the audience to activate the work and their body:[119] "The visual vocabulary of my work has become more and more reduced, and I think that change reflects a change in me as an artist; I'm less concerned with performing competency in an ableist world. It's also an attempt to circumvent the ableist insistence of the visual in the realm of art. There are many ways to register and experience artworks. My practice has become more responsive to the audience and to the site of reception."[120]

FIG. 2.2 A still image from Carolyn Lazard's CRIP TIME, depicting a human hand holding red pills above seven daily pill organizers. Courtesy of Carolyn Lazard.

Lazard's and Canaries' works reject the normative ideas of the universal spectator and, instead, attend to the differences between human bodies. Within this framework, Lazard's CRIP TIME could be read as an open invitation to practice and explore compression, redundancy, waiting, repetition, and other nonlinear temporalities. Shot on HD video, this ten-minute film consists of a static frame depicting an embroidered tablecloth and a weekly pill organizer separated into daily compartments (see fig. 2.2). As Lazard's video caption describes, "The labels on the organizer have been partially worn off through repeated use. A set of brown hands with gold nail polish emerges from the top of the frame and begins to separate and open the compartments. As hands open the bottles, the interiors of the bottles are made visible to the camera."[121]

Throughout its duration, not much happens. To that extent, CRIP TIME, much like Snow's WVLNT, is an endurance test. It asks the viewer to patiently watch a long shot while letting go of their inherent desire for narrative, causality, and character development. Many viewers might choose to speed watch this work. Such compression, however, will result in the creation of an entirely new work, since CRIP TIME is a careful study of the temporal experience of a body whose ongoing existence depends on pharmaceutical products. Slowly and methodically filling up containers labeled "Morning," "Noon," "Evening," and "Bedtime" reveals a different relationship with time. Instead of chrononormativity, with its reliance on linear sense of progression, the muscle memory guiding these hands is the product of repetition. The medications themselves, while remaining unknown to all but those fellow patients who might identify their color and texture based on their own medical regimens, tell the story of endless waiting rooms, medical appointments, insurance claims, and hours lost to side effects, symptoms, exhaustion, as well as temporal (and fiscal) debt. While the data contained in CRIP TIME could be easily extracted in 2× or even 3× playback speed, its call for affective embodiment by which the user's discomfort and boredom are strategically invoked is achieved via framing and pacing. When watched on Vimeo, the viewer can play this work at different speeds, implying that cripping time should not be confused with slowing it down.

While the hands rapidly move across the different organizers, the audio track cuts against the anxiety that medications and sickness might produce. With its quiet, repetitive clunking of opening and closing plastic bottles and organizers, the sonic effect resembles Autonomous Sensory Meridian Response (ASMR) clips designed to soothe and help viewers unwind.[122] Without dialogue or soundtrack, these sounds are simultaneously pleasant and stressful, and this tension imbues the work with a disturbing, uncanny quality.

CRIP TIME is invested in what Liat Ben-Moshe calls "epistemic humility": "the process of knowing what you don't know and of maintaining humility about the knowledge you do have, especially in regards to others' experiences."[123] Lazard strategically leaves the following questions open: Can we assume that the person arranging the pills is also the patient to whom these pills were prescribed?[124] What medical condition are these pills prescribed for? Are the pills effective in treating this condition? Do they have side effects? Are the side effects worse than the medical condition being treated? Not being able to answer any of these questions leaves the viewer in a state of disorientation.

These open questions are crucial in reconceptualizing access apart from compliance, technological fix, or standardization. They help us think of accessibility not as a replica aiming for clarity and coherence but rather as "access to the incoherency of the experience of art."[125] For Lazard, this rejection of a narrow definition of accessibility is crucial for collective work: "There are so many incredible disabled artists who are thinking through definitions of accessibility that don't necessarily evolve from Western frameworks of rationality or intelligibility, but are focused rather on the idea of being together, of collectivity and care, grappling with the real challenges of accessibility rather than this sanitized idea of transparency."[126] This is in line with John Lee Clark's "Against Access," where he forcefully rejects the normative understanding of access as simplifying a work of art to its most tangible elements.[127] Instead of asking how we can "make it more accessible," Clark urges his readers to ask, "What feels beautiful?"[128] Speed watching, with its libidinal and cognitive pleasures, can open up a new terrain of beauty.

With this call for ambiguity, subjectivity, and openness, CRIP TIME is a durational work that could be watched at various playback speeds. When accelerated, it draws our attention to the negotiation between speed and immersion without embracing a moral stand claiming one mode of engagement is inferior to others. With its repetitive hand movements and logic of accumulation, CRIP TIME practices "an aesthetic of redundancy" that invites viewers to engage with the film on their own terms.[129] If I choose to speed watch this film, I won't be able to do so without confronting my own affective reactions to sickness: Am I speeding because I'm too anxious, too bored, too uncomfortable to contemplate what life with chronic illness might feel like? Or, as many disabled spectators might ask themselves, am I too triggered by a realistic depiction of the weekly routine I know all too well? CRIP TIME does not force us to watch it at its intended speed, but it reveals a mostly unconscious decision-making process. Employing access as an "aesthetic practice," Lazard moves beyond ideas of a stable meaning that must be extracted at a predetermined pace.[130]

This work also plays with the idea of access as a sacrifice that able-bodied spectators are asked to make for the sake of others. In a reversal of this assumed dynamic of power and powerlessness, CRIP TIME is a film easily understood by chronically ill people, and it is the able-bodied spectator who might be in need of access—to more context, more explanations, more scaffolds that can help them make sense of what is depicted.

In this sense, CRIP TIME challenges one of the main motivations of speed watching: the pleasure of finitude and the dopamine rush of completion. While the ten-minute film could be consumed in half the time, the activity it describes is repetitive by nature. Weekly pill organizers, as their name suggests, must be refilled on a regular basis. In this sense, the actions it chronicles will truly end only when the patient dies. Lazard thus confronts us with an adulthood of dependency, where a temporal structure of perpetual repetition has come to replace the illusion of predictable, sickness-free future when one can fully control one's body, pacing, and creativity.

A disability-oriented theory of speed watching is useful as it highlights the tension between a design feature meant to provide a sense of agency and the crip temporalities of pacing. At the end of CRIP TIME, the daily compartments are closed up and stacked on their side, Sunday through Monday. The scaffolding part has ended, a new week is about to begin. Even with this careful preparation, its time is forever uncertain; a calibration is needed.

Conclusion

The digital super-user described by Rezab is only one possible interpretation of the popularity of speed watching. That this prominent stereotype of a viewer who treats their body like a relentless machine owes a historical debt to disability activists is one of the many ironies explored in this book. In the reading offered above, the super-user is not an accelerationist whose body and its limitations are both universalized and denied by capitalist demand; it is also the blind or deaf user accustomed to listening or reading faster than the imaginary sighted and hearing user.

The struggle around the ideal playback speed is over a century old, dating back to early film projection and its relation to danger and mortality. Writing in 1916, Münsterberg was deeply concerned that cinematic speed would wreak havoc on modern society. "The subtle sensitiveness of the young mind may suffer from the rude contracts between the farces and the passionate romances which follow with benumbing speed in the darkened house. The possibilities of psychical infection and destruction cannot be overlooked," he warned his readers.[131] Over a century later, this alarmist account of the movie house seems archaic. The kids, who now speed watch at home or on their way to school, are more likely to find "the darkened house"—with its predetermined pace and a single screen, rather than multiple ones—to be too slow and demanding. Domestic spectatorship now offers speed watching, second-screen viewing (e.g., watching Netflix on a smart TV while browsing TikTok on one's phone), and features like autoplay, skip intro, and play something, which I explore in the next chapter.

With its connotation of efficiency and reliance on training, speed watching provides a glimpse into the future of cognitive capitalism. It can be seen as nothing more than a model of labor and value extraction that recasts neurobiological limitations as mountains to be conquered. For decades, the celebration of a pure cinematic experience has been set up in binary opposition to accessibility. The importance of speed-reading by the deaf and hard of hearing and of speed listening by blind users complicates this understanding and opens up alternative histories, motivations, and pleasures.

The next chapter, which focuses on the autoplay feature, pushes this argument further by taking a close look at the temporality and affect of watching many hours of content via continuous screen engagement. This analysis once again moves the discussion from questions of storytelling (genres, the star system, aesthetics) to questions of agency and control. Netflix asks its subscribers,

"Are you still watching?" as part of a cognitive capitalism that sees the eye and the brain as essential to the human motor and separated from the rest of the human body. Declaring a war on sleep, the autoplay habituates users to ignore their biological needs. By studying the history of automating video on streaming platforms and advancing a theory of the unbingeable, I further unpack the multiple meanings of access. How can the disorientation explored in television shows such as *I May Destroy You* (BBC and HBO, 2020) reorient users to resist the sedative, built-in power of the autoplay? And should we again read this resistance as a much-needed mode of self-preservation?

AUTOMATING TRAUMA

On Autoplay and the Unbingeable

I made Netflix automatically play the next episode of the show you are watching. Sorry?
—SOFTWARE ENGINEER AND TECH FOUNDER ROBERT SWEENEY'S LINKEDIN PROFILE

In 2016, Netflix added a feature to its interface: previews autoplay, also known as "inline playback," which starts playing a preview when you hover your cursor over a thumbnail image of a film or a show that catches your eye or, on some devices, simply open the home page. The company explained that autoplay was designed to make it "faster and easier for our members to find titles tailored to their tastes."[1] Yet not everyone appreciated this new feature, and the inability to disable it led to a backlash. In 2019, a Netflix subscriber named Melissa Bryant started a petition calling for the streaming giant to remove its "previews autoplay" or at least to let users decide whether to use this feature.[2] "On some platforms, you don't even have to start scrolling. The moment you log into the application, Netflix begins playing their latest-and-greatest trailer," Bryant complained.[3]

This might sound like a minor inconvenience easily solved by muting your laptop, phone, or smart TV. Still, according to Bryant and the 124,351 supporters who signed her petition, it is more harmful than it seems. "As Netflix continues to release more and more hard-hitting shows, their unstoppable previews have gone from annoying to triggering," the petition explained. "Netflix's new shows, *Making a Murderer* and *Don't F**k with Cats: Hunting an Internet Killer* include content that is graphic, sickening, and real. It plays unprompted for people who have no interest—and it can't be turned off."[4] Bryant went on to propose a solution: disabling advertisements for "frequently-triggering content" like murder, sexual assault, animal cruelty, and suicide. Expressing similar notions of discomfort, other Netflix subscribers created browser extensions specifically designed to block previews autoplay.[5]

By writing code, taking to social media, and starting a petition, these users were pushing against an alarming trend media scholar Nicolette Little describes as "platform violence."[6] She introduced this term in her analysis of Facebook Memories, which automatically shows users photos and posts they uploaded to their account months or years earlier. Based on interviews with domestic abuse survivors who unexpectedly encountered photos of their abusers via Memories, Little demarcates this algorithmic feature as triggering and, in some cases, "re-traumatizing."[7] For "user-survivors," these old photos and posts effectively "extend abusers' intimidation back into their lives" by "unintentionally supporting perpetrators' aims: to scare, isolate, and punish their targets."[8] By focusing on the non-average user of social media, Little demonstrated how a feature designed to deepen attachment to the brand by reminding people of their personal archives can in fact produce negative and painful reactions.

A Netflix subscriber can never fully predict which preview will automatically play once they open the home page. More disturbingly, platform violence can become more pervasive once the content library from which a video is selected extends far beyond the user's private archive. A design feature like previews autoplay can abruptly transform a pleasurable experience aimed at relaxation or distraction into an anxiety-inducing, agonizing encounter with one's "ghosts."[9] Applying Little's theoretical framework to streaming platforms, this chapter studies autoplay as part of an amalgam of design features that, for some users, produces debilitating effects.

Netflix is not the only company automating video streams. To fully understand how autoplay has come to shape on-demand culture, we must first distinguish between its three prominent variations: *embedded or default autoplay*, which automatically plays videos or audio once a user opens a new tab or enters a website, leading to the rise of ad blockers in the early 2000s;[10] *postplay*, which automatically plays the next item in a content library as soon as the previous one ends, a feature embedded into Netflix, Spotify, YouTube, Hulu, and countless other services since the early 2010s; and *inline playback*, which automatically plays a video when a cursor hovers over a thumbnail, as in the case of Netflix's controversial previews autoplay.

Each of these variations potentially excludes users with disabilities. The default autoplay, for example, is incompatible with screen readers, pushing leading standardization bodies to recommend not using it in HTML5 and to disable it on commercial platforms.[11] As explained by Michael McWatters, director of product design at HBO Max, since screen readers audibly announce everything on the page, the noise of the video drowns out any other sound, making default autoplay "the equivalent of someone scrawling in Sharpie over the book they're trying to read."[12] Automating the play of video or audio effectively prevents screen readers from helping non-sighted users to navigate the platform—including finding the setting menu and the button that can disable this feature (assuming such button exists to begin with).[13] Default, automated ads, previews, or videos are not only notoriously annoying. They also transform many websites into gated digital spaces inaccessible to anyone who uses a screen reader.

This chapter, however, focuses on postplay and inline playback as case studies of digital debility because these features push users to ignore their physical and emotional needs. This happens in two distinct ways. First, previews autoplay unwittingly exposes subscribers to potentially triggering content, from sexual violence and animal cruelty to cannibalism, without warning and without providing an easy way to opt out. Second, the postplay feature, which automatically plays the next episode without requiring users to engage with the interface, conditions users to prolong their viewing sessions by "binge-racing" through entire seasons in one sitting or by quickly moving from one cliffhanger to the next, even when the content is disturbing, violent, and anxiety-inducing.[14] This not only prevents or, at the very least, inhibits the ability to process difficult feelings; it also conditions users to ignore their physical and emotional needs and limitations.[15] As I will show, the ability to disable autoplay was a late addition to popular interfaces and resulted from users' complaints and the growing popularity of browser extensions programmed to block the automated play of videos.

Those who pay the highest price for autoplay are non-average users who suffer from post-traumatic stress disorder. My analysis draws on public accounts by sexual assault survivors whose PTSD symptoms, including avoidance, catastrophizing, intrusive thoughts, and trouble sleeping, were triggered by autoplay. Because these chronic conditions are invisible, they are often ignored by both media and disability scholars.[16] By blurring the lines between disability and ability, these user-survivors open up conversations about "whose needs are considered access needs."[17] The fight to make Netflix's interface more inclusive by allowing users to disable autoplay demonstrates how access is commonly understood as a "checklist" of demands.[18] Adding an option to disable a feature, however, is not the only way to enact change. In fact, as Kelly Fritsch reminds us, "such efforts [to get people in] remain incomplete without a critical assessment of how those exclusions first came to be and how they continue to function."[19] By closely studying how autoplay has come to shape media consumption in the past decade, this chapter explores how users, creators, and platforms promote and negotiate various definitions of access.

Using Netflix as a case study, this analysis explores two possible solutions to the problem of platform violence: Little's "trauma-informed design," which pushes companies to customize and tweak products to make them more inclusive, and disability scholar J. Logan Smilges' "access thievery," which draws on the idea that access can be a form of attack.[20] In *Crip Negativity* (2023), Smilges argues that non-average users should hack systems or steal access rather than wait for institutions or companies to accommodate their needs.[21] When employed with respect to Netflix's autoplay, this can take the form of downloading a browser extension to block it or of actively seeking streaming platforms that reject addictive design. Exploring these different solutions to platform violence, I crip our relationship with mainstream media platforms and ask which platforms and content are worth fighting for.

Like every other feature I explore in this book, autoplay can be debilitating or helpful, depending on the context. The postplay feature, for example, offers multiple benefits: It can deepen our engagement with fictional worlds by eliminating ads, waiting time, and elements such as credits and opening sequences; it helps users identify and savor the recurring tropes, aesthetic choices, and musical cues of their favorite shows; it can expose users to new content they might not otherwise choose to watch; and it supports the spectatorial model of bingeing, which has proven to be a powerful distraction from pain, depression, and anxiety.[22]

With Netflix touting over 232 million subscribers in 2023, the growing attachment to commercial streaming platforms makes their design decisions more significant.[23] When so much of the cultural conversation takes place online, users are less and less likely to opt out of using Netflix, YouTube, or similar services. This attachment, as I will show, is produced and sustained by addictive design tools aimed at increasing the user's "dwell time" and other "captivation metrics."[24] By supporting a platform that "flows by default," autoplay produces digital debility experienced as addiction, lethargy, and muscular pain.[25]

"Our Most Successful Feature": How the Autoplay Changed Streaming

In 2010 Robert Sweeney, then a software engineer in the Xbox team at Microsoft, met a Netflix recruiter. "At the time I was a Netflix's subscriber, doing their DVD-by-mail, so I was familiar with the company but didn't really think about them as a tech company," Sweeney told me in an interview I conducted with him in early 2023.[26] "I just thought that they are an old-school mailing DVD company. They recently launched their streaming service, but I wasn't very interested in working there till I met their recruiter, who emphasized their commitment to creative freedom and personal accountability—which was very different from what life was like in Microsoft at the time." Frustrated with Microsoft's "bureaucratic and highly hierarchal" management philosophy, Sweeney joined Netflix in the hope of being a part of a company with "a lot more freedom to experiment." After introducing its streaming service in 2007, Netflix measured every new design feature using two "key performance indicators" (KPIs): hours watched and retention. The first was based on accumulated streaming time by the platform's subscribers; the latter was defined as the number of subscribers who paid for the service for over ninety consecutive days.

The introduction of streaming proved a watershed moment for on-demand culture, enabling Netflix to convert the viewing experience into an endless source of "data points."[27] Streaming pushed Netflix to reinvent itself as a data-driven tech company instead of a logistics mammoth dependent on the US postal service. It replaced explicit metrics, like the five-star rating system, with implicit behavioral data and used this data to improve its recommendation algorithm.[28] This was achieved by expanding its set of criteria to include not only the micro-tags sorting every title into categories like "genre," "emotional complexity," or "dark ending," but also the day and time in which subscribers signed into the service and whether they paused, rewatched a scene, or skipped forward.[29]

This was not just a technological shift. As Nick Seaver observes, this paradigm shift was part of a broader "captological turn," through which recommendation systems were reframed as "tools for captivation," instead of ways to help people manage increasingly large online catalogues.[30] Drawing on behavioral science, such as B. F. Skinner's theories of reinforcement and conditioning, streaming companies invested millions to make their interfaces into "traps" in which users are likely to stay longer than they intend.[31] The rise of captology aimed at increasing "dwell time," the industry term for the time a person spends in a single session before leaving the website.

The focus on dwell time contributed to radical changes Netflix made to its content library. Soon after the company introduced streaming-on-demand, it started prioritizing serialized content over cinematic titles. Netflix was founded as a service for cinephiles, but the data showed that subscribers tended to watch television shows more often than films. Since 2010, therefore, Netflix has focused its efforts on producing and promoting serialized content, often by pressuring content creators to succumb to the "Netflix stretch," a demand to reimagine a feature film as a multi-episode or even a multi-season show.[32] According to media historian Gina Keating, the economic rationale is clear: "Each TV series produced tens of hours of viewing, compared to the two or three hours for each film—resulting in greater rates of subscriber usage and satisfaction."[33] Furthermore, with the emergence of many competitors, from Amazon Prime and Hulu to Max and Disney+, investing in television shows is a crucial weapon in the streaming wars, as it encourages users to return to Netflix again and again in search of new seasons of beloved programs, enhancing their brand loyalty. This is only one example of how recommendation systems effectively create a feedback loop. By documenting viewing habits and consumption patterns, algorithms gradually change these very same activities. Thus, a service initially marketed as the ideal home for movie lovers turned into the digital equivalent of cable television.[34]

Streaming taught Netflix two important lessons: Its subscribers prefer TV shows over films, and its key performance indicators—retention and hours watched—are closely correlated. The more time subscribers spend on the site, the more likely they are to keep their subscription. The idea that a streaming platform would measure its success based on hours watched might seem obvious, but this is not necessarily the case for a company required to pay internet service providers (ISPs) for broadband, and—until 2022—promising to never sell ads.[35] Initially, Netflix's ideal subscriber might have been someone who signed up, watched one or two titles per month (enough to justify the monthly subscription fee, which was cheaper than a single movie ticket), and didn't require many resources in terms of servers and internet traffic. The story of how this imaginary subscriber turned into a heavy user engaged in "binge-racing"—completing a new series on the same day it is released—cannot be told without close attention to autoplay.

Sweeney's stint at Netflix proved pivotal to this story. Shortly after he was recruited, he was paired with a designer to work on a new feature called "post-play." The goal was simple. Once a subscriber finished watching a movie or an episode, Netflix would invite them to watch something else from its content library. Surprisingly, increasing the number of hours watched was not the only goal of this new feature. Initially, Netflix saw it as a tool for improving A/B testing. By presenting users with various selected recommendations and analyzing which ones they continued to watch, Netflix could better decide which recommendations to roll out to its entire user base. A/B testing has since become crucial to its brand as a data-driven market leader that calls its engineers "innovators" who move "incredibly fast" while building and testing one prototype after another.[36]

In the early days of streaming, improving A/B testing was vital for solving what is known in the streaming industry as the "cold start problem": When a new user tries out the service, the company has no data on their behavior and preferences and therefore cannot provide any personalized recommendations that might get the user hooked and turn them into a returning customer.[37] The common solution is to introduce the biggest hits in the content library, the star-studded films or television shows other users have been watching. Yet the faster a platform can ascribe a taste profile to a user, the faster its recommendation system can spring into action and start producing more personalized results.

As Sweeney stresses, he built the postplay feature in order to recommend cinematic titles from the Netflix library as soon as a user finished watching a title of their choice: "The design for movies was based on the idea of shrinking the credit roll into the top left corner of the screen and show[ing] you three other suggestions of films you could watch that were similar." This initial design minimized decision fatigue by asking subscribers to choose from a small number of algorithmically recommended options. It also turned the user into a de facto Netflix employee. With each click, they trained the algorithm by telling it which recommendation best aligned with their taste preferences. Unlike the now-defunct five-star rating system, which required users to watch a DVD, mail it back, and then log on to the website to rate it (often days or even weeks after they watched the title), autoplay streamlined the feedback loop, enabling the company to instantly compare clicks from different groups of users. This A/B testing paved the way to other forms of personalization, such as using different images and thumbnails based on the user's viewing history or determining the order of recommendations on the home page, leading the company's engineers to publicly announce that "everything is a recommendation!"[38] Within this system, even a "no-choice" like leaving the browser is a data point, as it implies that the recommendations were not accurate enough.

Autoplay, however, didn't come without risks. Once subscribers didn't have to return to the home page or search for the next title to watch, the accuracy of the data collected diminished. Netflix worried its users might fall asleep or leave the room while content continued to play for hours unwatched. To

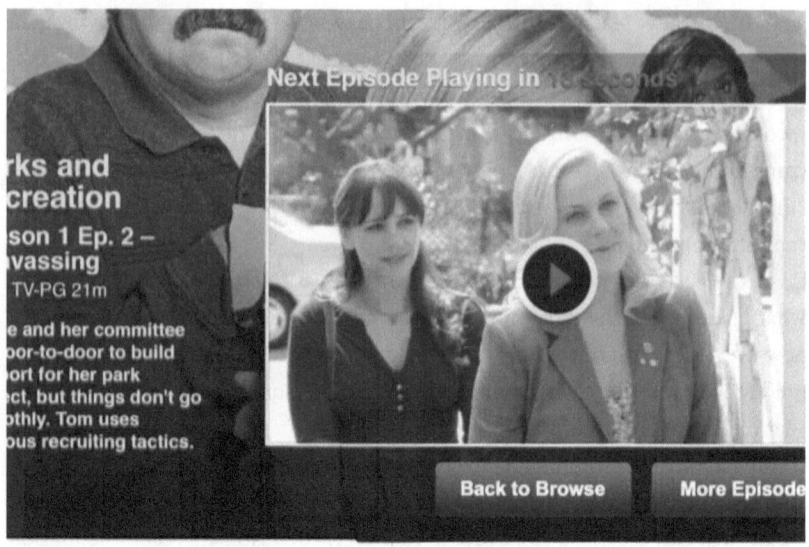

FIG. 3.1 A cropped screenshot of Netflix's initial design of its postplay feature, circa 2013, consisting of a countdown and a thumbnail image from the next episode. (Source: Netflix)

mitigate these concerns, Sweeney and his team added another new feature, "Are You Still Watching?," which prompted the user to engage with the platform after watching two or three consecutive episodes. Taken together, autoplay and Are You Still Watching? introduced a set of negotiations between the interface and its user. While the first produces a sense of passivity, the latter guaranteed that automating video streams wouldn't take a needless financial toll by overloading Netflix's data centers. Much like CAPTCHA and other digital features, Are You Still Watching? is part of a mounting digital ecosystem where human users are required to identify themselves to machines, proving that they aren't bots or AI systems.

As part of the autoplay-supported redesign, Sweeney and his team added a countdown clock and a thumbnail of the next episode, both appearing at either the right side or the bottom of the screen once an episode ended (see fig. 3.1). After testing multiple variants, including five-, ten-, and fifteen-second countdowns, Netflix concluded that fifteen seconds maximized the number of subscribers who chose to continue watching. This was since reduced to first ten and then five seconds as the newness of the feature gave way to diminishing user's waiting endurance.[39] The company also tested variations of the

FIG. 3.2 Netflix's postplay feature as seen on an Apple TV circa 2014, featuring "Play Next Episode" and "More Episodes" buttons, alongside an eleven-second countdown to the next episode, which is presented via a thumbnail image and a plot synopsis. (Source: Netflix)

postplay design, including an Apple TV–supported interface that presented a countdown, a thumbnail, and a plot synopsis of the next episode (see fig. 3.2).

As of 2023, the countdown clock has been replaced with a five-second progress bar simply stating "Next Episode" (see fig. 3.3). The user can also choose to click on a small button called "Watch Credits." However, they are unlikely to do so, as they have become habituated to skipping them (especially because Netflix's credits often include a tedious list of dubbing credits for multiple versions, adding a minute or more to each episode). The user's fear of empty time—whether imagined by the company or real—led Netflix to also introduce features like "Skip Intro" and, as I studied in chapter 2, the ability to adjust playback speed.

According to Netflix senior engineers Carlos Gómez-Uribe and Neil Hunt, the interface is designed to "minimize the amount of time that users spend deciding what content to watch."[40] Netflix aims to achieve the maximum number of "moments of truth"—that is, when a customer chooses to watch a specific title within seconds of logging in.[41] For media scholar Vicente Rodríguez Ortega, the race to minimize decision time resulted in a continuous flow of customized content "that is designed not only to keep users in front of multiple screens, but also to interact with their life rhythms and moods, effectively penetrating their

AUTOMATING TRAUMA   93

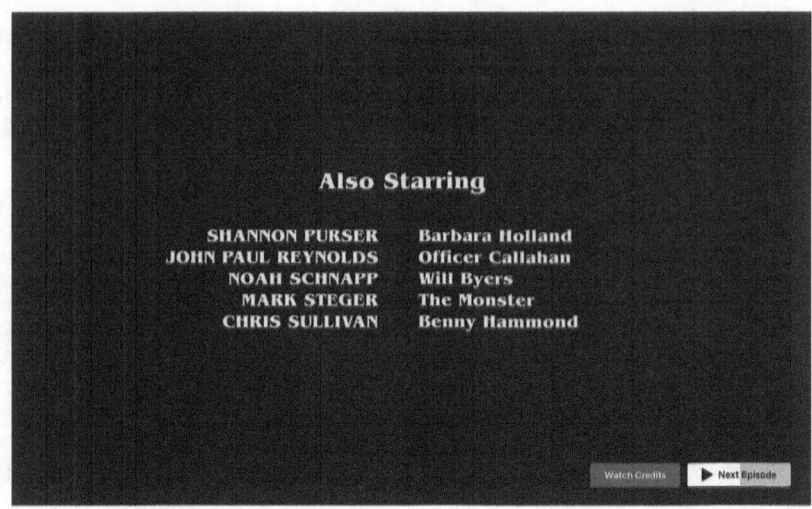

FIG. 3.3 A screenshot of Netflix's postplay in 2023, consisting of a "Next Episode" progress bar of several seconds in the right bottom corner of the screen, as well as a "Watch Credits" button. (Source: Netflix)

everyday and becoming ubiquitous as they navigate the contours of the social fabric."[42] To this end, Netflix not only automated its video streams, but also introduced features like "Downloads for You," which automatically downloads shows that the app infers a user may like to watch while offline. This led Ortega to conclude that Netflix "has almost completely taken users' choices out of the equation."[43] What started with the automation of recommendations in 2011 has developed, over a decade later, into the core business of Netflix. This, for Ortega, implies a future "with no more browsing, searching or even choosing, simply the relentless consumption of the content Netflix curates, 'allegedly,' for each of us."[44] While, as I argued elsewhere, predictive personalization is a promise never fully fulfilled, the company's interface design has been carefully employed to produce and sustain it.[45]

The myth of endless choice and the idea that the Netflix "profile" is a private, intimate diary documenting the user's shifting desires, fantasies, and fears have proved key to the global success of this brand. Netflix exploited that sense of intimacy as a marketing strategy, most famously in a 2017 tweet on its official account: "Love is sharing a password."[46] Years before the company rebranded password sharing as a premium service, it marketed this option as a way to deepen subscribers' relationships by providing one's partner a glimpse into one's algorithmically mediated stream of consciousness. However, algorithmic systems do not offer intimate, in-depth knowledge of each individual user.[47] Instead, they segment users and assign them taste clusters.[48] Impressive feats of calculation and abstraction that they are, algorithms cannot predict which content might be triggering, painful, or re-traumatizing.

Since it was implemented, autoplay has supported a bingeing model hailed in Netflix's marketing campaigns, its tech blog, and its public statements.[49] As described by Netflix CEO Reed Hastings as early as 2011, two years before the company drop-released the first season of *House of Cards* (2013–18), "Netflix's brand for TV shows is really about binge viewing. It is . . . to just get hooked and watch episode after episode. It's addictive, it's exciting, it's different."[50] It is in this early embrace of bingeing that the distinction between hours watched and retention seems to collapse; for Hastings, addictive design is key to the Netflix brand. It is the tension between passivity and activity, between autoplay and Are You Still Watching?, that has made Netflix the market leader in the streaming wars. In 2010, investors evaluated the company at around $10 billion. The figure had grown to $50 billion five years later.[51] This capitalization growth can be attributed in part to the introduction of autoplay in 2011 as part of a redesign of the home page, making it, according to Sweeney, "the most successful feature in the company's history."

Sweeney left Netflix in 2012, a year before the company started pushing binge-watching as its most recognizable spectatorial model. Reflecting on the impact he had on digital media consumption, he told me that "it was years later till it dawned on me how big of an impact it had. All of the other platforms—Hulu, YouTube and HBO—autoplay now because of the work we did at Netflix. . . . I think I invented binge-watching." Yet he has since developed an ambivalence about his time at Netflix. On his LinkedIn page, Sweeney summarizes his tenure at the company as follows: "I made Netflix automatically play the next episode of the show you are watching. Sorry?" When I asked whether his decision to include the word "Sorry?" is ironic, Sweeney replied, "I don't feel a lot of guilt per se because I think it would have been done by somebody. But I don't like that feature. I hate the impact that it had on me and the kids when I think about how much sleep loss has been caused by autoplay and how that is correlated to depression and anxiety and poor work performance and family issues and all sorts of these negative effects." Despite the feature's unprecedented success, Sweeney left the company shortly after it was launched, citing the shift from viewer retention to hours watched as central to his disillusionment: "One of the big reasons I ended up leaving was because that goal we had to get people to watch more Netflix is not a noble goal. It doesn't

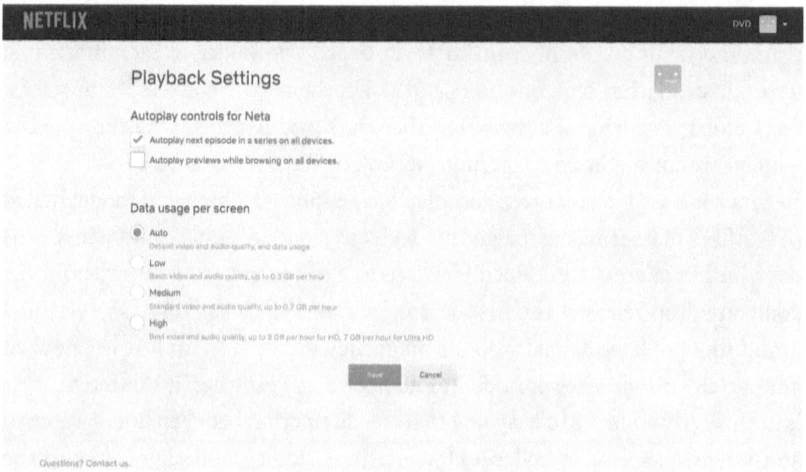

FIG. 3.4 A screenshot of Netflix's playback settings in 2023, where subscribers can disable the postplay and previews autoplay features by clicking a box. (Source: Netflix)

make the world a better place to have people spend more time watching TV." He now supports regulating tech companies, for example, by outlawing autoplay.

Such an attempt at regulating addictive design was recently made by US Senator Josh Hawley of Missouri.[52] Hawley's Social Media Addiction Reduction Technology Act, or the SMART Act, sought to limit the use of "dark patterns" by outlawing autoplay and endless scrolling.[53] As Hawley told *The Verge*, "Big tech has embraced a business model of addiction. Too much of the 'innovation' in this space is designed not to create better products, but to capture more attention by using psychological tricks that make it difficult to look away."[54] While the SMART Act never made it into a law, similar bills and laws have since tried to restrain tech companies' efforts to prolong engagement or upsell services.[55]

Part of the reason these features are so captivating is that they are introduced into the interface as default options. Initially, Netflix subscribers could not disable postplay, making it the new standard of spectatorship. Even once an opt-out was added in January 2014, it was hidden in the settings menu, leaving many subscribers unaware of the change and prompting endless blog posts teaching people how to disable autoplay (see fig. 3.4).[56]

Like Sweeney, other web developers and software engineers faced the autoplay dilemma in the early 2010s. Google-owned YouTube was quick to adopt this feature, which eventually helped make YouTube a key site for the spread of misinformation.⁵⁷ Whistleblower Guillaume Chaslot, a former Google engineer who worked on YouTube's recommendation algorithm, told the *New York Times* that "the idea was to maximize watch time at all cost. To just make it grow as big as possible."⁵⁸ In the mid-2010s, automating content turned YouTube into a platform where users accumulatively watch "a billion hours per day."⁵⁹ While Netflix introduced a model of ad-free "insulated flow," promising endless bingeing via their drop-release model, YouTube used autoplay to display algorithmically selected ads and collect behavioral data, supporting "the $500 billion attention industry."⁶⁰ As I studied elsewhere, YouTube's decision to automate its recommended videos had far-reaching implications, among them an "infodemic" of fake news and COVID denial during the early months of the pandemic and exposing kids and young viewers to graphic violent and pornographic images via the YouTube Kids app.⁶¹

Today, most streaming platforms utilize autoplay. Yet not every video or audio platform has embraced this feature, signaling that digital standardization is an ongoing, multilayered process. Web designer Michael McWatters explains that, after he studied the practice of autoplaying online videos in 2014, he decided not to build the feature into the platform for TED, where he worked at the time.⁶² Later, once he became the director of product design at HBO Max, he brought his autoplay skepticism to the prestigious network. In an essay titled "Autoplay Blues," McWatters clarifies that his aversion results from usability and accessibility issues, since autoplaying videos and ads disrupts screen readers by creating constant noise.⁶³ In his attack, McWatters also lists the issue of forced bandwidth consumption, which pushes users to pay higher fees to stream content they don't choose to consume and forces international websites and companies to pay more for bandwidth.⁶⁴

This growing demand for bandwidth has alarming infrastructural and environmental consequences. As Sweeney himself recounts, one of the concerns surrounding postplay was that, if subscribers used it en masse, it "could potentially melt down the entire internet." Autoplay threatened to further complicate the already tenuous relationship between streaming platforms and internet service providers because it sharply increased the demand for bandwidth and constant connectivity. While the internet did not melt, the bandwidth load caused by streaming proved harmful during the lockdowns of the COVID pandemic, pushing Netflix, YouTube, and other streaming companies to intentionally lower their video resolution.⁶⁵ As recent studies demonstrate, the greenhouse gas emissions attributable to streaming video are on the rise because of the need for more data centers and expanded broadband infrastructure.⁶⁶ While it is hard to calculate precisely the carbon footprint of platforms like Netflix, the scholarly consensus is that video-based platforms are exceedingly taxing for the environment.[67]

Despite its exclusionary and harmful effects, autoplay is here to stay. Dwell time has become both a means *and* an end. The longer a subscriber uses a service, the more data they provide the recommendation system and the less likely they are to cancel their monthly subscription by stopping their automated credit card payments. Users find themselves forced to navigate an addictive digital ecosystem prioritizing prolonged consumption over their mental and physical well-being.[68]

Still, users are more than helpless and passive consumers. By focusing on two case studies—the Netflix high-school drama *13 Reasons Why* (2017–20) and an online petition asking the company to dismantle the previews autoplay—I demonstrate how Netflix subscribers were able to resist the tyranny of default features. That these case studies center around self-described "edge users" who struggle with PTSD, anxiety, and suicidal ideation can help us imagine crip alternatives to the automation of video and audio streams.[69]

"YOU'RE THE SLOWEST ONE YET": ON NETFLIX'S *13 REASONS WHY*

What happens when the narrative and aesthetic conventions aimed at creating a bingeing experience are employed to tell serialized stories about suicidal ideation and "rape culture" targeting young viewers?[70] Netflix's *13 Reasons Why*, the first season of which became "2017's most tweeted show" while causing a heated debate among parents, educators, and mental health specialists, is a useful case study for understanding the history of Netflix's autoplay. The public pushback against the show forced the company to take steps supposedly meant to limit the binge-ability of its four seasons, in order to allow its mostly young viewers the time to process and share their feelings between one episode and the next.[71]

The series, adapted from a 2007 novel by the same name by US author Jay Asher, follows seventeen-year-old Clay Jensen (Dylan Minnette) as he tries to find out why his friend Hannah Baker (Katherine Langford), with whom he was secretly in love, took her own life. In the first season, seven cassette tapes that Hannah recorded shortly before her desperate act detail thirteen reasons that promise to shed some light on the last year of her life. Clay and several other students have access to these tapes, and he is pushed by his peers to listen to them as fast as possible. Listening to Hannah's retelling, however, proves to be a daunting challenge due to the tapes' increasingly disturbing depiction of sexual assault, rape, bullying, and social isolation. Despite its contemporary setting, the show is surprisingly ripe with analog media. In the world of high school rivalry and online bullying, defunct technologies such as the Sony Walkman and cassette tapes enable Clay to break the automated pattern of excessive consumption and, instead, allow him breaks crucial for his grieving and healing.

The irreversibility of Hannah's death is contrasted with the analog potential of rewinding and relistening. The show's obsession with analog media enables its creators to explore ideas of linearity and "finishability." In his paean to the analog, David Sax defines finishability as central for media such as a novel, a magazine, or a vinyl record.[72] For Sax, the ability to get to the end of the story by engaging with a physical object is preferable to the constant stream of digital content, as it provides the satisfaction of a linear progression from beginning to end. Despite the popularity of pandemic memes jokingly declaring, "I finished Netflix," it is impossible to consume an ever-changing, vast content library designed to autoplay similar shows and films. Autoplay denies finishability by delaying it ad infinitum, leading viewers to continue their search for instant satisfaction at the expense of their sleep and well-being.

By indulging in analog nostalgia, *13 Reasons Why* also reminds its young viewers of other material conditions of viewership or listenership they have never encountered, such as the scarcity of material copies (as opposed to the speed and scale of online and smartphone-enabled bullying), the pleasures of tactility (as manifested in Clay's attachment to the paper map left for him by Hannah), and the affordances of a technology like the Walkman, which is able to play and record audio, leaving the visual realm to the listener's imagination.[73]

Despite its investment in careful, deliberately slow modes of consumption, *13 Reasons Why* was initially marketed as a binge-worthy serialized drama. The first season consists of thirteen one-hour episodes, and its promotional posters positioned the "play" icon next to the title to suggest viewers will likely want to continue watching this engaging story, while also invoking the iconic "play" button of the Sony Walkman, targeting older viewers vis-à-vis analog nostalgia (see fig. 3.5). The show itself encourages bingeing by ending each episode with a cliffhanger, making its first season an immediate hit and spurring three more seasons. Its viral success and extensive media coverage also inspired endless memes nudging Clay to "just get it over with"—echoing his friends' pleas to listen to Hannah's tapes faster, as well as a more alarming notion of the kind of bullying that pushed his friend to kill herself. Both fans and television critics agreed that Clay's deliberate slowness was designed to extend the original novel into multiple episodes and seasons. The *New York Times*' Mike Hale called Clay's hesitation to binge-listen to the tapes "unbelievable" and wrote that "it makes no sense as anything but a plot device, and you'll find yourself, like Clay's antagonists, yelling at him to listen to the rest of tapes already."[74]

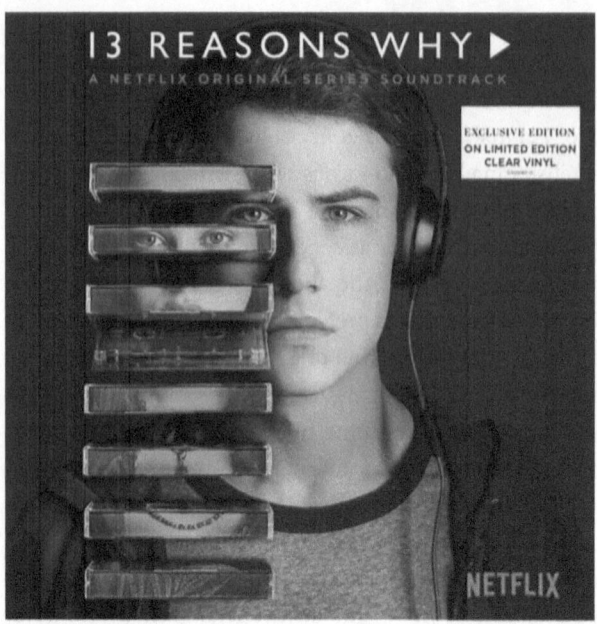

FIG. 3.5 Promotional poster for *13 Reason Why*'s original soundtrack, featuring the protagonist, Clay, wearing headphones and a "play" icon next to the show's title. The soundtrack cover design employs analog nostalgia by also including the seven cassette tapes recorded by Hannah. (Source: Netflix)

Clay's negotiations of the ideal pace for interacting with difficult content, however, are central to the success of the first season. In fact, his hesitation and slowness serve two supposedly contradictory goals: On the one hand, they extend the original novel into a thirteen-hour emotional roller coaster, instead of the single feature film originally pitched to Netflix, giving it the "Netflix stretch" and making users more likely to binge it.[75] On the other hand, his deliberation opens up a meta discussion of the potential downsides of bingeing by emphasizing the psychological need for processing difficult stories. In episode two, for example, Clay's friend Tony faults him for being "the slowest one yet" and asks, "What is taking you so long?" Explaining his aversion to binge-listening to the tapes, Clay responds, "It's hard. To listen." Throughout the show, the classmates who received Hannah's tapes—each of which traces her misery to one of their actions, making them partially responsible for her tragic death—tell Clay that they listened to them all "in one night," while some even chose to relisten almost immediately. Yet Clay stubbornly insists that he must take extended breaks from Hannah's horrific tales in order to maintain his own sanity. "I can only listen in bits and pieces or I . . . I freak out," he tells his friend Alex. "I feel a panic attack coming on."

This hesitation stands in contrast to Netflix's efforts to market the show as bingeable. The binge-ability of the first season also contributed to a widespread critique of its graphic depiction of multiple rape scenes, online and offline bullying, and Hannah's suicide. The US National Association of School Psychologists, for example, warned that "many teenagers are binge watching [the show] without adult guidance and support," which could "lead impressionable viewers to romanticize the choices made by the characters."[76] The juxtaposition of flashbacks and events occurring months after Hannah's death, these warnings argued, is problematic because it keeps her alive through her beyond-the-grave narration, which often ends each episode and opens a new one. As argued by Tanya Horeck, Mareike Jenner, and Tina Kendal, the "dead white girl" trope is key to the bingeability of "complex TV," and *13 Reasons Why* has employed it throughout its entire first season, romanticizing and idealizing Hannah and her actions through Clay's adoring and regretful gaze.[77]

The wave of criticism led to several empirical studies, one of which found a sharp increase in suicides among children and teens in the month following the show's release, while another reported a sharp increase in Google searches of suicide-related terms.[78] While mental health professionals warned it is impossible to determine a direct link between a single show and suicide rates, these studies convinced Netflix that the binge-ability of *13 Reasons Why* is a threat—if not to viewers' well-being, then to the company's wholesome brand.

Following a barrage of warnings by schools and parental groups, Netflix announced a set of actions designed to make their hit more suitable, and potentially less bingeable, for young audiences. First, they commissioned and produced a short warning that "will automatically play before each season."[79] Starting in 2018, a subscriber trying to play the opening episode of any of the four seasons of *13 Reasons Why* is forced to watch this warning, where the main actors introduce themselves by their real names and the names of the characters they play. Drawing attention to the fact that the show is a fictional story about difficult topics such as sexual assault, substance abuse, and suicide, the clip goes on to warn potential viewers who "are struggling with these issues right now" that "this series may not be right for you." A clock in the right bottom corner counts down fifty seconds until the opening credits begin (see fig. 3.6).

Netflix also ordered a study that looked into how teens and parents responded to the show, leading the company to launch a website with mental

FIG. 3.6 A still image showing actor Alisha Boe, who plays Hannah's friend Jessica Davis, warning potential viewers that *13 Reasons Why* might be triggering, in a clip produced by Netflix that automatically plays before each season. (Source: Netflix)

health resources, such as a list of emergency hotlines in dozens of languages.[80] The company produced an after-show special called *Behind the Reasons*, hosted by cast members, mental health experts, and the show's producers. In July 2019, Netflix also announced that it had edited out Hannah's suicide scene in the first season's finale, citing "advice from medical experts."[81] This decision is noteworthy because it stands in contrast to the company's decade-long commitment to creative freedom. As Netflix publicly stated, its creators are never censored or pushed to change plotlines.[82] Yet *13 Reasons Why* suggests that subscribers have some power over the streamer's storytelling when it comes to controversial and violent content—a point I will return to in the next section.

The outburst of true crime docuseries and dark, disturbing content on Netflix, however, implies that the company's response to the *13 Reason Why* controversy was first and foremost aimed at stopping a PR fiasco in its tracks. That the company only announced these steps months or even years after the first season was released attests to its reluctance to introduce any feature that might interfere with postplay, even when it comes to a dark and violent drama specifically targeting teenagers and young adults.

Netflix's actions were unlikely to offset the ways in which the show resembles a video game "cultivated around successive levels of intensity," where users are invited to "unlock" the mystery of Hanna's suicide by piecing together the puzzle based on the tapes.[83] Critiquing its narrative hooks and cliffhangers, as

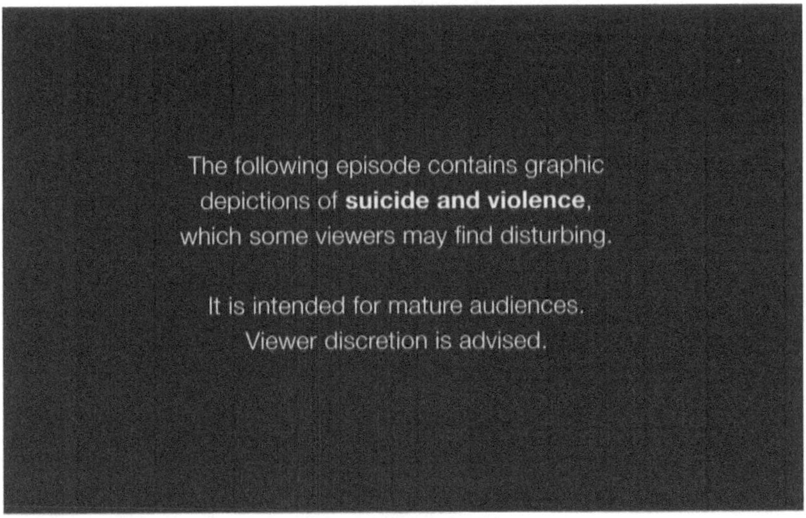

> The following episode contains graphic
> depictions of **suicide and violence**,
> which some viewers may find disturbing.
>
> It is intended for mature audiences.
> Viewer discretion is advised.

FIG. 3.7 Netflix's trigger warning for episode nine of the first season of *13 Reasons Why*. Similar warnings were retroactively added to other episodes. (Source: Netflix)

well as the decision to include two rape scenes in the final episodes, Horeck contends that "sexual violence is gamified in *13 Reasons Why* and is used as a structuring punctuation device for the full-drop season, which aims to keep viewers locked into Netflix's streaming interface."[84] Disturbingly, Netflix's decision to add explicit warnings to specific episodes contributes to the gamification of sexual violence, as it builds up anticipation and suspense while placing the responsibility for potential harm on the (supposedly mature) viewer (see fig. 3.7).

With the tapes as a central plot device, the show relies on autoplay as a digital punctuation of "and then," swiftly moving the viewer from one appalling event to the next by creating the impression *that one led to another*. In the case of a suicide of a beautiful, brilliant, and goodhearted seventeen-year-old girl, this linearity is especially troubling, for it assumes that the desperate act could be neatly explained by tracing the multiple traumas that caused it, ignoring both the complexity and variability of possible reactions to sexual violence, as well as the unpredictability of suicide. As revealed in episode twelve, Hannah chose to end her life shortly after she was raped by a wealthy, white athlete named Bryce Walker (Justin Prentice), who, as we learn in episode nine, also raped her friend Jessica after she passed out during a house party. Due to its binge-ability, the show quickly moves from Hannah's rape to her failed attempt to seek help

AUTOMATING TRAUMA 103

from the school's counselor. Disappointed by his response, Hannah returns to her house, where she cuts her wrists in the bathtub and bleeds to death in a graphic scene that Netflix was eventually pushed to remove.

The sense of causality by which Bryce's actions, as well as other harmful actions by Hannah's high-school peers, directly lead to her death does not reflect the complex set of factors that contribute to teenage self-harm. Yet it is depicted in the show as the only explanation for her desperate act. This is demonstrated by the show's title, which takes the form of a listicle, as well as by a conversation between Clay and the school counselor in episode twelve. Confronting the counselor, Clay asserts that it is possible to know what went through Hannah's head because she recorded her reasons on the tapes. He then passes the tapes to the counselor, supposedly providing him with the smoking gun explaining all that went wrong in Hannah's life. Even with yet another suicide attempt hooking viewers to stay tuned for the next season, the mystery of Hannah's suicide is supposedly solved, framing Bryce, the archvillain of the show, as not only her rapist but also her assassin. This clear-cut solution, however, doesn't help young people understand how these atrocities could have been prevented or why Hannah chose to take her own life while her friend Jessica, also raped by Bryce, was able to move forward.

This sense of causality is pleasurable for viewers because it recasts them as detectives. Capitalizing on the promise to solve yet another mystery, season two's promotional campaign included an actual scavenger hunt "for clues of what happened to Hannah across the US."[85] As Horeck summarizes, "The packaging of suicide and sexual violence as engaging, interactive mysteries to be 'solved' by viewers sits rather uncomfortably alongside the somber public service framing of *13 Reasons Why* as an educational series that 'breaks the silence' and 'opens up conversations.'"[86] This "somber public framing" is in fact even more suspicious considering Netflix's amalgam of addictive interface design features, which effectively limit the user's ability to reflect and converse. The company's decision not to dismantle the automated postplay and the five-second countdown effectively positioned the first season as a thirteen-hour spectacle best consumed in one sitting.

If automated warnings before each season, a resource-filled website, and re-editing the first season's finale all failed to deter young viewers from bingeing *13 Reasons Why*, what could be a more successful approach to balance autoplay culture with triggering content? What happens when subscribers are exposed to graphic violence and suicidal ideation as soon as they open the home page because of the previews autoplay feature? And what are the most useful strategies to reshape a media landscape through the lens of trauma-informed design?

"PLEASE STOP": NETFLIX'S PREVIEWS AUTOPLAY AS "PLATFORM VIOLENCE"

Netflix's content library has radically changed since the company implemented autoplay. Since the 2010s, the company has become one of the biggest production studios in the world, investing billions in original content. In recent years, Netflix produced dozens of multipart true crime docuseries, while some of its biggest hits include dark, violent dramas like *13 Reason Why*, *Squid Games* (2021), *Monster: The Jeffrey Dahmer Story* (2022), and *Baby Reindeer* (2024). These high-profile shows are heavily marketed via the automated playing of previews. The home page was also redesigned to include "Top Ten Netflix Shows" and "Popular in Your Area" recommendations, so that someone seeking to binge *Seinfeld* or *Friends* will likely encounter a preview for a shocking retelling of a true crime story.

That Netflix chose to use its platform to push its original content should not come as a surprise. However, there are several key differences between the previews autoplay and the century-old movie trailer industry. While "red-band" movie trailers depicting gore, graphic violence, and other R-rated content have become increasingly popular in the last decade, no movie theater would screen them before a PG-13 film.[87] Instead, most trailers that are shown in cinemas in the United States come with a green-band label, meaning he MPAA have rated them acceptable for viewers of all ages. Furthermore, both cable networks and movie theaters have financial and regulatory obligations ensuring that daytime viewers and children would not be exposed to disturbing and graphic content during commercial breaks on television or the movie house's "coming attractions." Netflix, on the other hand, is a subscription-based service built on the promise of personalization and global access to niche content. Its subscribers tend to ascribe a sense of safety, familiarity, and intimacy to Netflix's brand of narrowcasting. To that extent, repeatedly encountering a triggering Netflix preview at any hour of the day is potentially more harmful as it might happen to those who didn't chose to buy a ticket to a gory horror film or to watch an R-rated crime procedural late at night.

More disturbingly, Netflix subscribers were initially unable to disable the automated play of both sound and video as soon as they log into the platform. The decision to make the previews autoplay a default feature, I argue, has proven harmful for some of its users. As described by American writer Lisa Martens, the previews autoplay frequently triggered debilitating symptoms ranging from anxiety to insomnia.[88] This was the case, for example, when she logged into Netflix in February 2021 and a preview for the newly released *Crime*

Scene: The Vanishing at the Cecil Hotel automatically began to play. Directed by Joe Berlinger, this four-part docuseries examines multiple violent crimes that took place in the Cecil Hotel in downtown Los Angeles, especially the 2013 disappearance of Elisa Lam, a Canadian college student whose untimely, unexplained death is the main hook of the show.[89]

The automatically played preview for *Crime Scene* included snippets of surveillance footage depicting Lam as she hesitates to leave the hotel's elevator shortly before she disappeared. For Martens, this grainy footage was highly triggering. "I froze. I couldn't even reach for the remote control," she writes. "The entire trailer played, and the part that really got me . . . and by got me, I mean ruined my ability to sleep, take an elevator, and even stand to brush my teeth . . . was the hotel footage of Elisa Lam moving in and out of the elevator, her hands looking particularly disjointed."[90] These images proved particularly triggering for Martens because the preview's fast-paced editing implied a connection between Lam's mysterious disappearance, her abnormal body language in the elevator footage, and her diagnosis as bipolar. For Martens, this stigmatized depiction of a mental illness invoked some of her deepest fears: "Immediately, I began to catastrophize. If someone killed me, then people would blame my mental state. They would pour [sic] over my blog posts looking for evidence. My own words, the way I express myself, would be used against me."[91] Even without watching the show, this brief trailer had an immediate harmful effect on Martens.

As Martens herself stresses throughout her post, she is not "the ideal user." Instead, she describes herself as an "edge case" because of her painful experience navigating video platforms in the autoplay age. As she concludes, "I know autoplay isn't going away. But it really, truly messes with my mood. Seeing the wrong thing, even just a trailer, is enough to trigger catastrophic thoughts and anxiety for days."[92] She ends her account with a plea to companies and web designers to make the internet feel "a little more safe for me . . . not with Trigger Warnings from other users, but with product decisions that prevent these warnings from being needed to begin with."[93] This dismissal of trigger warnings as potential antidote to the risks posed by autoplay is an important reminder that a seconds-long title or subtitle cannot compensate for the inability to disable such features. What users need, Martens argue, is not a textual summary of the atrocities about to be depicted on their screen—"nudity, substance abuse, violence" and so forth—but a simple way to opt out from automated previews as soon as they log into the platform.

Martens' account joined similar complaints by Netflix subscribers on social media, as well as Bryant's petition mentioned above, which asked the company to "please stop!" playing previews.[94] While the tens of thousands of subscribers

FIG. 3.8 A screenshot of Netflix's tweet announcing the company will enable subscribers to turn off autoplay previews, in response to a tweet by Sarah Hollowell complaining about this feature. (Source: Twitter/X)

who signed the petition or posted complaints listed various shows as potentially triggering, they seemed to agree that the first step in solving this issue was to add the option to disable the previews autoplay. Focusing on unpredictable, debilitating effects, these personal stories return us to Little's analysis of platform violence. Forced to encounter narratives of sexual violence, murder, and suicide, many subscribers were pushed to limit their use of the platform in order to protect their mental health.

While Netflix initially ignored users' complaints, in February 2020 it took to Twitter to announce that the autoplay previews would be made optional (see fig. 3.8).[95] This small victory, which came only after public pressure, should not distract from the ways in which Netflix's autoplay has been key to the company's global success. Even when disabling previews autoplay, Netflix subscribers are less likely to disable the postplay between one episode and the next due to its drop-release model and ever-shrinking countdowns.

But how else can companies like Netflix make the internet safer for edge users? Despite the differences between social media and streaming platforms, Little's proposed solutions could be applied to the autoplay feature: adding the option to *opt into* this feature rather than *opting out*, introducing filters that can help users block content that they would prefer to avoid, and altering the interface to enable the immediate flagging of problematic content. This "trauma-informed design" can replace the default settings and open up more inclusive ways to interact with digital media.[96] Instead of implementing a default feature, this model reframes the interface as a site through which users can potentially limit or extend their exposure to content based on their shifting needs, experiences, and sensitivities. To this end, a trauma-informed design could improve the experience for a variety of users, including children, survivors of domestic abuse, or those with PTSD or a low tolerance for graphic content.

While trauma-informed design pushes companies to consider how non-average users might experience new features, critical disability scholars provide us with alternative ways to resist, or at the very least limit, platform violence. For Smilges, "access thievery" is an alternative to existing ideas of accommodation.[97] To steal access is to take it without asking for permission or waiting for an adaptation to be implemented. In the case of Netflix's previews autoplay, this can entail installing a plug-in or a browser ad-on that prevents automated video play, similarly to ad-blockers. Before Netflix added the option to disable the automated previews, some of its tech-savvy subscribers installed an open-source Google Chrome extension called "netflix-stop-autoplay." After they downloaded a ZIP file from a developer platform like GitHub, this browser add-on automatically deactivated videos on Netflix's home page and, instead, showed still images similar to the thumbnails that advertised content in the days of yore. As a 2019 tech blog concluded, "'netflix-stop-autoplay' makes navigating Netflix quick and also saves you some internet charges."[98] By saving time and money, such hacks imbue users with a renewed sense of agency and choice, yet they are limited to those who possess the digital literacy and know-how to navigate a platform like GitHub. In this case, the user is not asking Netflix to introduce the option to disable a default feature; they simply disable it without permission, by overriding its proprietary code.

An open-source browser extension is only one possible weapon in the uphill battle against platform violence. For non-average users, access could mean pushing commercial platforms to consider trauma-informed design and to hire and promote engineers, designers, and testers from diverse backgrounds. If, however, we frame access as an attack, rather than a request for accommodation, it can also involve canceling one's subscription and finding platforms that reject addictive design and the business model of captology, such as the art-house cinema streamer MUBI or the streaming platform Kanopy, which is available via public and academic libraries. As Smilges stresses, access thievery is not only desirable, but often necessary in order to survive in a deeply ableist world. Advancing this model of activism, Smilges writes that "sufficient access should include access to the lives we want for ourselves.... It's not only that we are stealing access but also that we are redefining what access means in the process."[99] As online platforms are deeply invested in captivating their users, it is left to the user to ask themself what kind of access is worth fighting for. "The lives we want for ourselves" may or may not include Netflix, YouTube, or Disney+, but the ubiquity of such platforms often occludes our ability to explore our needs, sensitivities, and desires.

When it comes to invisible, fluctuating, and unpredictable conditions like PTSD resulting from sexual trauma, requesting accommodation is particularly challenging. In her study of academics with disabilities, Margaret Price warns that the legal language of accommodations is limited, in that it "relies on the assumption that disability is stable and knowable, not only in moments—for example, when confronting a step or a time limit or an uncaptioned video—but in *predictive* ways."[100] She therefore recommends replacing "access" with "adaptation," which can better assist institutions and companies to respond "to an access need as it emerges."[101] Price's critique of accommodation-based access raises three important questions: "Who can identify their own access needs in an understandable manner? Who can predict what sort of accommodation they'll need tomorrow, or next week? And ... who cannot?"[102] As I discussed in chapter 2, Netflix marketed its playback speed feature as an accessibility feature for blind and deaf subscribers who rely on audio descriptions or closed-captioning. Yet when it came to the company's previews autoplay feature, the public announcement about making it optional was intentionally opaque, stating that "some people find this feature helpful. Others not so much." Despite Bryant's petition and dozens of users who publicly reported that they found this feature triggering, the "others" remained unspecified. This implied that, in the highly competitive market of digital services, some access needs are recognized, publicly addressed, and—in the case of the playback speed—used for "cripwashing" controversial design decisions, while others remain contested and unnamed.[103]

Instead of finding ways to make a product more inclusive, Price, Smilges, and other disability scholars working within the emerging field of "critical access studies" bring us closer to an understanding of access "as an ongoing and shifting process rather than as a mode of solving individualized problems."[104] Framing access as an attack on the cultural and economic logic of autoplay opens up a new set of questions: Should users actively seek to expand and extend access to commercial platforms, even if the content they distribute is often sexist, ableist, and invested in tokenism? And how can media and disability scholars use such moments of friction to explore collaborative ideas of thriving and living outside capitalist norms (for example, by developing new production models or distribution platforms)?

Smilges's account implies that leaving a platform altogether might prove more beneficial for someone's mental health than trying to redesign it. Applied to Netflix, it helps us understand this market leader as a double-edged sword: While it initiated a streaming revolution that made it easier than ever to watch global content made by diverse creators from the comfort of one's home or on one's phone, its captivating design features contribute to digital debility and put some users in harm's way.

The risk of platform violence is increased by the idea that *every* show is bingeable. Some content creators, however, have pushed against this assumption by asking which stories are best served by the drop-release and autoplay model. As I explore below, Michaela Coel's *I May Destroy You* (BBC One/HBO, 2020) illuminates these negotiations between platforms and creators. Coel, a British screenwriter and actor, became the first Black woman to win the Emmy Award for outstanding writing for a limited series, movie, or dramatic special, for her work on the show, which she wrote, co-directed, executive produced, and starred in. By rejecting Netflix and its drop-release model, Coel and her work allow us to explore the idea of the unbingeable. *I May Destroy You*, I argue, is a feminist-of-color attack on both the autoplay business model and the serialized depictions of rape culture popularized by Netflix shows like *13 Reasons Why*.

ON THE UN-BINGEABLE (OR, SAYING NO TO NETFLIX)

In the ninth episode of *I May Destroy You*, ironically titled "Social Media Is a Great Way to Connect," Arabella (played by Coel), an up-and-coming writer whose claim to fame is her debut book, *Chronicles of a Fed-Up Millennial*, takes to social media to encourage sexual assault victims to speak up and share their stories. As she struggles to piece together what happened to her during a night in which she was drugged and raped in a London bar, Arabella assumes a public persona of a vocal, judgmental crusader, becoming gradually more aggressive both online and offline. Shortly after finding out that the police closed her rape investigation without arresting any suspects, her downward spiral bottoms out in a drunken live stream during which she encourages her social media followers to publish the personal information of their attackers, a controversial strategy called "doxing."

Despite Arabella's commitment to drawing attention to very real issues by employing the "hashtag activism" popularized by the #MeToo movement, her posts fail to communicate the ambivalence, grief, and confusion resulting

FIG. 3.9 A still image from episode nine of *I May Destroy You*, featuring Arabella, played by show creator Michaela Coel, in her therapist's office. (Source: HBO)

from her sexual assault.[105] Dozens of likes and heart emojis later, Arabella finally calls the emergency line and is able to meet her therapist, Carrie (Andi Osho), who strongly recommends that her distraught patient quit social media. When Arabella insists that "it's important that [sexual assault victims] speak," Carrie responds: "The business models of these networks incentivize us to behave in certain ways. In ways that promote speaking, often at the cost of listening." She then reminds her of the "three R's" mentioned earlier in the show, when Arabella started therapy following her assault: "Rest, reflect, rejuvenate" (see fig. 3.9). "If you can't abandon it altogether, take a break," Carrie suggests in a soft voice. When Arabella groans and rolls her eyes, her therapist continues, "We take breaks. We don't work weekends. We break for half-term. Even a cantor has a sabbatical. And it's good for our mental health."

Drawing on Coel's sustained attacks on binge-watching during the PR campaign for her show, I wish to read this dialogue about social media as inviting viewers to reflect more broadly on their relationships with their screens. Coel is not the first creator to reject the drop-release model popularized by Netflix.[106] Other leading figures in the television industry, from Damon Lindelof to Joss Whedon, have voiced similar concerns.[107] However, in *I May Destroy You*, Coel offers a more sustained and complex exploration of the unbingeable by incorporating the three Rs into every layer of her creative process.

I May Destroy You explores consent, sexual trauma, and healing by following the stories of three working-class, Black British millennials: Arabella, Terry (Weruche Opia), and Kwame (Paapa Essiedu). Coel wrote the series' twelve episodes, during which each of the main characters is forced to struggle with complex questions of consent after being sexually assaulted, as a way to process her own rape.[108] While most television shows about sexual violence feature white victims, *I May Destroy You* explores the intersection of sexism, racism, and homophobia by detailing the friendship between three Black Londoners.[109] It depicts complicated situations where consent is given based on information or impressions later proven to be incomplete or false, blurring the lines between victims and perpetrators and revealing how an initial attack reverberates throughout the community in a cycle of aggression and miscommunication.

In her reading of Coel's work, Caetlin Benson-Allott suggests that it "explores healing as much as it does trauma. Its elliptical, associative approach to narrative mimics the a-linear process of recovery, while its broadcast schedule allowed viewers to appreciate how victims become survivors."[110] Benson-Allott refers here to a feature of Coel's deal with BBC One and HBO. Netflix, which drop-released Coel's debut series, *Chewing Gum*, in 2016, reportedly offered her $1 million for *I May Destroy You*, but she instead chose to work with the BBC and HBO in order to retain creative control over production and distribution.[111] Based on their agreement, BBC One broadcasted two episodes per week from June 8 to July 14, 2020, while HBO aired one episode per week from June 7 through August 24. Coel explained her rejection of Netflix's offer as pertaining to copyright, yet she also framed it as a denunciation of binge culture.[112] In a series of interviews promoting the show, she stated, "I am not too into bingeing" and questioned the very nature of this spectatorial mode: "Just look at what the word means—when you binge food, you barely taste it and it's a hedonistic rush. You don't get to chew and enjoy the flavour. You should let it go down, wait for the next bite."[113] For those reasons, Coel did not want *I May Destroy You* to drop-release on the BBC iPlayer. As she told the UK-based *Broadcast*, "I explained my reasons [to the BBC's executives] and they got it."[114]

In so doing, Coel rejected the cultural logic of seamlessness and autoplay on multiple levels, reshaping industry standards. As the show was partially based on her own sexual trauma, the notoriously demanding shooting schedule was carefully designed to ensure Coel got eight hours of sleep, could take time off when needed, and had time for walks, meditation, yoga, and on-site therapy.[115] Coel is not the only female or queer-identified creator to push against the stressful demands of ever-shrinking network deadlines in the age of streaming wars, but her consistent, public effort to reshape production to enable rest and reflection invites a reading of *I May Destroy You* through the framework of the unbingeable, both as a spectatorial mode and as a mode of production. Cripping industry standards, this temporality emphasizes calibration, collective work, and rest as alternatives to the temporality of compression and accumulation associated with bingeing.

True to the three Rs, *I May Destroy You* offers its viewers twelve episodes that can function as separate, stand-alone stories. As opposed to *13 Reasons Why*, which lures viewers with cliff-hangers, dark secrets, and increasingly violent scenes, each episode of *I May Destroy You* is a self-contained narrative implicitly inviting people to practice the three Rs alongside Arabella. Jumping back and forth in time, including an episode that mostly takes place during Arabella and Terry's adolescent years, the show imitates the nonlinear process of healing from sexual trauma.

This narrative rejection of linearity enables Coel to explore the cultural and social demands pushing her characters to heal by neatly following the seven stages of grief. Both in the show and in Coel's real life, the rapist was never caught, preventing the possibility of closure and challenging one of the most common tropes in police procedurals and true crime dramas: the idea that justice, even if delayed, will eventually be served. As one of Arabella's friends tells a sexual assault survivors' support group in episode six, "One in every two women is a survivor, yet eighty-nine percent of trials end in exoneration."[116] This sobering statistic points to the ways in which sexual assault survivors are invisible. For the tech industry, survivors might seem like a small minority comprised of "edge users," yet Coel reminds us that gender-based violence is painfully common.

If bingeing obeys the logic of linearity, accumulation, and personalization, Coel's refusal to embrace it develops a deeper understanding of the weekly release model as potentially supporting serialized stories that explore difficult, disturbing, and complex storylines. In the season finale, however, Coel imagines how an alternative version of the autoplay might look like by offering three possible endings that automatically play one after another. Instead of a closure providing a clear-cut, whodunit explanation as in *13 Reasons Why*, Coel brings Arabella's story arc to its (speculative) end with a genre-bending montage. In one scenario, she confronts her rapist, drugs him, beats him until he loses consciousness, and eventually hides his body under her bed. Seconds later, however, Arabella is back in the London bar when she was attacked, and the episode begins again. This time, Arabella finds herself gently tending to her rapist after he confesses his sins and starts swearing and attacking himself, blurring the line between victim and perpetrator. This "abundance of closures" enables viewers "to appreciate how ambivalent the concept really is."[117] Coel is less invested in why she was raped than in how she might recover and whether recovery is even possible in a rape culture monetizing the traumas sustained by female-identifying and queer people of color.

Yet another ending consists of Arabella's triumphant launch of her new book, titled *January 22nd*—the date of her assault. In this plot twist, Coel replaces what Stephanie Patrick calls "the (post) feminist logic that frames vengeance as female empowerment" with an embrace of friendship, creativity, and fragmented, open-ended testimony.[118] As such, it brings us closer to crip and queer understandings of nonlinear healing, where the ultimate goal is neither cure nor closure, but rather forming "care webs" that can sustain us overtime.[119] By exploring the friendship between Arabella, Terry, and Kwame, Coel highlights how emotional, physical, and libidinal needs are constantly in flux, leading her viewers to recognize how "care should be distributed across a community."[120] It is ongoing care, rather than cure, that Coel's characters seek.

That Arabella was able to finish her book does not imply a life devoid of posttraumatic symptoms. Rejecting medical categories such as "cure" as Western and ableist, disability scholars have long warned that ableism, racism, and sexism can retraumatize even those who were supposedly able to heal.[121] They also show how the medical-industrial complex often confuses healing with productivity, measuring a patient's well-being and recovery solely based on their capacity to work.[122] Both Coel's ability to fictionalize her attack and Arabella's successful struggle to finish her book are presented at the very end of an emotional roller coaster exploring the nonlinear, often counterintuitive nature of healing. The show's investigation of multiple ways of healing, including friendship, exercise, therapy, and writing, as well as more controversial coping strategies such as substance abuse and sexual exploration, moves us beyond a one-size-fits-all, prescriptive idea of cure. This echoes Leah Piepzna-Samarasinha's "cripped definition of healing," which "include[s] *anything* that supports someone's disabled body/mind."[123] Such "care webs" can take the form of a walking cane, a friend's garden bench, a heating pad, Zoom captions, or the disabled parking spaces at the Grocery Outlet, as long as they "ensure my or someone else's chances of an excellent disabled life."[124] For Piepzna-Samarasinha, cure might consists of "a million hours of *The Office* cued up on Netflix," whereas for Coel it might require exploring the three Rs with a close friend—reminding us that cure can take many different forms.[125]

With its queer characters, multiple plotlines of sexism and racism, and fragmented narratives of trauma, grief, and survival, *I May Destroy You* is a show deemed unbingeable by its creator. In a 2020 interview with Louis Theroux, Coel once again stressed her need for rest, explaining that, instead of pitching or developing a new project, she lets herself grieve while indulging in what she half-jokingly describes as her "post-writum depression."[126] Refusing to succumb to the relentless expectations of constant productivity, she described dedicating time to running, seeing friends, and spending time with her family, as well as going to therapy. De-automating recovery, productivity, and creativity, Coel demonstrates how creators can resist profitable business models.

Coda: The Death of Bingeing?

In 2021, Netflix started testing alternatives to its familiar drop-release model. It announced that the fourth season of the hit show *Stranger Things* and the final season of *Money Heist* would be released in two parts, and the horror trilogy *Fear Street* would debut weekly.[127] In 2022, Netflix also introduced ads for those interested in paying less for their monthly subscription.[128] These changes position the California-based company, which once "disrupted" the DVD rental market, as a digital equivalent of old-fashioned cable television. History repeats; first as a default, then as a premium service.

Things could have been different. When I spoke with Sweeney, he stressed that autoplay was not intended to make Netflix more addictive. Things changed only once the data showed that "the hours you watch are correlated with the money you spend." Without this correlation, Sweeney contends, "there wouldn't be an incentive to keep you addicted because you're a paying subscriber, and you should have total control over how you consume Netflix." If the postplay's definition of success had been retention rather than hours watched, perhaps the feature could have "helped users maintain a healthy balance in their lives by introducing time limits." Looking back, Sweeney concludes that "consumers seem to like when companies care for their mental health. So if they have been watching for a while, we could tell them, hey, it's time to take a break."

Sweeney's ambivalence about his involvement in launching autoplay culture is part of a broader trend in which senior tech workers use their experience to shed light on the dark patterns designed and deployed by the companies they once worked for. Since he left YouTube, former Google engineer Guillaume Chaslot became a vocal crusader against the use of automated video streaming, warning of the spread of misinformation.[129] Similarly, Tristan Harris, a former Google product manager, co-founded the Center for Humane Technology, which he promoted on Netflix's hit documentary *The Social Dilemma* (2020).[130] Other high-profile examples include Silicon Valley blogger and entrepreneur Nir Eyal, whose 2014 bestseller *Hooked* played a crucial role in the rise of captology, and B. J. Fogg, who founded the Persuasive Technology Lab at Stanford University.[131] According to Seaver, these public mea culpas attest to the extent to which more and more former tech leaders "have come to emphasize their own captological expertise as a resource to help *resist* such engineering, not only to build it."[132] Yet these voices, sincere as they may be, have so far failed to reverse the addictive trends they helped set in motion. That the digital ecosystem still heavily relies on endless scrolling and autoplay stresses the need to explore access thievery, unbingeable production and distribution models, and consumer activism.

Because of the established correlation between hours watched and retention, it is too early to eulogize bingeing or to downplay the importance of algorithmic recommendation systems. Even if Netflix and other streaming giants eventually alternate between different release models, the cat is out of the bag. American users are habituated to consume bottomless streams of content supported by internet service providers and supposedly immaterial digital infrastructure. While day-to-day experience might confront them with friction, buffering, and disconnection, the ubiquity of autoplay across video and audio platforms is crucial for sustaining the illusion of seamlessness.

As autoplay is likely to remain key to the system of anticipation and prediction fueling surveillance capitalism, it is imperative to study its evolution, standardizations, and failures. Seen through the framework of digital debility, autoplay directly contributes to maximizing screen time, increasing the risk for physical pain, sleep deprivation, and addiction. Introducing trauma and emotional distress into this analysis, I argue that this feature is especially harmful when it unwittingly exposes users to graphic and sexual violence or prevents them from taking time to process difficult topics that might be best discussed by reaching out to others. In these cases, enhanced accessibility can entail adding easy opt-outs or removing a feature from the interface design. The access-as-attack approach, on the other hand, utilizes these frictions to reject the underlying logic of commercial media platforms and to ask which content they choose to invest in, distribute, and aggressively promote. Shifting the emphasis from an accessibility checklist to a discussion of "care webs" and how to build digital worlds we would like to inhabit, this kind of collective access offers radical ways to rest, reflect, and rejuvenate.

Martens, who describes autoplay as potentially debilitating, cannot simply turn off her screen. In fact, she uses the "background sound" of her television to fall asleep, which is why she can't leave Netflix or YouTube on as she fears it might play a video "that will scare me."[133] If autoplay-supported streaming is unpredictable, sleep apps promise to provide the user with uninterrupted white noise that can play all night long. Both industries, the next chapter argues, foster an unhealthy dependency on screens that can worsen fatigue and insomnia. As we shall see, autoplay works in tandem with Apple's Night Shift and other tools designed to convince users to take their personal electronics to bed. These technologies perpetuate an ecosystem by which triggering, disturbing, or incendiary content can keep users up at night. That the very tools aimed at improving the quality of sleep in fact normalize behaviors proven to hinder it is one of the paradoxes the next chapter unpacks.

"LOG IN, CHILL OUT"

"Horizontal Media," Night Modes, and Sleep Apps

> How do you throw a brick through the window of a bank if you can't get out of bed?
>
> —JOHANNA HEDVA, "SICK WOMAN THEORY"

Night Shifts

Born with facial paralysis, I am unable to fully shut my right eye. To fall asleep, I must use an eye mask, blackout blinds, or some other tool or technique to create an entirely darkened environment. When traveling, I have used furniture, towels, pillows, T-shirts, houseplants, books, and, less successfully, pets to block out light. Large windows freak me out. They are the first thing I notice when entering a bedroom. My level of fatigue, or, to borrow a popular concept among disability scholars, the number of "spoons" or energy reserves available to me on a given day, is correlated directly to my ability to sleep in a dark room.[1] Sources of light such as Bluetooth headphone chargers, smartphones, tablets, or any kind of digital screen are unwelcome disturbances in my bedroom. Years before "sleep hygiene" became a self-care industry of endless books, listicles, and products, I removed every electronic device from my surroundings before going to bed and disconnected appliances in "standby" or "sleep" mode, which, despite their misleading names, still draw power and often include light-emitting indicators.[2] To avoid nocturnal flashes caused by calls or notifications, I charge my phone outside the bedroom.

My screen-free bedtime experience is the exception to the rule. In 2010, more than 65 percent of American adults and 90 percent of young adults reported falling asleep "with their phone on or right next to their bed."[3] The pandemic, which reshaped remote work and pushed white-collar workers to turn their bedrooms into makeshift offices, further accelerated this trend.[4] When in bed, soporific features like Apple's Night Shift or the sleep app Calm assume a fatigued media user relying on their electronics to improve the quality of their sleep. The imagined "drowsy" user of sleep apps is someone like American columnist and author Pagan Kennedy, who uses her smartphone and noise-canceling wireless headphones in bed to create a calming, personalized cocoon.[5] Kennedy, who has struggled with chronic insomnia for decades, describes how listening to audiobooks while sleeping with headphones transformed her condition from debilitating to manageable, providing "literary medicine" via a "library we can stumble through in the dark."[6] Technology proved therapeutic for two reasons: Her smartphone provides a "lullaby of digital media," helping her to stop ruminating and drift off, and online forums enable her to gather with fellow insomniacs and share insights, breaking the silence around their invisible condition.[7]

Many users of soporific media would find that Kennedy's account speaks to their experience. As part of a broader wellness industry valued at over $120 billion, the soporific media industry includes hundreds of products, from light calibration tools like dark mode and night mode to noise-canceling "sleep headphones," from sleep trackers and ASMR "bedtime stories" to "smart lights" and "sunrise" apps, as well as apps promising to monitor and alleviate medical conditions like insomnia and sleep apnea.[8] Many of these apps and devices require constant tracking.[9] The Runtastic Sleep Better app, for example, "can help you keep track of your sleep apnea by not only tracking your sleep, but also moon phases, lifestyle choices like exercise or alcohol consumption, and other things that have an impact on sleep."[10] Yet the promise to use technological tools to improve the quality of sleep has so far produced limited and contradictory results, as monitoring sleep via wearables or smartphones has been shown to increase stress and anxiety, undermining sleep quality.[11] While users can choose between an ever-growing number of sleep-supporting products, four out of five Americans struggle with sleep problems at least once a week and wake up feeling exhausted, and one in ten American adults suffers from chronic insomnia.[12] The problem of sleep, hindered by ubiquitous screens, doomscrolling, and remote work, demonstrates how technology companies develop new products to solve problems they themselves created.

While new soporific products enter the market at a staggering speed, the very same companies that manufacture them deny the extent to which screen-based life is likely to worsen the user's exhaustion. As explored in the introduction, fatigue is one of the three most prevalent manifestations of digital debility, alongside physical pain and addiction. I therefore study soporific media as part of a broader ecosystem built on addictive design features such as the refresh (chapter 1) and autoplay (chapter 3). Scripted online environments and what I call *ascetic technologies* compete with the user's circadian rhythms by training the user to either ignore or to push past their bodily and emotional limitations.

Exploring the soporific media industry as both a poison and a cure, I follow the logic of "technopharmacology," which has been coined and developed by Joshua Neves, Aleena Chia, Susanna Paasonen, and Ravi Sundaram to "expand media theoretical inquiry by attending to the biological, neurological and pharmacological dimensions of media."[13] Soporific products, I argue, reveal a tension between a promise to cure prevalent sleep disturbances and medical conditions like insomnia, and a demand for premium subscriptions and constant surveillance. Blurring the lines "between big data and big pharma," these apps and features monetize the quest for convenience.[14] The tech-based cocoons they offer deem it necessary to transition from wakefulness to sleep by eliminating inconvenient cognitive, emotional, or optical factors such as rumination, anxiety, noise, or daylight. By drawing on a medical discourse touting the benefits of destressing and rest, such products have become conducive to the user's sense of comfort and well-being.

As an ever-growing, billion-dollar industry, soporific media remind us that digital users are often recast as medical subjects in order to test the human limits of engagement, attention, and retention. To that extent, I theorize the transition from sleep as "the great human affront to the voraciousness of contemporary capitalism" to sleep as a site of value production.[15] Sleep, Jonathan Crary contends, is passive, nonproductive, and composed of empty time. It "requires periodic disengagement from networks and devices in order to enter a state of inactivity and uselessness. It is a form of time that leads us elsewhere than to the things we own or are told we need."[16] This description, however, fails to account for the myriad ways in which sleep has become labor. The sleeping body has been studied and monetized by pharmaceutical companies since the rise of "sleep labs" in the 1970s, while the domestic sphere has been more recently expanded into a makeshift sleep laboratory with the help of Wi-Fi–connected technologies.[17] Sleeping bodies are increasingly connected to headphones, smartphones, and tracking devices that turn circadian rhythms into data streams sold to third-party companies. An early ad for the wearable tracker Fitbit culminated with a close-up of a woman sleeping with the device on her wrist, promising to optimize "even inactivity."[18] Sleep or awake, profit can be made.

This chapter argues that night modes, sleep apps, and other soporific products promote a technological solutionism habituating users to associate sleep with their personal electronics while denying the effects of digital debility on their bodies. Framing sleep and its absence as an individual problem, these tools depoliticize the broader structural, financial, and sociological issues that might chase away sleep or serve to explain why some bodies are allowed and encouraged to recharge while others are prevented from doing so. I closely study Calm's "sleep stories" to reveal how they co-opt racial and ableist histories as scripts for relaxation and somnolence. These stories are central for the success of Calm and other sleep and meditation apps that, as argued by Lida Zeitlin-Wu, cater to "overwhelmingly white and affluent consumers."[19] Calm promotes "sleep stories" about the lives of artists of color like Frida Kahlo and Jean-Michel Basquiat, to suit the assumed preferences of a mostly white clientele while diversifying its brand and content library.

That sleep apps rely on the user's exposure to blue light, which has been correlated with sleep disturbances, is one of the paradoxes of the soporific media industry. To resolve this problem, technology companies like Apple enthusiastically design and manufacture new products promising to mitigate the adverse effects of late-night exposure to self-illuminating screens. Features like night mode offer users more control over the color and brightness of their display while normalizing the idea that they should take their personal electronics to bed. To change the color scheme in correlation with the local time, Apple's Night Shift requires access to the device's location. This tracking requirement was downplayed during the 2016 launch of this feature, which Apple touted as a tool for self-care.[20]

By comparing night modes and sleep apps, I argue that they are less effective in improving the quality of sleep than the claims made in their promotional campaigns. Why, then, do users still find them beneficial? Because they "nudge" them to change their bodily posture from standing or sitting to reclining or lying down, improving their likelihood of falling asleep.[21] I argue that both night modes and sleep apps are content-agnostic; the first filter blue light, and the latter filter rumination and obsessive thoughts. This analysis of "anti-content" opens up new ways to examine how interface design challenges existing notions of mediation.[22] Soporific media teach us how a service's value and meaning are being produced via an intersection of embodiment, interface, and—to a lesser extent than users might assume—content.

Promoting an understanding of postural ways to engage with media, I argue that a handheld digital interface is crucial to sleep technologies because it is horizontal-friendly. I explore the shift from vertical and sedentary media to what I call *horizontal media*: devices, apps, and interfaces strategically designed to be used while lying down. We need a theory of horizontal media for three reasons. First, much of media theory is invested in studying "seated spectatorial positions" by focusing on reading, theater, film, and television and ignoring "folded," injured, or bedridden embodiments.[23] Second, existing accounts of ideal bodies and viewing positions fail to isolate technologies that habituate the user to shift from one posture to another. Third, these forms of media are significant because so many of us consume videos, websites, and audio while supine, creating a need for a critical account that asks not just what content the user consumes, but also what bodily position is assumed by the interface through which the content is accessed.

Drawing on critical disability studies and the work of people who struggle with insomnia and chronic fatigue, I demonstrate how horizontal media can help a user reflect on their relationship with both technology and their body. I read crip artworks made by bedridden filmmakers and artists as invitations for communal reflections on the political conditions that enable or limit sufficient rest. Sleep itself cannot be used to challenge power structures, as the chronically fatigued subject simply doesn't have enough stamina, time, or resources to fight for their rights.[24] But the case studies I draw on introduce an "hydraulic system of labour"—to return to Carolyn Lazard's crip and queer art collective explored in chapter 2—by which some can rest while others work, in order to create a more sustainable system of care. Such crip horizontal media include the mobile app #SelfCare, designed for people who struggle with depression and insomnia, a desktop film directed from bed by chronically ill filmmaker Hannah Bullock, and a collection of short videos chronicling Canadian artist Dayna McLeod's interrupted sleep during the pandemic.

If Night Shift and Calm habituate users to rely on their laptops and smartphones to improve their sleep, these interventions invite us to repoliticize sleep by reflecting on the conditions under which it is limited or deprived. What can we learn from focusing on media that prompt us to transition from one bodily position to another? How can crip horizontal works help us rethink the meaning of both rest *and* resistance by drawing on longer histories of disability activism?[25] And can these works replace an individual emphasis on "sleep hygiene" and "strategic naps" with communal and collective rituals of recharging and daydreaming?[26]

In Pursuit of a "Good Night's Sleep": On the Rise of Night Modes

Launching its operating system iOS 9.3 in 2016, Apple promoted a new design feature it called Night Shift with the promise to improve users' quality of sleep. As an early ad explained: "Many studies have shown that exposure to bright blue light in the evening can affect your circadian rhythms and make it harder to fall asleep. Night Shift uses your iOS device's clock and geolocation to determine when it's sunset in your location, then it automatically shifts the colors in your display to the warmer end of the spectrum. In the morning, it returns the display to its regular settings. Pleasant dreams."[27]

This ad, which establishes a connection between personal electronics and the user's sleep routine, fully embraces Silicon Valley solutionism by telling a familiar story: Existing technology might be harmful, yet new technology can mitigate its harm.[28] It also transforms surveillance into self-care. If only we would allow Apple to continuously track our location and time zone, we could enjoy a good night's sleep. At the time of its launch, Night Shift was only compatible with newer Apple products, such as the iPhone 5s or the sixth-generation iPod Touch, pressuring users to upgrade their current device as part of the planned obsolescence business model that helped the company reach an unprecedented market value of $3 trillion by 2022.[29]

An enthusiastic review of this feature posted by the popular YouTube channel AppleInsider shortly after the iOS 9.3 launch depicted a young man lying in bed and using Night Shift while browsing the web on his iPad. The male narrator explains that changing the color tones of the display to a warmer hue "is backed by actual science: research has shown that lights with blueish hues help to keep you awake at night by suppressing the production of melatonin."[30] AppleInsider is a channel solely dedicated to glowing reviews of Apple products, and as such its endorsement of Night Shift should not come as a surprise. As I will later show, however, the "actual science" exploring the connection between blue light, melatonin, and sleep is in fact much more confounding and contradictory than these promotional materials make it sound. The review, for example, fails to distinguish between light emission and other cognitive and psychological stimulation produced by exposure to online content. Restating Apple's promise that this feature contributes to "a good night's sleep," this clip's aesthetic and narrative choices disclose who is the imaginary user of the night mode. By casting a young man as the ideal Apple consumer and announcing that "power users" can customize the feature via their "display and brightness" menu and schedule when it will turn on and off, this early review of Night Shift echoes Apple's decades-long practice of promoting its products by casting white, able-bodied men in its commercials and tutorials.[31]

In this ninety-second review, the user's face is lit by the warm hue of the screen, creating a handheld, customizable light source in the midst of an otherwise darkened bedroom. We cannot initially see what this man is looking at, but his somber and focused expression suggests that he is engaged in a work-related activity. This shot is a visual representation of a marketplace in which the bedroom functions as an office, and work hours extend into the night. Increasing numbers of corporate employers recognize that embracing the "chrono-diversity" of their employees is key to maximizing productivity, for example, by allowing workers to limit their office hours or to work weekends instead of weekdays.[32] The shift to flexible work, however, has disproportionally benefited "racially classed 'white' workers and managers," while others are still asked to work in predetermined shifts.[33]

As a classed, gendered, and racial privilege, the co-option of chrono-diversity should not be read as a rejection of chrononormativity.[34] This temporal framework, which I explored in chapter 2, structures the neoliberal life around a predetermined set of milestones and accomplishments, from graduation to procreation. Confusing human worth with quantifiable productivity manifested as income, assets, marriage, and children, chrononormativity assumes an able-bodied subject who, ideally, only requires care and communal or state support in infancy and old age. As we have seen throughout this book, disabled scholars and artists have long challenged chrononormativity, revealing its hidden workings and disastrous effects on those whose bodies, desires, or needs do not neatly align with this narrative of seamless progression from one stage to the next.

Enabling white-collar workers to work from home, which can potentially improve the lives of chrono-diverse employees, fails to acknowledge or resist the ableist assumptions supporting a culture of endless productivity masquerading as hybrid work. Instead, companies like Apple tap into a techno-solutionist zeitgeist according to which technology can make the fragile, weary human body more compatible with 24/7 capitalism. For Crary, the consequential example of the effort to medicalize and technologize sleep is the effort to produce a "sleepless soldier."[35] By testing the limits of human biology, the US military hoped to minimize its soldiers' need for rest without diminishing their muscular and cognitive abilities.[36] I argue, however, that ubiquitous design features like the night mode are not aimed at minimizing the hours dedicated to sleep by creating a super-user; instead, such light calibration tools promise to make the screen display more compatible with the human optical nerve and circadian rhythms. According to this marketing logic, limiting exposure to blue light can mitigate potential disturbances to sleep, tweaking technology to better align with biological limitations and the natural environment. As the unnamed user in the AppleInsider's review reads on his iPad, "Night Shift's warmest setting approximates the color of the setting sun." Still, while natural darkness helps the human body prepare for prolonged rest, light-emitting screens—even when their blue light production is limited and filtered—are likely to contribute to sleep deprivation. By catering to users' sense of agency and self-control, this customizable design feature encourages them to prolong their screen engagement, increasing their risk of addiction, muscular pain, and, most disturbingly, fatigue.

This analysis draws on Dylan Mulvin's theorization of "media prophylactics," that is, "the techniques, technologies, and design choices that are made on behalf of or by users to preempt the ill effects (whether imagined or concrete) of media use, participation, or environmental exposure."[37] As media prophylactics, light calibration tools promise to reduce the harm caused by artificial light. For Mulvin, the night mode is the most recent attempt to return humans to a "more harmonious relationship with their environment" by allowing users more control over the "artificial but socially necessary" relationship between themselves and their self-illuminating screens.[38]

Night Shift is a tool designed to reduce screen-induced harm. As such, it recognizes fatigue as a source of suffering and as "a chronic and pervasive bodily condition" that can supposedly be limited by employing innovative design features.[39] Yet instead of helping users to identify the conditions, institutions, and demands that limit their ability to rest and care for their bodies, media prophylactics invite each user to solve the problem of sleep by simply customizing their display settings.

Apple did not invent the idea that a softer color could help users fall asleep. Night modes were preceded by dark modes, which enable users to change the contrast of their screen display by switching the default white background of the graphic user interface (GUI) to a white text over a black background. Both night modes and dark modes are based on scientific explorations of how artificial light might disrupt sleep. Tracing the war on artificial light to the 1980s, Mulvin draws on a famous study that showed how exposure to light was able to reprogram the "internal clock" of human subjects.[40] The claim that artificial light could disrupt sleep patterns, however, gained popularity only in the early 1990s, when US and Canadian newspapers began to cover the new public health menace of working night shifts and staring at television and computer screens for long hours each day.[41] The threshold reported for the amount and kind of light capable of hindering sleep changed considerably over the last few decades: "Whereas in the late 1980s a very bright light was believed necessary to disrupt a person's circadian rhythms, by the early 2000s *any screen* was now a potential antagonist."[42] As a result, tech companies like Apple and Samsung were pushed to address the problem of sleep loss by marketing "science-based" tools designed to block blue light.

The imagined user of the night mode, as seen in Apple's promotional materials, is an able-bodied, sighted "power user" who is likely to work from bed. Ironically, however, Night Shift could not have been invented without blind test subjects—the very population unable to use it. Much like the blind students who hacked the playback speed of early audiobooks (see chapter 2), blind people have played an important, if surprising, part in the story of light calibration features. A small group of test subjects who lack "normal" human optical systems eventually helped scientists in the early 2000s to discover the light-perceiving cells being activated by artificial light and self-illuminated screens. Experimenting on blind people lacking rods and cones, Farhan Zaidi and others were able to identify a photoreceptor that operates separately from the image-forming parts of the eye.[43] This discovery eventually led to the invention of night modes and other media prophylactics aimed at helping sighted users to better calibrate their bodies with their artificially lit environments. Despite the fact that the research included only a small subset of blind people and did not include sighted test subjects, it helped establish the connection between artificial light and sleep for nonblind users. As Mulvin summarizes, "This discovery repeated a well-worn research method where the exceptional bodies of people living with disabilities are used to isolate physiological functions."[44] This is in line, for example, with how the science of hearing loss and the encoding of an imaginary, distracted listener were crucial for early telecommunications and have shaped compression-based audio formats such as MP3.[45]

Yet it is still unclear whether Night Shift and similar light calibration tools in fact help sighted users improve their sleep. A 2021 study published in the scientific journal *Sleep Health* concluded that Apple's Night Shift failed to achieve its stated goal.[46] Dividing 167 study participants into three groups—one who didn't use their iPhones at all, one who used their iPhones without Night Shift enabled, and another who used their iPhones with Night Shift enabled—the researchers found that "[t]here were no significant differences in sleep outcomes across the three experimental groups."[47] The only improvement in sleep quality measured in the experiment involved those users who were randomly asked not to use their smartphones at all. The researchers explained this finding by referring to the mental stimulation produced by phone use, rather than to the light emitted by the device. This can explain why night modes, despite limiting the exposure to bright light, can in fact hinder sleep as they make it more tempting, and therefore more likely, to doomscroll or engage in other activities that aggravate rumination, rage, and anxiety—the affective states chasing sleep away.

Still, the soporific media industry promotes design features, sleep-inducing content, and hundreds of mobile apps as potential cures for the very problems that bedtime exposure to screens exacerbates. Much like light calibration tools, sleep apps promise to better harmonize users with their electronics by employing the sonic—rather than the visual—affordance of handheld devices. Apps like Calm invite paying subscribers to choose a sleep story or a soundscape, each of which begins with a soft, whispering voice inviting them to lie down, take a deep breath, and close their eyes. If night modes are designed to mitigate eye strain, the minimalist interface of sleep apps nudges the user to change their bodily posture from sedentary to horizontal. This moment of transition, as well as the invitation to close one's eyes while listening, is crucial for embedding the app into the user's bedtime behavior. That the user is lying down in bed is more important than the content they choose to engage with. Closely reading Calm's sleep stories, I argue that sleep apps rely on narrative, haptic, and sonic methods to promote a content-agnostic attachment to the handheld device. In bed, we listen.

KEEP CALM AND REWRITE HISTORY: SLEEP
APPS AND HORIZONTAL MEDIA

In 2011, American web designer Alex Tew built a website called "Do Nothing for 2 Minutes" (donothingfor2minutes.com), which enabled users to look at a photo of an ocean sunset and listen to the sound of waves while a clock counted down two minutes (see fig. 4.1). If, however, one succumbed to the desire to move one's mouse, click, refresh, or type, the black clock turned into a red sign stating "try again," and the countdown began anew. At the end of two minutes, an email prompt appeared, asking those who mastered the challenge to sign up. In just two weeks, over a hundred thousand people did so. As told by *Business of App*'s history of the company Calm, "A few months later Calm.com was founded, with the intention of building on Tew's website success."[48]

Cofounded by Tew and Michael Acton Smith in San Francisco, Calm has since grown into one of the most popular sleep and meditation apps in the world. According to company data, Calm made an estimated $200 million in 2020 and was valued at $2 billion.[49]

FIG. 4.1 A screenshot of the website donothingfor2minutes.com, inviting users to stare at a sunset and "just relax" for two minutes. (Source: donothingfor2minutes.com)

The app promises "to help you manage stress, sleep better and live a happier, healthier life" thanks to "hundreds of hours of original audio content available in seven languages." Once a subscriber downloads the app and pays the annual membership fee, they can engage with an ever-changing library of "sleep stories," "meditations," "soundscapes," and "playlists." More than a hundred million users now have Calm on their smartphones, after downloads surged by a third in the pandemic's early days.[50] New users are now recruited via their employers. Through the company's "Calm Business" program, ten million American workers have free access to the app as a mental health benefit.[51] The company's growth, in terms of both venture capital and paying subscribers, has pushed it to become a "wellness empire," with an HBO television show and an ever-expanding line of products, including an $80 meditation cushion and a $272 weighted blanket.[52] The rapid growth in paying subscribers during the pandemic enabled the company to announce an expansion into tourism through Calm-branded resorts, demonstrating how it might use its user base to market new, nondigital products.[53]

As I seek to explore the gaps and frictions between the stated goal of a new technology and its short- and long-term effects, it is useful to examine the entrepreneurial mindset that birthed Calm. An alternative origin story, as told by the *Atlantic*'s Annie Lowrey, stressed how the co-founders were drawn to the idea less by their desire to help users de-stress and improve their sleep and more by the business opportunity presenting itself when the domain name Calm.com came up for auction.[54] As described by Acton Smith, "We saw it and thought, Wow, what a domain! Should we try and buy it? We can build the world's most incredible brand."[55] Both Acton Smith and Tew were twenty-something entrepreneurs whose early online ventures included selling a shot-glass chess set and launching Moshi Monsters, an online game for kids that grew into a successful franchise.[56] This might explain why Tew named one of Calm's beta versions "Log In, Chill Out"—aptly implying that this brand was more invested in strengthening users' attachment to their devices than in inviting them to reflect on the nature of this human-machine relationship.

While Tew describes himself as "a dedicated meditator," Acton Smith had no prior experience with or knowledge of meditation before he lunched Calm.[57] In fact, he was only convinced that a meditation and sleep app might be a valuable product after Tew recommended books and articles describing the benefits of a daily meditation practice. According to Acton Smith, he got on board once he realized that "this is actually neuroscience" and "a way of rewiring the human brain."[58] In other words, this origin story—if we are to believe the company's co-founders—reveals the extent to which even meditation and sleep apps encode techno-utopian ideas of striving to optimize the human body rather than attending to its limitations. Calling itself "the Nike of the mind," the app rewards users for extending a meditation or sleep "streak" every time they listen to content. Through these design decisions, Calm makes the pursuit of better sleep a competitive and stressful endeavor. This can lead to an obsessive quest for optimal sleep, a condition called "orthosomnia" that was identified in 2017 and attributed to the use of sleep trackers and apps.[59]

This notion of "rewiring" or "hacking" the brain returns us to the ideal of the super-user as explored in my analysis of the speed watcher (see chapter 2). Tech founders often imagine this digital *Übermensch* as a wealthy, white, and able-bodied man. In her critique of the "wellness-industrial complex," Zeitlin-Wu contends that this multibillion-dollar industry "caters to overwhelmingly white and affluent consumers, often through the appropriation and decontextualization of non-Western spiritual and curative practices like Ayurveda and traditional Chinese medicine."[60] In the techno-utopian spirit of the early 2010s, entrepreneurs like Tew and Acton Smith collapse optimization and enlightenment. By promising users to improve their sleep and nudge them to take strategic breaks throughout the day, Calm seeks to enhance their productivity.

For millions of users, Calm is a source of pleasure because it associates sleep with an intimate voice whispering into their ears, returning adults to

FIG. 4.2 A screenshot from the Calm app, depicting a thumbnail of the sleep story "Dreaming with Frida." (Source: Calm)

the childhood ritual of the bedtime story. Since it was launched in early 2013, Calm's most popular content has been its "sleep stories."[61] These include readings from classic literature, children's stories, original stories about taking a train or visiting a city, descriptions of birds or mammals, and many other ten- to thirty-minute audio segments inviting subscribers to fall asleep wrapped in fantasies of a slow-paced world devoid of climate change, natural disasters, racism, or borders. In the vein of "slow TV" shows and YouTube videos savoring a ten-hour train ride or a five-hour fishing escapade, Calm's sleep stories offer an antidote to an audiovisual culture based on fast-paced editing, viral TikTok videos, and cliff-hangers ensuring bingeability.

While the rise of slow TV and the allure of nature films have drawn scholarly attention, I wish to focus on a subcategory unique to the Calm app: sleep

FIG. 4.3 A screenshot of the credit page of Calm's "Dreaming with Frida." (Source: Calm)

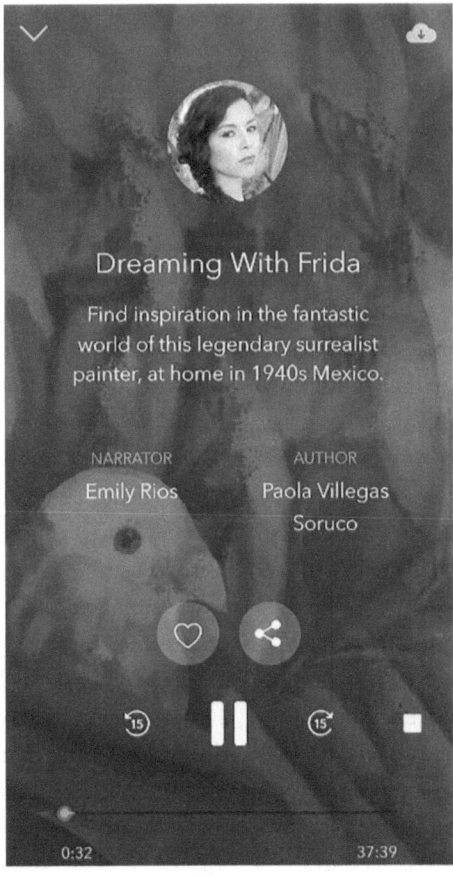

stories portraying the lives of famous artists.⁶² "Dreaming with Frida," for example, is a thirty-eight-minute sleep story pushed to new subscribers with a thumbnail consisting of a colorful portrait of the artist Frida Kahlo. The easily recognizable iconography includes the famous painter wearing a blue shirt and a hair ribbon decorated with three pink roses. Her relaxed torso emerges from a jungle-like garden, with a yellow parrot on her left and a green butterfly to her right (see fig. 4.2). As to be expected from an app designed to put users to sleep, this thumbnail projects tranquility and harmony between Frida—presented here only by her first name—and the natural world. The story, written by Paola Villegas Sourco and read by Mexican American actor Emily Rios, is noteworthy for the ways it recasts the surrealist painter as a protagonist of a fairytale taking place in 1940s Mexico (see fig. 4.3). The bedtime story introduces Kahlo as a fierce warrior, who "never apologized for who she was," and whose paintings

"LOG IN, CHILL OUT" 131

explored recurring themes "including her marriage, her chronic pain, and her love for Mexico." The listener is then invited by Rios's soft voice to close their eyes, take a deep breath, and "dream with Frida." For the next half an hour, Rios walks us through an imaginary day in Kahlo's Casa Azul in the Colonia del Carmen neighborhood of Coyoacán in Mexico City.

Rios briefly reminds her lethargic listeners that, at age forty, Kahlo suffered from injuries that kept her mostly at home, and "she often painted while lying in bed." But today, she continues, Kahlo is filled with ambition and desire to step outside and paint. Talking slowly—in an app that does not enable its users to use a playback speed feature—Rios takes ample time to describe Kahlo's delight in feeding exotic animals, including monkeys and parrots, and walking around her beautiful house. The "sleep story" glosses over the years-long torturous relationship between Kahlo and painter Diego Rivera, saying "their love, sometimes stormy, runs deep." The result is a sentimental depiction of an artist who bravely challenged rooted conceptions of the disabled female body that only mentions her injury and pain as a vague aside—"her imagination conquered all." By the time Kahlo selects a few papayas from "her favorite tree" and gazes at "a flock of butterflies" that gently land on her shoulder just as the earth "wraps around her like a soft embrace," the listener should be already fast asleep. "She has everything she needs within these walls," Rios whispers, painting an image of a five-star resort, rather than a woman confined to her bed for years following a spine injury and a series of complicated surgeries. The story ends when Kahlo leaves the house to purchase a new brush and, upon returning to her studio, is inspired to paint one of her most famous self-portraits, *Roots* (1943), depicting her wearing an orange dress with vines growing out of her body into the ground. As described by Rios, this painting is a celebration of nourishment and hope, two recurring concepts in the sleep stories lexicon.

With their close attention to colors, textures, flavors, flowers, and natural rhythms, Calm's sleep stories provide relaxing soundscapes designed to function as white noise and shield the listener from bedtime anxiety and rumination. Employing techniques such a soft, slow voice and clean, simple design, sleep and meditation apps offer a horizontal media experience that has grown in popularity over the past decade.[63]

"Dreaming with Frida" repackages the lifelong health struggles of a pioneering, disabled Mexican artist as a soothing lullaby for overworked phone users. Yet, at the same time, I argue that the content of horizontal media is less important than its form. In his analysis of Night Shift, Mulvin differentiates between media prophylactics that are "content agnostic," including ear plugs, air purifiers, and night modes, and those that are "content partisan," like safe search algorithms or the use of commercial content moderators in platform governance.[64] These tactics, as different as they may seem, are all designed and marketed to filter part of the user's sensory environment: noise, smell, light, or graphic content.

The idea that Calm and other sleep apps are content-agnostic might seem counterintuitive considering the costs of recruiting Hollywood stars, copyrighting beloved audio segments from works like *The Joy of Painting*, and marketing their premium subscriptions by touting an ever-growing content library. Yet users are unlikely to listen to "Dreaming with Frida" because they are eager to learn more about the history of modern art. In fact, if they stay awake long enough to discover that the day described by Rios led to the creation of one of Kahlo's most celebrated portraits, then the app failed to achieve its stated goal of putting them to sleep. Indeed, once Rios is done reciting this tale, the app disappointedly asks, "Still awake?," against a dark-blue background, immediately offering the insomniac listener another sleep story. A sleep app that draws too much attention to its content might keep its users awake out of interest, curiosity, or suspense. The imaginary user of Calm is not the fully awake universal spectator of apparatus theory; rather, they are the "somnolent" or "drowsy" spectator-turned-auditor who liberates themself "from the directives of the text and its system of meaning."[65] The app's users are likely to be lying down rather than sitting, and as such they differ from the sedentary moviegoer who purchased a ticket in the hopes of being immersed in a fictional world.

Decades before Calm recruited Benedict Cumberbatch and Matthew McConaughey to gently whisper in the ears of its premium subscribers, the movie theater was theorized as a "dreamscape" replicating the bedroom with its low lights, comfortable seating, and an invitation to retreat into the liminal sphere of the unconscious. In apparatus theory, which heavily drew on psychoanalytic discourse, sleep often served as a metaphor, connecting "the construction of dreams with the formal elements of storytelling."[66] From Jean-Luc Godard to Christian Metz and Jean-Louis Baudry, the movie theater was conceived of as a space in which the immobile spectator can "sleep with their eyes open."[67] When used by filmmakers like Apichatpong Weerasethkul, Abbas Kiarostami, or Béla Tarr, sleep is recast as a desirable, intentional mode of engagement rather than a distraction or disturbance.[68] Kiarostami described the films "that put their audience to sleep in the theater" as "kind enough to allow you a nice nap," while Weerasethkul invited audiences to rent a bed and spend an entire night with his twenty-hour site-specific film installation, *SLEEPCINEMAHOTEL* (2018).[69]

The somnolent spectator, Jean Ma writes, simultaneously embodies "the model and counter-model of spectatorial attention."[70] This moviegoer is crucial for developing a more nuanced model of absorption and attention. Even slow cinema, which is often read as subversive and critical of capitalist modes of acceleration and linear progress, "turns to the familiar ideal, that of the active spectator, and advocates for a return to concentration as a privileged form of attention."[71] This active spectator is key to reception studies, as they need to maintain their engagement in order to perform the functions afforded by the cinematic dispositive: identification, critique, and knowledge production.

The movie theater, however, is far from an ideal dreamscape: It requires sedentary rather than horizontal engagement, with changing light, sound, and exposure to the bodily movements, whispers, and smells of strangers. Even when achieved, the spectator's sleep is limited by the length of the film. Unlike the bed, the theater's architecture and design have historically privileged an able-bodied spectator, preventing wheelchair users and people with above-average height and weight from comfortably joining this communal ritual.[72]

Sleep apps challenge this history of sedentary engagement with media in two ways: first, by replacing the prescribed seated posture with the horizontal; second, by moving us away from the representational and aesthetic questions that have come to dominate film theory. Instead of focusing on narrative structure, mise-en-scène, editing, pacing, soundtrack, casting, and so forth, sleep apps can best be explored as "anti-content."[73] It is not the content of sleep apps' recordings that explains their immense success, but rather the sonic and affective affordances of their interface design. Embracing the inattentive user, what these apps offer is an ambient human voice strategically recorded to be listened to in a liminal state between wakefulness and sleep.

In a favorable review of Calm, *New York Times* columnist Amanda Hess recounts how she listened to the exact same recording every night for many weeks, falling asleep and developing a "strangely intimate relationship" with the app's popular meditation guide, Tamara Levitt.[74] For Hess, Levitt's soft voice functions as a "sound tranquilizer" crucial for her daily sleeping ritual.[75] The fact that Hess listens to the same recording every night suggests a unique attachment to both the content and the narrator. Yet this repetition, which, over time, might become compulsive ("I tapped into Calm at night without thinking much about what I was doing," Hess writes) has more to do with Hess's familiarity with her smartphone, the app's interface, and Levitt's voice than with the recording itself. That Hess never bothers to describe the content of her chosen segment strengthens the idea that it is Calm's interface and voice-based library, rather than its stories, that convince millions to pay for subscriptions. As Hess concludes, "Half of the programming is stuff designed to fall asleep to: If it's working, you don't hear it."[76] Here it is the passive—or, even better, the snoring—user who is the imagined ideal of the app, rather than the active spectator of film theory. If it achieves its goal, only the first few minutes might be recalled by the user-turned-listener.

If earplugs filter unwanted noise, air purifiers filter unwanted smells, and night modes filter unwanted blue light, what do sleep apps filter? One possible answer is that they filter unwanted thoughts. It is often one's stream of consciousness that chases sleep away. Ruminations, to-do lists, and feelings such as abandonment, jealousy, and fear arise more frequently and intensely at nighttime because of a lack of distractions. To counteract them, Calm offers something to put one's mind toward. Drew Ackerman, the founder and host of the popular sleep podcast *Sleep with Me* and a self-described insomniac, explains that he launched his show in 2013 "to tame the vigilant, overactive 'guardian' in the brain that feels it must stay awake to worry."[77] Over one thousand episodes later, Ackerman told the *New York Times* that he finds listening to be therapeutic, as it prevents him from ruminating all night long.[78]

Despite the growing popularity of sleep podcasts and apps, these soporific tools are not as successful as they often claim. A research study analyzing 369 sleep apps available on Android phones and iPhones found that the majority of apps failed to include components that have proved beneficial for those seeking to improve the quality, duration, and regularity of their sleep.[79] While researchers found that the apps were easy to navigate and use, they concluded that there is much room for improvement, as "only a minority of the apps included features that support behavior change."[80] Only four apps described to their users habits that can interfere with sleep and worsen insomnia, such as drinking caffeine or alcohol before bedtime.

This is not to say that sleep and meditation apps do not offer benefits. When asked to reflect on their use of personal electronics during the many months of pandemic lockdown, my undergraduate students at Colgate University frequently mentioned how sleep apps helped them maintain a healthier routine when studying from home—anecdotal data supported by empirical studies.[81] A meta-analysis of over 1,500 peer-reviewed articles published in 2010-22 concluded, "Existing studies have proved the initial validation and efficiency of delivering sleep treatment by mobile apps; however, more research is needed to improve the performance of sleep apps and devise a way to utilize them as a therapy tool."[82] Yet it is important to emphasize that sleep apps might be successful not because of their content libraries and endless loops of ocean waves, but thanks to how they encourage their users to shift from the sedentary use

FIG. 4.4 Frida Kahlo, *Without Hope*, 1945, depicting the artist as she is lying in bed and being force-fed. (Source: www.fridakahlo.org)

of media (bingeing Netflix, writing emails, working at their desk) to horizontal use consisting of mostly audio, limited visual cues, and dark, ad-free interfaces.

Sleep apps gently nudge users to lie down and be metaphorically tucked in by their electronic devices. This creates a very different relationship to the horizontal than that invoked by Kahlo's painful paintings. Kahlo's self-portraits, in many of which she is lying down, reject the association of horizontality with tranquility or sleep. In paintings such as the aforementioned *Roots* (1943) and *Without Hope* (1945), the artist's horizontal figure brings her closer to earth and the natural world but also to death, sickness, pain, and paralysis. These paintings convey vulnerability, intimacy, and an injured female body in desperate need of rest.

If "Dreaming with Frida" can ease us into sleep by using ASMR effects like the gentle sound of butterfly wings, *Without Hope* is a work of art chasing sleep away (see fig. 4.4).[83] A visual nightmare, this oil painting was painted while Kahlo was bedridden after a failed operation intended to straighten her damaged spine with a bone graft and steel support. Because she lost her appetite during her recovery, she was force-fed through a funnel.[84] Drawing on these traumatic experiences, the back of the painting carries the following inscription: "Not the least hope remains for me . . . everything moves in tune with what the belly contains."[85]

Desperate, bedridden, and in constant pain, Kahlo painted a self-portrait in which a painter's easel hovers above her bed. Instead of a canvas, it "suspends a gristly funnel delivering dead-eyed fish, plucked chicken, bloody shanks of meat and pendulous entrails, directly into Kahlo's mouth."[86] According to art critic Reed Enger, each of the objects draws on Kahlo's ongoing struggle with sickness and surgeries confining her to bed, from her hospital bed during her post-surgery recovery in New York to the oddly shaped easel created by her father to allow her to paint while bedridden.[87] The oversized funnel, Enger explains, was inspired by Alfonso Toro's engravings of the Spanish Inquisition's water torture from Kahlo's own copy of *La Familia Carvajal*.[88]

This horizontal portrait cannot be easily transformed into a "sleep story." The oil painting is a two-dimensional interface owing its existence to a simple hack: an easel that could be used for painting while lying in bed. The result is disturbing, even shocking. It conjures longer histories of force feeding and other forms of violence targeting hospitalized patients and incarcerated convicts, many of whom were female.[89] "Dreaming with Frida" replaces these personal and collective struggles with a soothing female voice and an infantilized depiction of Kahlo as a happily married woman in complete harmony with her natural environment. If Calm enhances the user's agency by gamifying and personalizing sleep, *Without Hope* depicts the excruciating pain of losing one's autonomy over one's body.

By depicting the very apparatus needed to create the painting—Kahlo's oddly shaped easel—*Without Hope* draws attention to the labor and unique tools needed to sustain the creative act while bedridden. This makes the horizontal orientation of recumbent labor an important theme of this work. Calm's content creators, on the other hand, are heavily invested in masking the conditions under which they work. Levitt, one of Calm's most popular narrators, told Hess that for two years she "regularly worked 12-hour days" to fulfill the growing demand for original content."[90] Much like Kahlo, Levitt's work requires an easel. When she records guided meditations or sleep stories for Calm, she uses "a paisley-printed easel fitted with an iPad (for her script) and an iPod (for keeping time), and a footstool crowded with beverages."[91] While Kahlo's father helped her to configure a scaffolding device aligning her injured body with her creative ambition, Levitt and Calm's other narrators are asked to align themselves with growing demand by using technological tools and nutritional support that override their need for rest and the limitations of the human vocal cords. This returns us to disability scholar Alison Kafer's description of crip time: "Rather than bend disabled bodies and minds to meet the clock, crip time bends the clock to meet disabled bodies and minds."[92] Kahlo's embrace of the horizontal is a crip call to bend the domestic environment to meet the injured body instead of forcefully feeding it into health. Calm's sleep stories, in both their demanding production schedules and ableist narratives of cure, provide mass-scale "sound tranquilizers" that can help users meet the 24/7 relentless clock.

Rios's "Dreaming with Frida" is part of the company's attempt to cater to its growing user pool by commissioning celebrities and voice actors of color to read sleep stories about nonwhite people and communities. Other examples include Vietnamese voice actor Anthony Phan's "A Day in Da Nang," NBA star LeBron James' "Train Your Mind" series, and African American former radio announcer Timothy Alexander White's "Basquiat in New York." What these recordings all have in common is an attempt to downplay racial and social tensions even while telling stories about people whose lives and struggles are shaped by colonial, ableist, and racist histories.

Calm's rewriting of history can also be found in "Basquiat in New York," in which White glosses over Jean-Michel Basquiat's chaotic life. While briefly mentioning the Black communities who populated Lower Manhattan, the story focuses on how Basquiat joyfully wandered the city's bohemian streets and collaborated with Andy Warhol, David Bowie, and other white artists during the 1980s. Working in his studio, Basquiat "smiles till he enters what scientists call 'a flow state.' ... As he reaches for transcendence, he does what he was put on earth to do." What is missing from this sleep story is not only Basquiat's drug addiction and untimely death at the age of twenty-seven, but also how he used his paintings to express rage, pain, and trauma as a Black man living in America. Much as the self-portrait *Without Hope* might confound and shock listeners of "Dreaming with Frida," Basquiat's self-portraits and morbid iconography, including his obsession with skulls and masks, convey anger, fear, and vulnerability entirely missing from the celebratory "Basquiat in New York." Using name dropping, ASMR techniques, and, once again, an ambient voice listing different colors and hand movements comprising each painting, this sleep story ignores what curator and art historian Chaédria LaBouvier describes as Basquiat's "awareness of the constant menace of policing to young black men like him, and the psychic burden that came with it."[93] This is apparent, for example, in his painting *Defacement (The Death of Michael Stewart)*, which depicts two policemen in blue uniforms, one baring pointy teeth, with batons raised over an all-black silhouette—a work painted after Basquiat learned about the violent death of the twenty-five-year-old Black artist Michael Stewart in police custody in September 1983.[94] Police brutality has nothing to do with the inspiration-filled day designed to tuck Calm's listeners into bed.

Whether you choose to listen to a sleep story about Basquiat or Kahlo does not matter much, as the app is designed to put you to sleep before you might be inclined to Google their names or ponder what is missing from the fictionalized depictions of their lives. An assembly line of relaxing voices, Calm invites users to "log in, chill out" by producing "anti-content" that helps filter out disturbing thoughts—including thoughts about the structural inequalities that make some human bodies matter more than others. The resulting irony is that the specific stories Calm includes, if told more truly, could cost users some sleep.

Reliant on users to renew their monthly or annual subscriptions, Clam is a postural technology associating horizontality with enhanced productivity. Yet *Without Hope* suggests that being horizontal might allow us to critique ableist ideas about health and wellness. What happens when we focus our analysis of soporific media on those who either are not allowed or are otherwise unable to sleep? And how can artists living with depression, chronic fatigue, or other disabilities open up new ways of understanding horizontal media?

RECONFIGURING #SELFCARE

For both Apple and Calm, night modes and sleep apps double as surveillance technologies, as the user willingly provides data points related to their habits, locations, and patterns of sleep and wakefulness. What forms of sleep, if any, can remain more resistant to capitalist optimization in the age of hyperconnectivity? Is it possible to offer a crip sleep app that highlights the tensions between activity and passivity, resistance and refusal, instead of deepening an unhealthy dependency on light-emitting electronics and mobile apps? If Calm habituates users to take their smartphones to bed, the mobile app #SelfCare opts to improve sleep and ease anxiety by reconfiguring and de-automating the user's relationship with their screen. As such, it offers a crip alternative to the soporific media industry.

Launched in 2018 by the Toronto-based studio *TRU LUV*, #SelfCare is a free app with no advertisements.[95] The app, which the studio called a "companion" to differentiate it from for-profit sleep and health apps, is intentionally simple. It consists of several short pastimes, among them a slow breathing exercise, petting a cat by gently stroking the screen with one's fingers, or idly sorting a digital

FIG. 4.5 A screenshot of the home page of the app #SelfCare. (Source: #SelfCare mobile app)

laundry basket. The home page portrays a domestic scene familiar to any mobile user: a person lying in bed, tucked under a white blanket, with a single hand gently resting on the pillow while a cat lies on the left bottom of the bed (see fig. 4.5). The bedroom, which is seen from a bird's-eye view, is bright and minimally furnished with a white rug, a laundry basket, and two bedside chests with flowers, cards, and several other items. A smartphone is tossed on the left pillow, barely out of reach from the half-asleep, half-awake protagonist.

While users can change the skin color of the sleeping protagonist via the settings menu, the default color is dark, differentiating #SelfCare from other products of the soporific industry. The app's imaginary user, as described by its developers, is someone who struggles with insomnia, anxiety, or depression. At the same time, its minimalist design and relaxing, scoreless games can help a plethora of users reassess their relationship with their phones. This is achieved by asking the user to pet a cat vis-à-vis "tapping" or caressing the screen, and

FIG. 4.6 A screenshot of a word game featuring the word "insomnia" from the #SelfCare app. (Source: #SelfCare mobile app)

then put their phone away so they can gently tap their own body. A user who gets bored with a breathing exercise and attempts to leave the app by pressing the menu in the top right corner instead encounters a screen suggesting, "Let's stay here a bit longer." While it is still possible to leave the app, these design decisions break the automated bodily reactions to boredom and frustration. After a few short games, the app encourages the user to turn off their phone entirely—an alternative sleep-inducing approach to that of Calm and other sleep apps, which offer an endless stream of sleep stories and white noises requiring keeping one's phone at arm's length.

If Calm rewrites personal histories of pain and sickness as bedtime lullabies for weary bodies and minds, #SelfCare normalizes depression, fatigue, and burnout by offering a single home page featuring an insomniac person hiding under the covers and tossing from side to side. As the app tells us, this person "refuses to leave bed today." The mostly hidden protagonist is not a tranquil and healthy user about to rest and recharge. This human body is bound to remain horizontal as long as the app is turned on. For Canadian game designer and disability scholar Kara Stone, the choice not to include a script of waking up or going to work is what makes the app successful: "#SelfCare has not set out to cure all debility or negative feelings, but to change our relationship with our phones."[96] In *TRU LUV*'s parlance, this is achieved by degamifying the more familiar health and sleep apps: "Our goal is simply to feel better. There's no winning, no failure, no score. No difficulty, no ads, no notifications. There is just us and our feelings."[97] These feelings, the app tells us, might entail "I don't want to get back to my emails" or "I feel disconnected." It then invites the user to recognize these feelings, for example, by playing a word game in which they are asked to complete words such as "is_lation" or "insoma_ia," only so the user can sit with them for a while instead of clicking their pain away (see fig. 4.6). #SelfCare's call to "stay home today" crips the sleep apps' promise to help users calibrate their schedules and energies with capitalist rhythms. As Stone argues, "The goal of the game is not to overcome depression, a common narrative arc concerning disability, but to create rituals that make life sustainable."[98] One such ritual could be putting one's phone away after briefly reflecting on how it might disturb sleep. By depicting an image of an insomniac person who tosses from side to side next to their phone, the app associates phone use with sleeplessness, providing an alternative to Calm's interface. Here, to fall asleep, one must first get rid of one's phone and be reminded of one's bodily needs, even when these needs might invoke undesired sensations such as pain and rumination.

Still, #SelfCare promotes individual, rather than communal, behavioral change, and as such it participates in the soporific media industry while dismantling its mechanisms. It leaves us wondering what a communal and political soporific tool might look like.

LASSO OF TRUTH: CRIPPING HORIZONAL MEDIA

By offering reflection, rather than distraction, as a way of preparing for bed, #SelfCare employs disability-inspired caring rituals that are designed to be enacted for just a few minutes before (hopefully) turning away from one's personal electronics. #SelfCare tries to produce not adrenaline and dopamine but, if successful, melatonin. This free app was designed for people whose pain and chronic illness prevent them from falling asleep. For these users, chronic fatigue might result from autoimmune syndromes, long-term insomnia, or, in recent years, long COVID.[99] One of the challenges of living with constant fatigue is that both loved ones and medical professionals may not believe one's account of pain and exhaustion. Film scholar Alex Juhasz, who was unable to see a doctor during the early weeks of the pandemic despite suffering from

COVID symptoms, writes that "many of the untested may not be known to those who are counting the infected and determining the official number of those constituted as recovered. *How do we care for the recovering [of those] who were never known to be ill?*"[100] The denial and dismissal of long COVID testifies to the extent to which chronic fatigue is a condition not easily recognized, treated, or diagnosed. By chronicling her life, which often consists of prolonged periods in bed due to chronic sickness, Toronto-based filmmaker Hannah Bullock explores this tension between the subjective experience of pain and exhaustion and the limitations of diagnostic tools offered by medical professionals.

Shot entirely on Bullock's MacBook's desktop, *2020-09-16 at 11:19:28 AM* opens with the familiar default image of a sandy mountain and clear blue sky.[101] The nine-and-a-half-minute video essay merges the dwindling energies of the fatigued body of the filmmaker-turned-subject with that of the machine. It begins when the battery icon stands at 20 percent, raising a concern as to whether the film might abruptly end once the battery dies. With the desktop's meticulous arrangement of folders and icons carrying foreboding names such as "MRI," "PCC_patient_questionnaire," and "Medical Records," the decision to create a work without charging the laptop beforehand cannot be accidental. This collapse of the interface and the sick body makes the viewer painfully aware of the dependence of one on the other, raising the question of who might die first (see fig. 4.7). It also creates an immediate sense of intimacy, as Bullock simultaneously invites us into her bedroom, her personal computer, and her decade-long medical archive.

The film's desktop aesthetic and the phone-based shots of Bullock in bed take us away from the fetishized movie theater and into the intimate realm of horizontal media. This work asks: What kind of vulnerability does lying down enable? How can we invent and employ crip tools to replace the diagnostic logic of the medical model? And how does the machine's fragility, its ever-dwindling battery life, allow us to reconnect to, or at the very least to recognize, our own vulnerability rather than ignoring it?

Bullock plays with vertical and horizontal juxtapositions as she clicks on several vertical, rectangular videos files shot with her phone camera. As these short recordings start playing, her desktop screen is divided into several planes of action, while Bullock narrates her story of living with undiagnosed pain since 2009. Stuck in bed for extended periods of time, Bullock developed a makeshift hack resembling Kahlo's easel: By tying a wire to her waist and connecting a black pen to its other end, she is able to use the movement created by her breathing abdomen to "draw" on a white paper she attached to the wall at bed height. "I'm trying to teach myself that I can still make valuable work

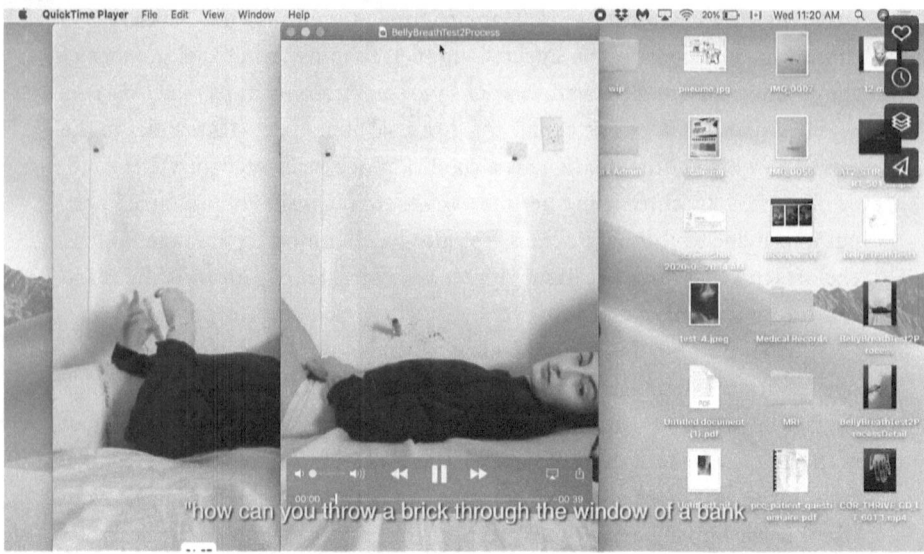

FIG. 4.7 A still image from Bullock's *2020-09-16 at 11:19:28 AM*, depicting the filmmaker lying in bed and using her breath to paint as well as her desktop. Courtesy of Hannah Bullock.

without getting out of bed," she explains. She then cites Johanna Hedva's "Sick Woman Theory," a love letter to the creative and political potential of rest as resistance and of bedridden creativity.[102] "I'm trying to unlearn that my body is apolitical if I can't manage to lift it out of bed," Bullock continues, alluding to Hedva's inquiry: "How do you throw a brick through the window of a bank if you can't get out of bed?"[103]

In her manifesto, Hedva answers this question by describing the anticapitalist potential of communal care. Inspired by support systems funded and sustained by disability activists, this can take the form of "sharing our stories of therapies and comforts, forming support groups, bearing witness to each other's tales of trauma, prioritizing the care and love of our sick, pained, expensive, sensitive, fantastic bodies."[104] This emphasis on communal infrastructure, rather than tech-based individual solutions, aims at reframing fatigue not as a problem to be solved but rather as a condition whose disproportionate effects on different bodies need to be publicly discussed and acknowledged.

For the chronically ill and fatigued, horizontal media take on a sense of urgency. For both Hedva and Bullock, lying down is not a choice; it is a survival technique and a bodily position that has come to define their existence. Drawing on Hedva's manifesto, Bullock describes how "sitting up feels like a workout" due to debilitating neck and head pain. This pain isolates her because others, even loved ones, find it hard to believe that she lacks the energy or ability to get out of bed. "As if it wasn't infantilizing enough, now I need to prop up my own head," Bullock quietly says, connecting horizontally to regression and fears of dependency.

This enforced horizontal orientation not only limits the body, but also changes the notion of space and time. American author Laura Hillenbrand, who wrote her best-seller *Seabiscuit* while ill with chronic fatigue syndrome, describes how she could only write a paragraph or two a day as a result of dizziness and fatigue: "When I could no longer stand the spinning, I'd take a pillow into the yard and lie in the grass.... When I was too tired to sit at my desk, I set the laptop up on my bed. When I was too dizzy to read, I lay down and wrote with my eyes closed."[105] For the chronically fatigued, the entire world is a makeshift bed. Instead of the imaginary power user of night modes, Hillenbrand helps us to imagine a human body in need of prolonged periods of support and rest in order to enjoy brief moments of creation. Her account is also a reminder that chrono-diversity, apart from being a corporate buzzword, might limit one's ability to engage in creative and social activities.

For disability writer and scholar Ellen Samuels, fatigue turns crip time into "vampire time," that is, "the time of late nights and unconscious days, of life schedules lived out of sync with the waking, quotidian world."[106] Samuels' genetic disease, while endangering her joints, tendons, and heart due to the lack of collagen, also makes her look younger than her age because of its effects on the smoothness of the skin. Much like Bullock, this lack of visible signs of sickness induces a crisis of disbelief. For Samuels, "being a crip vampire spins me back into that whirlpool of time travel. I look 25, feel 85, and just want to live like the other 40-somethings I know. I want to be aligned, synchronous, part of the regular order of the world."[107] This desperate plea to synchronize oneself with others might explain the success of the soporific media industry and its promise to improve one's sleep.

Bullock directly engages this mistrust by depicting a self-made, improvised "pneumograph," marketed by its inventor as "the original lie detector." This tool consists of a wire that, by means of Bullock's irregular and abnormal "belly breaths," moves a pen and creates drawings on a white piece of paper hanging on the wall next to her bed. Bullock explains that the resulting artworks might provide evidence for the sickness ravaging her body. "I realized that I made a super simplified and shitty version of a pneumograph," she tells us. "Still trying to detect the truth of my own illness, still interrogating my own body, still looking for evidence. Fun fact: The guy who invented the pneumograph lie detector also invented Wonder Woman. Maybe I made my own lasso of truth. I doubt it, though." This improvised "lasso of truth" is a different kind of sleep tracker; it is employed not to optimize sleep but rather to mediate the havoc that chronic fatigue wreaks on one's body to doubtful others. This is especially crucial for someone like Bullock, whose MRI scans fail to detect abnormalities. What Bullock is striving to develop is not a cure but rather a way of "getting better at feeling like shit." This is a modest, yet highly ambitious, goal.

While Bullock is alone throughout this piece, her pursuit of a "lasso of truth" demonstrates that the dismissal of fatigue and its effect on one's well-being is no less debilitating than the symptoms of sleep deprivation. There is real suffering in not having enough energy to leave one's bed, and individualizing this pain by promoting tech fixes like night modes or sleep apps is a limited strategy destined to worsen the social consequences of sleep loss by putting this burden on the employee, the sick, and the insomniac, instead of pushing for a world in which one's value is not solely measured based on one's productivity.

Coda: COVID Nightmares

My hypersensitivity to light makes me more prone to fatigue. When woken up by artificial or natural night, I am seldom able to fall asleep again. In the resulting moments of forced wakefulness, leaving my bedroom and turning on my phone amounts to surrender, an embracing of the fact that the night is lost. Transforming the individual act of sleep into a communal reflection on the conditions that hinder or support it, I wish to conclude this analysis of the soporific media industry with another recent artwork.

In *COVID Sleep*, an art piece comprised of fifteen short videos, Dayna McLeod produces night-vision surveillance footage of herself and her girlfriend sleeping (or failing to sleep). The project was conceived as part of a virtual residency inviting ten Canadian artists to reflect on the idea of "being alone together" during the pandemic lockdowns, and the footage was shot over the course of the sixty-day residency from April to May 2020. As McLeod describes it, "I've always had sleep disturbances like nightmares, sleepwalking, and night terrors, but [I] didn't realize their extent and frequency until I started these recordings.... I gasp, yell, talk, scream, and otherwise ask questions while asleep."[108] While the project was originally presented as a gallery installation, the fifteen video pieces are available on YouTube. The short segments, which last between ten to forty seconds, capture McLeod as she wakes up from a

FIG. 4.8 A screenshot from Dayna McLeod's *COVID Sleep–April 9, 2020*, depicting McLeod as she abruptly wakes up from a nightmare at 4:06 a.m. Courtesy of Dayna McLeod.

nightmare, involuntarily moves her arm, and talks in her sleep. As such, they present us with a depiction of a vulnerable, restless human body (see fig. 4.8).

With its glimpses of McLeod's sleeping girlfriend, whose body is farther away from the camera and is often concealed by McLeod's torso and facial expressions, this project intentionally draws on previous cinematic explorations of queer intimacy. Durational works like Andy Warhol's *Sleep* (1964) famously inquired what might happen to this most intimate act when exhibited in public, depicting a nonsexual mode of care and vulnerability.[109] Such documentations of the sleeping body frame it as a screen onto which viewers are invited to project their own fears and desires.

In her artist's statement, McLeod explains she employs night vision as its aesthetic features consist of "pixilation, blurriness, perspective distortion, grain, and lighting."[110] This low-resolution aesthetic reframes McLeod's abrupt movements as shots from a horror film. It is not just queer intimacy that McLeod invokes but rather the suspenseful, uncanny sense of a living creature being caught on hidden camera in the dead of night. I read McLeod's work as an attack on surveillance capitalism and the notion that, to improve one's quality of sleep, we need to subject ourselves to technologies that monitor our circadian rhythms.

In *COVID Sleep*, McLeod is in full control over the personal data she decides to share. She uses this footage to connect with others whose sleep is disturbed by involuntary twitches and nightmares. As such, she joins Bullock and other artists who use sleep in their work to recognize it—in line with Crary's analysis—as a social issue. Yet, by creating this work as part of an artist's residency and presenting it in a gallery space, McLeod helps us to theorize sleep as a means for value production, rather than as the last untouched zone of nonproductivity. Shot during the early months of the pandemic, this documentation of sleep provides a different kind of glimpse into the intimacy of one's bedroom than that enforced on white-collar workers who had to switch to remote work. As Shannon Mattern reminds us, during the pandemic-induced lockdowns, "a mere glimpse of a bed in the background of a Zoom screen could be deemed unprofessional."[111] The decision to incorporate the bed into artworks, Twitch gaming sessions, or ASMR videos, on the other hand, demonstrates that some sleepers can turn their sleep into a source of profit.[112]

McLeod's cramped bedroom conveys claustrophobia and paranoia. It features multiple technologies, from a television screen in the very back of the frame to an iPad McLeod holds before going to bed, as well as a phone on her nightstand and, of course, the camera documenting her and her partner throughout the night. Yet these personal electronics all fail to provide what McLeod seems to seek: an undisturbed night's sleep, allowing her body to fully rest and recharge. Watching her nocturnal struggles to go back to sleep reminded me not only of my own sleepless nights but also of the limitations of the design features promising to tuck me into bed.

Inviting us to reexamine our dependency on screens, crip horizontal media offer radical interpretations of vulnerability, care, and rest. McLeod, Bolluck, and the #SelfCare app all help us reflect on the anxieties associated with sleep and its lack—aging, sickness, pain, vulnerability, and uncertainty. They provide a framework of communal interdependence replacing the surveillance industry tracking users' sleep and wakefulness patterns. The soporific media industry, with its growing number of apps, design features, and products, worsens insomnia and, as a result, increases digital debility, by making people obsessed with optimizing their sleep and achieving "the perfect slumber."[113] Rejecting the impulse to pathologize sleep, crip horizontal media consider how this basic human need is shaped by medical, psychological, sociopolitical, and environmental conditions.

The interface fiction produced by night modes and sleep apps is that users inevitably strive to be more aligned with 24/7 capitalism. Yet crip time teaches us that misalignment can sometimes prove crucial for creativity, healing, and new orientations from which to see the world. It recognizes chrono-diversity not as a corporate means to maximize productivity by allowing some workers to work on their own schedule, but rather as an ever-changing spectrum of abilities, sensitivities, and needs.

If the design features this book explores—refresh, playback speed, autoplay, and night modes—have something is common, it is the way they assume a universal user and, at the same time, push users to ignore their bodily limitations and biological needs. While these features are sometimes beneficial for some users, taken together they support a scripted online environment based on addictive design. Sleep, the epitome of the inherent limitations of the human body, is a key site for meaning production and for recentering varying modes of embodiment within media theory and interface design.

CODA

Digital Debility and the Normalization of Fatigue

Zooming In, Zooming Out

A woman, a man, and two children hold a screaming contest in Marilene Oliver's *Whoever Screams the Loudest*, a five-minute video artwork shot on Google Hangouts and uploaded to Vimeo in January 2021, at the height of the pandemic (see fig. C.1). The goal, as Oliver explains in a short description, is "to scream the loudest in order to try and steal the Google Hangouts spotlight."[1]

The result is a depressing, amusing, and mostly unwatchable manifesto against the videoconferencing technologies that have come to shape the lives of millions. The video, much like the pandemic's lockdown that inspired it, is an endurance test. The four family-members-turned-coworkers forsake the social norms of online communication for a desperate cry for attention. They practice self-harm; as the con-

FIG. C.1 A screenshot from Marilene Oliver's *Whoever Screams the Loudest*. Courtesy of Marilene Oliver.

test progresses, they become visibly exhausted as they gasp for air. The series of screams ends with the sound of coughing. Everybody lost. While desperately shielding themselves from a new viral threat by staying home, the intergenerational group of screamers endures exhaustion and pain.

Oliver drew inspiration from "medieval religious rituals of crying and screaming to be heard (and thus saved) by God," as well as from Edvard Munch's *The Scream* and Marina Abramović and Ulay's 1978 performance *AAA-AAA*. Yet there is something disturbingly timely about her work. How many times have you wanted to scream at your screen during yet another remote meeting? How many cries have you alchemically transformed into a polite nod, a comment in the chat, a wry smile? How much rage or fatigue can a human body hold?

Videoconferencing platforms are a productive end point from which to evaluate how interface design reshapes human bodies. The four design features and spectatorial modes I explored throughout this book introduce an interdisciplinary theory of digital usership and its somatic temporalities of waiting (chapter 1), compression (chapter 2), endurance (chapter 3), and drowsiness (chapter 4). As different as these states seem to be, they all produce and sustain an unrecognized friction between the interface and its real-life user. Reassessing the early press coverage of "Zoom fatigue"—a set of symptoms ranging from migraines to muscle pain associated with the extended use of the popular platform—can reveal how digital debility has been normalized. This "consensual impairment," to return to Sterne, has been endured en masse as millions grew reliant on Zoom, Google Meets, and similar tools for virtual meetings and hybrid or remote work.[2] According to Tung-Hui Hu, Zoom fatigue and digital burnout not only have been accepted as common side effects of online living; they have become "a status symbol of overwork."[3] Hashtags like "#sotired," which grew in popularity since the pandemic, expand the chat room conversations in which tech workers recast pain and exhaustion as proofs of one's resilience, productivity, and efficiency.[4]

Early in the pandemic, schools and universities hastily trained their faculty to use Zoom for synchronous learning, and the company's stock price skyrocketed.[5] Established in 2011 as a video conferencing platform for global businesses, Zoom was recast as a heaven-sent solution for quarantine anxiety and an economy threatening to collapse. By making possible everything from yoga classes to psychotherapy sessions, Zoom promised much more than seamless video; it held out the possibility of normalcy, routine, and connection during a crisis characterized by limited mobility and lack of in-person social interactions.

Like other phrases from the pandemic lexicon that quickly entered Americans' colloquial language, such as "flattening the curve" and "sheltering in place," the term "Zoom fatigue" was popularized by the press during the early months of lockdown in March and April 2020. This side effect of online life included debilitating symptoms such as brain fog, migraines, and exhaustion. That the very same symptoms of Zoom fatigue are also often caused by long COVID demonstrates how similar physiological and cognitive conditions can be pathologized or normalized, depending on the context. Alarming headlines identified Zoom fatigue as a common side effect of videoconferencing, only to quickly reassure readers that this temporary, individual problem can easily be solved by "changing your remote work setting," "taking a ten-minute break," or "avoiding multitasking."[6] None of these listicles acknowledged the uncanniness of trying to focus on a conversation while your boss, colleague, or potential employer holds both a mirror and a camera within three feet of your face.

More disturbingly, the pandemic rapidly created a potentially fatal distinction between two groups of people: "essential workers" required to put their bodies at risk and remote workers asked to move their entire lives online. While many essential workers contracted the virus early on during the pandemic, white-collar workers enjoyed the safety of their homes. Working remotely, however, worsened the effects of digital debility by increasing users' risk of muscular pain, addiction, and eyestrain. It also normalized an increasingly unequal labor market in which some workers are able to work remotely while others are penalized if and when they demand the same flexibility. Even for tech and creative workers who enjoy the freedom to choose how often to work from their office, hybrid work might produce a sense of malaise leading to increased levels of stress and burnout. According to the *New York Times*, the increase in job dissatisfaction since 2022 can be attributed, in part, to how remote or hybrid work tends to "break up our work bonds," as "you might go in on a different day than your boss or than your closest work friend."[7] Severing organic, in-person meetings with one's boss or colleagues proved especially harmful for younger or junior workers who rely on networking and personal connections for their training, evaluation, and promotion.[8]

Remote work decreased or eliminated altogether the daily commute, while also limiting social and multisensorial interactions with others. Forced to sit in front of a computer monitor for hours, a body might scream for relief. For people with disabilities, videoconferencing is yet another example of how the digital interface might be experienced as both inclusive and exclusive. Zoom, for example, popularized the use of automated captions and made it relatively easy to add real-time captions by a human transcriber. The ability to customize and personalize the screen size of each speaker also makes it easier to use an ASL interpreter for those who prefer signing over captions.

Early in the pandemic, attendance at the New York Public Library's online programs targeted at blind and low vision people grew by 500 percent.[9] Describing her experience navigating the lockdown as a person with low vision, accessibility consultant Bojana Coklyat recalls how she and others used Zoom to create a multisensory, communal event:

> I always think about the first Zoom party I went to, called Remote Access. It was really early on in March 2020. I think it was organized pretty quickly, Kevin Gotkin was DJing, and Yo-Yo Lin showed some animations, kind of abstract patterns of color. What was so great was that they hacked Zoom in a way where, for audio description, I was able to call in. There was one link or phone number for the Zoom Meeting experience, with music and illustration, and then there was another Zoom link that I clicked onto with somebody doing live audio description. . . . There was a real sense of community, and I really appreciated it.[10]

Coklyat's description reminds us that videoconferencing platforms are incredibly helpful for people with disabilities, enabling them to engage in cultural, social, and political debates without having to navigate physical environments that might put them at risk. While similar accounts of Zoom as a lifeline abound, media scholars should be careful not to idealize these commercial platforms. As *Interface Frictions* makes manifest, design features should be studied through the lens of "access friction," in which "actions that increase access for some may limit or hinder access for others."[11] Those with speech impediments or a stutter, for example, might find videoconferencing platforms to be ableist spaces because of their data collection policies and profit-driven focus on efficiency, productivity, and verbal communication.[12] AI-generated captions, which are much more common than the use of professional transcribers, have also been repeatedly critiqued as unreliable. Speakers with non-Anglophone accents (such as myself) often find the automated transcription of their speech to be limited and lacking. This is the result of an ableist and Anglophonic voice-recognition industry, whose datasets often comprised a narrow sample of "standard" voices.[13]

The growing popularity of videoconferencing apps has had contradictory effects on many people with disabilities. Empirical data shows that, for many disabled students, remote participation "both exacerbated existing inequities and instigated new ones" by limiting access to resources, in-person communication, and social interactions with their peers and teachers.[14] Similarly, homebound people with myalgic encephalomyelitis (ME, also known as chronic fatigue syndrome) reported experiencing "greater isolation" during the pandemic despite the increase in remote access events.[15] Reminding us that people with ME have been socializing and organizing via videoconferencing platforms long before COVID-19, Harris Kornstein and Emily Lim Rogers reveal how homebound patients experienced a sense of "pandemic déjà vu" once the lockdown caused the nondisabled public to experience what people with ME have lived with daily.[16] Those longer histories of remote work and communication simultaneously made homebound or bedridden people more prepared for pandemic life while worsening the sense of isolation they had to endure long after the pandemic was officially over (according to federal and state agencies). While normalizing and increasing access to accommodations like captioning or telehealth, the pandemic also left people with disabilities with difficult feelings of resentment and neglect, creating a rift between the immunocompromised and the rest.

The rising popularity of videoconferencing platforms also pressures people with disabilities, especially those with invisible disabilities, to continue working and socializing even when they feel sick, depleted, or overwhelmed by the "temporal debt" of living in crip time (see chapter 2). In his analysis of "access thievery," J. Logan Smilges describes how he "stole" access by skipping a faculty meeting and canceling a class, telling his colleagues he had a "family emergency" and telling his students he had a stomach virus.[17] However, he explains, his family members were fine and he felt physically fit. The real reason for cancellation was his "sensory hangover" following a late-night dinner at a loud restaurant. As a neurodiverse person living in "crip/trauma/mad time," Smilges writes that a sensory hangover isn't something he can explain "to non-autistic and otherwise nondisabled people who more often than not find themselves *energized* rather than depleted by excessive sensory stimulation."[18] To translate his access needs into a language supported by a "hyperabled academic institution," Smilges came up with false excuses, stealing "the access I needed in order to flourish" by using a common and nonstimatized medical condition such as a stomach flu.[19]

Stealing access, however, is increasingly challenging at a time when many workers are expected to work from home even if they are sick or confined to their beds. And while many disability scholars and activists celebrate videoconferencing as an equalizer, it also produces a unique sense of disorientation and fatigue when the human brain is constantly asked to compensate for the micro-delays between audio and video signals.[20] This built-in latency is most noticeable in moments when the video stream freezes yet the audio remain intelligible, but it exists even when there aren't any connectivity issues. In an interview with the BBC, Gianpiero Petriglieri explained that being on a video call requires more focus than a face-to-face chat: "Video chats mean we need to work harder to process nonverbal cues like facial expressions, the tone and pitch of the voice, and body language; paying more attention to these consumes a lot of energy. Our minds are together when our bodies feel we're not. That dissonance, which causes people to have conflicting feelings, is exhausting."[21] While this dissonance can manifest itself as Zoom fatigue in neurotypical users, it might create an unbearable mental burden for neurodiverse people like Smilges.

The "Zoomtopia," in company parlance, also ignores the inherent latency of the digital infrastructure I studied in chapter 1 and the short- and long-term effects of screen-induced fatigue I explored in chapter 4. The ubiquity of internet trolls and the unexpected disruptions that pop into the frame in the form of pets, children, and partners makes videoconferencing more unexpected and anxiety-inducing than acknowledged by employers and tech companies alike. In fact, Zoom's ability to provide seamless video is now doubtful, as an exponential influx of users encounter buffering issues, frozen screens, and other forms of digital noise (see chapter 1). Worse, the privacy breaches of the product made Zoombombing ever more tempting as it spreads into public events and academic seminars.[22]

These oft-denied issues complicate the prevailing idea that videoconferencing is a digital equalizer. While commercial platforms are employed by many immunosuppressed or bedridden people, their design features neatly align them with chrononormativity and its emphasis on productivity. As I mentioned in chapter 2, Zoom is one of the only platforms that allows its user to speed up, but not to slow down, its video recordings. The embedded assumption of Zoom's playback feature is that some speakers or topics might be deemed too boring or slow. Adding the option to slow down the playback speed of recorded Zoom lectures or meetings could have easily made it more accessible for a variety of users, yet the platform's imaginary user is the abled-bodied, neurotypical neoliberal subject trying to cram content.

Yet another default feature of Zoom is the self-view, which users can remove from their screen by choosing and clicking the "hide self-view" option. As we have seen throughout this book, default features requiring the user to locate and navigate an opt-out option might be harmful for some users. If, as I studied in chapter 3, many users found Netflix's previews autoplay to be triggering or, in some cases, retraumatizing, Zoom's self-view might exacerbate self-hate and anxiety. This is the result of habituating users to stare at their image while trying to attend a class, meeting, therapy session, or job interview. Unlike looking at a mirror, staring at our digital image worsens the fatigue caused by the delay between sonic and visual cues. It also makes users painfully aware of how their facial expressions, clothes, and energy levels compare with those of on-screen others, paving the way to unhealthy obsession with one's appearance. As proven in the case of Instagram, such comparisons—made increasingly unrealistic due to the use of filters and AI tools—directly contribute to mental health risks, especially among young women.[23]

On Zoom, the close-up is not a vehicle for intimacy, admiration, and proximity, as famously theorized by early film scholars.[24] Instead of offering a sublime vision of a Hollywood star, the close-up framing of the self-view can worsen feelings of isolation and inadequacy. The medium close-up, which normally encompasses both the speaker's head and shoulders and their background, worsens class divides by setting expectations for well-organized, private domestic settings—leading to the rise of commercial companies offering curated bookshelves and virtual backgrounds designed to transform one's bedroom into a makeshift library.[25] In short, the uneven improvement of infrastructure and video compression has birthed a new set of standards and social norms, among them the expectation to maintain a professional, public-facing visibility even from one's bedroom.

By shifting events, conferences, lectures, and public gatherings online, videoconferencing platforms foreground many of the challenges of archiving digital cultures. *Interface Frictions* was written in part as an attempt to historicize and offer a decentralized archive of design features that radically shaped our media consumption over the last two decades. As partial and limited as it is, such documentation is needed since, as I explored in chapter 2, standardization is a process of forgetting and erasing. While digital archives like the Wayback Machine are a crucial source for studying the ever-evolving shape of the internet, they fail to capture error messages, minor changes to the interface, and personalized encounters between different users and their subscription-based platforms.

These limitations should also inform any analysis of videoconferencing platforms. With its built-in recording option, Zoom supposedly automates the creation of cloud-supported digital archives. However, such recordings are highly problematic: Users might lose access to old recordings once they switch devices or institutions; the recordings don't always include the chat and other data available to real-time participants (for example, the use of emojis or reactions like a thumbs up or an animated heart); and only the designated host gets access to the recording link. This results in dispersed, fragmented archives lacking a standardized set of regulations or best practices and failing to provide an easy way to access an accumulating plethora of content.

One recent attempt to record the ways in which people with disabilities have used videoconferencing is the Remote Access Archive initiated by the Critical Design Lab and its director, Aimi Hamraie, in 2023.[26] Reminding us that, prior to the pandemic, disabled people were often denied access to remote telecommunications based on the assumption that it was too financially or logistically burdensome, the lab seeks to document the ways in which homebound users pioneered, explored, and tweaked remote access tools. Aware of the many challenges of digital archiving, the team leading this effort called participants to send video recordings of online events, artworks inspired by or made via remote access platforms, but also "the times you asked for remote participation or access and were told 'no.'"

The Remote Access Archive not only helps us understand the pivotal role that people with disabilities have played in using digital tools, but also expands our definition of archives to include the entire interface as well as the improvised setups enabling users with various bodily capacities to interact with it. These can include a personal computer, web cam, microphone, lights, shades, and other elements, such as a standing or a bed-accustomed desk. Employing screenshots as an accessible tool for documentation, the Remote Access Archive also contains text messages, discussion boards, group photos, and event advertisements. This endeavor seeks to realistically portray "specific ways that disability communities, such as Autistic and neurodivergent people, Deaf and Hard-of-Hearing people, Blind people, Chronically Ill or Sick people, and mobility-disabled people, use remote access."[27]

In its call for submissions, the Critical Design Lab also asked videoconferencing users to share "ways you keep up with friends and loved ones at a distance,"

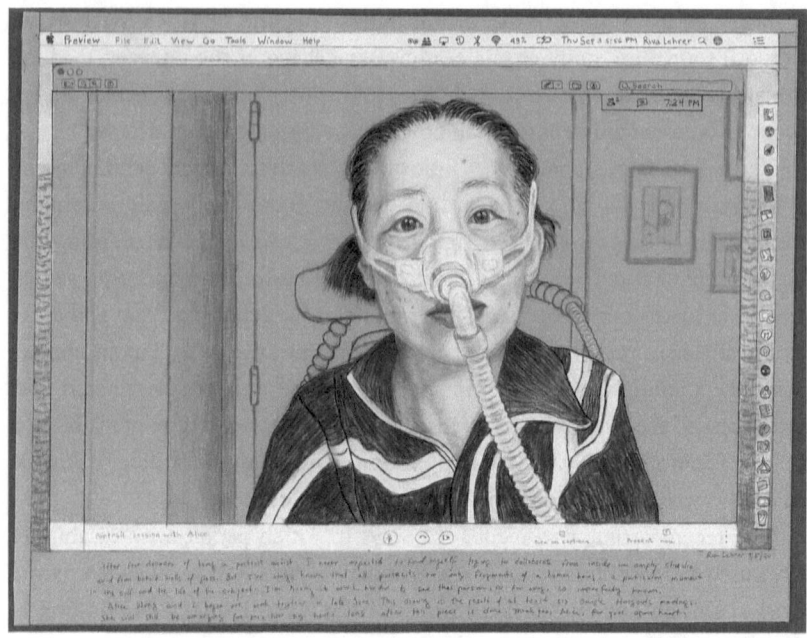

FIG. C.2 The painting *Zoom Portrait: Alice Wong* by Riva Lehrer. Courtesy of Riva Lehrer.

inviting people with disabilities to theorize these tools as crucial for community building, socialization, and survival. Riva Lehrer's *Zoom Portraits* series, which I explore below, celebrates such potential benefits while lamenting the loss of what cannot be accounted for by screen-based encounters.[28]

THROUGH THE (DIGITAL) LOOKING GLASS

Could there be another way to observe ourselves through the digital looking-glass? Once again, I find the answer in a work made by an artist with disabilities. In a 2020 collaboration between two prominent disability rights activists—Riva Lehrer, who is a painter, and Alice Wong, a writer and educator—Wong is seen at the center of a painting, wearing an oxygen mask (see fig. 5.2). It is a loving and gentle portrayal of a virtual encounter, complete with a desktop, open tabs, and other aesthetic elements that have come to frame our human-to-computer and human-to-human interactions. The use of color is striking, as Wong's face and torso are in full color, including her red lips, brown eyes, and white oxygen mask, while her background is in grayscale, revealing a closed door and a few photos on the wall behind her. The Google Hangouts screen featuring Wong does not occupy the entire painting, as Lehrer's desktop, which consists of what looks like a photo of ocean waves, peeks from both sides of her screen and creates a tranquil, blue framing. The hyperrealism of the painting invokes muscle memory; I am tempted to click on the open tabs and enlarge the videoconferencing screen so I could concentrate on Wong's face. Alas, I am left with a trembling, anxious hand.

The painting includes the Google Hangouts' familiar icons, with two notable icons presented on the right side of the interface: "captions on" and "present now," alluding to the access needs of the two collaborators. At the bottom of the painting, Lehrer included handwritten text that reads:

> After four decades of being a portrait artist, I never expected to find myself trying to collaborate from inside an empty studio and from behind walls of glass. But I have always known that all portraits are only fragments of a human being, a particular moment in the self and the life of the subject. I'm having to work harder to see this person, so far away, so imperfectly known. Alice Wong and I began our work together in late June. This drawing is the result of at least six Google Hangouts meetings. She will still be emerging for me, hour by hour, long after this piece is done. Thank you, Alice, for your open heart.

Lehrer painted Wong, a San Francisco-based disability activist born with spinal muscular atrophy, a neuromuscular disorder limiting her mobility, despite Wong being over two thousand miles away from Lehrer's Chicago studio. This encounter was enabled and sustained thanks to a videoconferencing platform, creating a collaboration that unfolded over "an unstable internet connection" during the isolating months of lockdown.[29]

Lehrer's decision to create a frame-within-a-frame encapsulates how videoconferencing might be experienced as a pharmakon, both a poison and a cure. Her love for her collaborator requires intense concentration, while no less than twenty-two apps—represented here by the colorful icons on the right side of the desktop—compete for her attention. This portrait reveals a desperate attempt to fully immerse oneself in the life of a distant other vis-à-vis an interface carefully designed to seduce us with color, icons, and notifications.

This duality between proximity and efficiency, collective healing and enforced isolation, was beautifully captured by Lehrer in a *New York Times* op-ed, where she reflected on the differences between her remote portraits and her studio work:

> Imagine that you're used to the cloistered privacy of the studio, just you and your collaborator. You've carefully composed the lighting, designed

the costuming and props. Imagine the hours of languorous conversation, the breaks for cookies and cocktails. And then imagine that in the midst of posing, your subject shifts or gestures and it's so unexpectedly beautiful that everything changes. That's the thing about real life; it can take your breath away.

Now, shrink all that down to a 13-inch-by-9-inch digital portal. I can see Alice's hallway behind her; a few framed pictures show me that she loves cats. My eyes aren't great, so it doesn't help that the lighting is dreadful and that the screen flattens any dimensional information and that all colors are distorted. Alice sends me pictures of herself in sunlight, so I can see the true shades of skin, hair and eyes, but those photos are so radically different that I fall back on what the laptop tells me, so that the feeling of Zoom won't be lost.[30]

I chose to linger on this portrait because Lehrer and Wong's collaboration conveys a sensitivity that *Interface Frictions* was set to develop. It is a gentle and complex realization that our interfaces open up infinite new ways to interact, deepen our social bonds, endure difficult periods of isolation, and engage in worldmaking. Yet these very same digital worlds, by assuming an abled-bodied, chrononormative subject, can debilitate bodies in gradual and persistent ways. When we normalize Zoom fatigue, carpal tunnel syndrome, lower back pain, eyestrain, migraines, wrist tenderness, text neck, and other muscular, cognitive, and postural issues, we too quickly give up on imagining technologies that better support our bodies and their varied, ever-shifting needs. Instead, our growing dependency on videoconferencing platforms minimizes the importance of touch, smell, and bodily intimacy. Tactile, disability-informed languages like Braille or Protactile, as I explored in chapter 1, can provide an alternative by reminding us how various body organs, from fingers to knees, are essential for communication.

Interface Friction explored the three most common manifestations of digital debility: chronic pain, addiction, and lethargy. Yet this brief analysis of Zoom fatigue reminds us that the selection of design features this book studies is meant to be representative rather than exhaustive. The parameters for digital debility I propose in the introduction create a cohesive and targeted analysis of a topic that often gets eclipsed by both users and media scholars. One of my main goals has been to articulate digital debility as a coherent term that can be employed in a plethora of interfaces and design decisions.

Rewriting the history of ubiquitous design features from the point of view of the non-average user opens up roads not taken and challenges the myth of interminable, linear progress. There are multiple, decades-long legacies of disability activism harnessing virtual tools by those who couldn't leave their beds or attend weekly meetings and protests.[31] These include using online forums to establish and support care webs across the United States and pushing for video- and phone-based telehealth years before COVID-19.[32] Writing about "activist fatigue," Emily Rogers distinguishes between the "performative, and immensely successful, actions of AIDS activists, whose legacy provides a longstanding model for disease activism," and activists "who face the same challenges of inertia, but in exhausted bodies and foggy minds that make such conventional activist tactics particularly inaccessible."[33] Not every human body can be put on the line; to scream, one must have functioning vocal cords, throat, and lungs.

Beyond the Interface

Exploring disability hacktivism and worldmaking, *Interface Frictions* does not include how-to design solutions or a clear road map that web designers can follow in order to avoid some of the pitfalls I studied. This intentional omission serves different goals. First, it enables me to complicate the prevalent narrative of crip creativity or "innovation from below" as yet another resource to be coopted by an otherwise ableist tech industry.[34] Such public embrace of improvised design solutions might too easily recast disabled, poor, or marginalized people as resourceful innovators whose survival techniques can and should be scaled for commercial products aimed at abled-bodied or affluent users. "Decentering innovation," as argued by Liliana Gil, means rejecting the idea that improvised, local, or community-based solutions should be used as templates and testing grounds for entrepreneurs.[35] In the context of interface design, solutions like disabling a default feature or ensuring compatibility with screen readers are important first steps, yet they have a limited impact on the political economy and media flows of an increasingly commercial internet based on surveillance. By using cripwashing, as Netflix did when implementing its playback speed feature (see chapter 2), companies might distract from the ableist content they produce and distribute or from the ways in which their global expansion is harmful for local film and television industries.

While this book does not provide technical manuals for web designers, it offers a sustained exploration of alternative models of human-machine interactions, including the multisensorial and tactile approaches to communication explored in chapter 1 or the trauma-informed design explored in chapter 3. These approaches demonstrate the benefits of moving away from a universal, able-bodied understanding of usership. Any design solution should be rooted in specific environments and technological infrastructures and affordances. As repeatedly argued by science and technology scholars, this goal cannot be achieved without including a diverse set of designers, engineers, and test users in every step of the process—a goal that is far from realization in a tech climate shaped and controlled by a majority of white, able-bodied tech workers.[36]

It is increasingly crucial to consider a vast variety of potential users as we move toward a techno-social ecosystem based on no-screen interactions via voice commands, biosensors, or neurological sensors. The interfaces explored in this book—the pull-to-refresh function on mobile apps, Netflix's playback speed and autoplay, and the dark mode and night mode features available on most operating systems—might lose their dominance or be replaced by other design features touting miniaturization, compression, and automation. The Internet of Things and embodied technologies like "wearables" or "hearables" are already being used to "imagine the ear and voice as the ultimate human-computer interface (HCI)."[37] This future, Mack Hagood argues, consists of a set of miniature electronics and biosensors housed in the body and enabling the user to communicate with their phone or connected appliances and devices via vocal communication.[38] Due to the rise of wearables, soon users will no longer navigate visual interfaces or click in order to refresh or change the playback speed. Such a screenless future, however, will not necessarily eliminate any of the frictions explored in this book. In fact, I argue, it might make digital debility more pronounced, as we will not be able to disconnect in any meaningful way from the internet. Revisiting the politics of "opting out" I explored in the introduction, I note that embodied technologies collapse the distinction between cognitive and information flows while denying the ubiquity of friction, decay, and malfunction in both biological and technical systems.

The utopian visions hyped by our tech overlords, from Mark Zuckerberg's Metaverse to Elon Musk's Neuralink, offer embodied interfaces only as a way to further cement consumers' attachments to their technologies. When asked how he might improve the smartphone, Musk replied that he would transform it from a rectangular box to an invisible neurological link: "the best interface would be a neural interface directly to your brain."[39] In a tech summit hosted by the *New York Times* in December 2023, Musk responded to criticism following reports of grisly deaths of monkeys in Neuralink testing facilities by insisting that the company's brain implant devices were installed on monkeys that were terminally ill and died of other causes.[40] In his attempt to change the topic, the billionaire was quick to point to the medical implications of Neuralink for people with disabilities, especially those who have lost their brain-body connection. These test subjects, Musk promised, will be able to "operate a computer or a phone faster than someone who has hands."[41] This celebratory description of a technology that, at the time of the interview, had yet to be tested on humans, draws on social imaginaries of the super-crip. In this framing, cutting-edge technologies can be used to unlock hidden capacities of injured bodies, making them not only whole again, but potentially more competent than able-bodied people. Musk extended this line of thinking by explaining how Neuralink would be able to cure those who lost their eyes or their vision, transforming them into "Geordi La Forge from *Star Trek*" by gifting them with the ability to control the frequency and resolution of their optic nerve.[42]

This utopia of blind people afforded "radar vision" by this no-interface bio-sensor has yet to materialize, yet it reminds us how people with disabilities are often used by tech companies to advance controversial or risky technologies. Used as test subjects and, later, cast as part of PR campaigns, blind or quadriplegic people are already at the forefront of a no-screen future. These attempts at cripwashing focus on people with disabilities to promote a "curative imaginary" in which technology can restore—and potentially improve upon—lost bodily functions.[43]

Even if we are heading into a future heavily based on voice- or neurological-based human-machine interaction, light-emitting screens and technologies conjuring limited postural affordances are likely to endure. By offering a nuanced understanding of how digital technology shapes our body, this book situates digital debility at the heart of media theory. Injured or sick bodies are ignored, while able bodies are forced to sustain and endure a plethora of techno-social forces that make it increasingly difficult to find rest or a path to recovery. Recognizing the frictions our interfaces are designed to hide is a crucial first step in dispelling their grasp on our bodyminds.

ACKNOWLEDGMENTS

I began working on this manuscript while sheltering in place in a small, rural town in Central New York during the early, anxious months of the COVID-19 pandemic, when exploring the entanglements between human bodies and ubiquitous screens provided a much-needed distraction and a sense of purpose. Those days of grief and isolation, however, also reminded me that writing and thinking are collaborative processes. A life lived almost entirely online felt both familiar and strange, but I was lucky enough to become a part of a lively, ongoing conversation between disability activists, writers, filmmakers, artists, and educators without whom this book could not have been written.

I first encountered many of these thinkers through my friend and mentor Faye Ginsburg, whose fierce intellect and endless generosity inform much of my thinking on embodiment, technology, and access. Since our early conversations in her classes at New York University, Faye gave me permission to bring my own lived experience into my theoretical work—and demonstrated how this can be done with grace, compassion, and rigor.

Both Faye and Mara Mills, the co-directors of New York University (NYU)'s Center for Disability Studies, introduced me and many others to the cutting-edge work in the emerging field of disability media studies. It was through the center that I learned about Joseph Grigely, Carolyn Lazard, Riva Lehrer, Alice Wong, and many other individuals whose art, scholarship, and activism is featured in this book.

Jonathan Sterne and the entire editorial team at Duke University Press believed in this project from its early stages. I'm deeply grateful for Jonathan's comments on drafts of this manuscript. His collaboration with Mara pointed me in new and exciting directions and proved crucial for my analysis of speed watching. His untimely death is a tremendous loss to his family, friends, and multiple scholarly communities. If I could share even a tiny fraction of Jonathan's intellect, humor, and generosity with my readers, the world would be a better place.

This work could not have been completed on time—or at all—without the patience and meticulousness of Duke's Courtney Berger, whose editorial insights and support were incredibly valuable. Laura Jaramillo, Bird Williams, and the whole production team offered detailed answers to my many inquiries, and I thank them for all their help.

The anonymous readers who reviewed this manuscript offered ideas and corrections that made it much stronger. I'm also indebted to the many friends and colleagues who read excerpts and brainstormed ideas: Caetlin Benson-Allott, Anat Dan, Ori Levin, Shannon Mattern, Laliv Melamed, Kartik Nair, Tasha Oren, Rachel Plotnick, Pooja Rangan, and Gerald Sim. My developmental editor, Ben Wurgaft, pushed me to improve every draft I sent him and patiently helped me to reframe the book's overall argument.

This book started to take shape when I was part of the Film and Media Studies Program at Colgate University. I'm grateful to Colgate for providing a research sabbatical, generous travel and publication grants, and for nominating me for a National Endowment of the Humanities summer fellowship that proved crucial for the completion of this book. I'm deeply grateful to the wonderful colleagues who always miraculously found a way to support my teaching and scholarship: Ashleigh Cassemere-Stanfield, Monica Facchini, Margaretha Haughwout, Lindsey Lodhie, Paul Lopes, Lakshmi Luthra, Ani Maitra, Lynn Schwarzer, Noah Shenker, Mary Simonson, and Meg Worley. A special thanks is due to Mary Simonson, a rare individual who is able to offer friendship, mentorship, and brilliance while running marathons and taking students to Brooklyn and the Cannes Film Festival. Thank you for being a role model and an inspiration, Mary.

When I came to Yale, I was greeted with more support, enthusiasm, and generosity than I could have wished for. For that, I'm indebted to my Film and Media Studies colleagues Alison Bechdel, Marijeta Bozovic, Francesco Cassetti, Oksana Chefranova, Marta Figlerowicz, Aaron Gerow, John MacKay, Charles Musser, Fatima Naqvi, John Durham Peters, Camille Thomasson, and Katie Trumpener. Thank you Marc Francis and Tony Sodul for making every screening idea come true. I would also like to thank Kathryn Lofton and Marc Robinson, who played a pivotal role in bringing me to Yale and have since been wonderful sources of helpful advice and institutional knowledge. Yale's Frederick W. Hilles Publication Fund generously aided the production and publication of this book.

My first intellectual homes in the United States, Columbia's MA program in Film Studies and NYU's doctoral program in Cinema Studies, shaped my interdisciplinary thinking and taught me how to read, and write, critical theory. For those formative years, I am forever grateful to Nico Baumbach, Jane Gaines, Richard Peña, and James Schamus at Columbia, and to Alexander Galloway, Faye Ginsburg, Anna McCarthy, Dana Polan, Natasha Dow Schüll, and Nicole Starosielski at NYU.

Many of the ideas in this book were workshopped and developed at the annual conferences of the Society of Cinema and Media Studies (SCMS), as well as at conferences held by 4S, CIGCIS, and the Society for Disability Studies. I first presented parts of this project in invited talks at the Boston Seminar of Film and Media, NYU, Stanford University, the University of Michigan, University of Pennsylvania, and Yale, and I wish to thank the organizers, staff, students, and audiences for their thoughtful engagement with my work.

This work studies—and is inspired by—artists and filmmakers exploring embodiment and difference. I would especially like to thank those who gave me permission to include excerpts or images from their work: Rebecca Baron, Hannah Bullock, Doug Godwin, Carolyn Lazard, Riva Lehrer, Dayna McLeod, and Marilene Oliver. Several web designers, tech bloggers, and accessibility consultants agreed to read excerpts and to share their insights, for which I am deeply grateful, and I'm especially thankful to Robert Sweeney, who generously shared with me his experience working on the autoplay feature for Netflix.

Like the artworks it studies, this book attends to disability and difference as a methodology and an epistemology. The disability activists I engage with pushed me to explore the importance of collective and communal forms of knowledge production. While this is a monograph, it bears the mark of the many surgeons, doctors, colleagues, friends, and family members who helped me to form networks of care across continents. These networks are beautiful, vast, and rich, and I won't be able to do justice to the many people and institutions that made them possible.

Of the many who sustained me through difficult moments, I wish to thank those who, without their love and friendship, this book could not have been written. Pooja Rangan was always there to encourage and inspire, her brilliance and endless imagination opening doors at every turn. Brynn Hatton and Amy Swanson made a small town feel like a home away from home, and A.K.M. Skarpelis and Manuela Ruckdeschel offered more moral support than I could have asked for. My parents, Gad and Elia Alexander, and my brothers, Eran and Uri, have always been my secret weapon against despair, self-doubt, and homesickness. And my therapist, despite a severe allergic reaction to critical theory, helped me to carve the space that made thinking and writing possible amid the chaos.

Finally, Bradley H. Kerr was forced to read, discuss, and edit these pages more times than anyone else, and he is the most gracious and loving partner anyone can imagine. That he mustered the patience to copyedit these overly lengthy acknowledgments is yet another testament to his resilience. I dedicate *Interface Frictions* to you, my love, and I promise that you will never have to read it again.

NOTES

INTRODUCTION: DISABLED/ENABLED

Epigraph 1. Mills and Sterne, "Dismediation," 368.
Epigraph 2. Jain, "Prosthetic Imagination," 33.

1. In the United States, rural towns suffered from lack of broadband that, amid the spread of COVID, limited people's ability to remain informed. Even tech workers in urban centers experienced more buffering during the early months of the pandemic: "As people have hunkered down to contain the spread of the coronavirus, average internet speeds all over the world have slowed. Some broadband providers are feeling crushed by the heavy traffic. And dated internet equipment can create a bottleneck for our speeds." See Chen, "Everything You Need to Know."
2. For a historical analysis of the rise of computer-inflicted pain and injuries since the 1980s, see Nooney, "Have Any Remedies," 416–34.
3. I borrow the term "disabled cyborg" from Laura Forlano. See Forlano, "Crip Futurity."
4. For a complete list of ReelAbilities' accommodations, see https://reelabilities.org/newyork/accessibility/.
5. See Nooney, "Have Any Remedies," 417.
6. Costanza-Chock, *Design Justice*, 47. For a critique and historical overview of the idea of the "average user" as a white, able-bodied user, see also Mulvin, *Proxies*.
7. The term "techno-chauvinism" was coined by Meredith Broussard to describe gender inequality in the tech industry and how it produces gender-based algorithmic biases. See Broussard, *Artificial Unintelligence*.
8. I here draw on Jain's critique of the assumption of a "normative" tech user in media theory. See Jain, "Prosthetic Imagination," 33.
9. For a historical analysis of internet-based access, see Ellcessor, *Restricted Access*.
10. Mills and Sterne, "Dismediation," 372.
11. Mills and Sterne, "Dismediation," 368.
12. For an overview and critique of these models of disability, see, for example, Ben-Moshe et al., "Disability Politics," 178–93.

13. See Ben-Moshe et al., "Disability Politics," 178.
14. For a critique of the curb cut as the model and the most prevalent metaphor for disability accommodation, see Hamraie, *Building Access*, 125–30.
15. Tracing biometric technologies to the branding of African slaves by their white owners in order to identify, control, and deter them from running away, Simone Browne studies the rise of digital and algorithmic-based biometrics as part of a longer legacy of racialized state violence. She suggests the concepts of "digital epidermalization" and "prototypical whiteness" to consider "what happens when certain bodies are rendered as digitized code." See Browne, *Dark Matters*, 109–16.
16. See Kafer, *Feminist, Queer, Crip*, 4–10.
17. Kafer, *Feminist, Queer, Crip*, 7.
18. See Browne, *Dark Matters*, 122–26.
19. In their critique of the social model and the "disability rights" framework that focuses on legislative protections from discrimination, for example, A. J. Withers and Liat Ben-Moshe contend that "rights frameworks in general can be described as assimilationist rather than radical (radical in the sense of transforming the root causes of oppression)." See Ben-Moshe et al., "Disability Politics," 179.
20. For an overview of the emerging field of "critical access studies," see Hamraie, *Building Access*, 13.
21. See, for example, Piepzna-Samarasinha and Lakshimi, *Care Work*.
22. The term "security theater" was coined by computer security specialist and writer Bruce Schneier for his book *Beyond Fear* (2003), but has gained currency in security circles, particularly for describing airport security measures. See Schneier, *Beyond Fear*.
23. For an analysis of the racism and sexism of face recognition technologies, see Magnet, *When Biometrics Fail*.
24. See Ellcessor, *Restricted Access*.
25. Ellcessor, *Restricted Access*, 11.
26. I borrow the term "ideal user position" from Elccessor. See Ellcessor, *Restricted Access*, 71–74.
27. For an overview of spoon theory and "spoonies," see Miserandino, "Spoon Theory."
28. Nooney, "Have Any Remedies," 416.
29. For an analysis of the "broken body" of computer programmers, see White, *Body and the Screen*, 177–97.
30. Livingston, *Debility and the Moral Imagination*, 234.
31. Puar, *Right to Maim*, xvi.
32. Puar, *Right to Maim*, xiii.
33. Basel Action Network and Silicon Valley Toxics Coalition, *Exporting Harm*, 31.
34. Basel Action Network and Silicon Valley Toxics Coalition, *Exporting Harm*, 31.
35. For an overview of the labor conditions in Amazon warehouses, see Hu, *Digital Lethargy*, 8–14.
36. Hamraie, "Universal Design," 1–22.
37. Hamraie, "Universal Design," 4.
38. Jain, "Inscription Fantasies and Interface Erotics," 219.

39. Nooney, "Personal Computer," emphasis added.
40. Screen time rocketed during the pandemic. One study showed the percentage of kids spending more than four hours daily on their devices nearly doubled, while another found the average screen time for teenagers went from 3.8 hours before the pandemic to 7.7 hours during the early months of lockdowns. See Berthold, "Adolescents' Recreational Screen Time"; see also Bernstein, "Window of Opportunity," 64–83.
41. For an overview of the growing overuse of technology and the inability to opt out, see Bernstein, *Unwired*.
42. Sterne, *Diminished Faculties*, 123.
43. Sterne, *Diminished Faculties*, 123.
44. Sterne, *Diminished Faculties*, 123.
45. For an overview of these trends, and especially the "slow computing" movement, see Kitchin and Fraser, *Slow Computing*.
46. Jain, "Inscription Fantasies and Interface Erotics," 220.
47. Jain, "Inscription Fantasies and Interface Erotics," 224.
48. Jain, "Inscription Fantasies and Interface Erotics," 224.
49. Jain, "Inscription Fantasies and Interface Erotics," 221.
50. Uncovering the century-long history of this sexist tendency, Jain writes, "Between 1950 and 1980 carpal tunnel syndrome remained unrecognized under worker's compensation in the U.S.; it was understood to be a disease of middle-aged women attributable to hormonal changes." In short, even when machine-induced pain has been common enough to be addressed, it was attributed to the female body—protecting designers and manufactures from having to compensate employees in case of injury. See Jain, "Inscription Fantasies and Interface Erotics," 245.
51. Jain, "Inscription Fantasies and Interface Erotics," 242.
52. For a discussion of how people with disabilities have employed remote access tools during the pandemic, see the conclusion. See also Mills et al., *How to Be Disabled in a Pandemic*.
53. As Natasha Dow Schüll suggests, time-on-device is the raison d'être of casinos: The more time gamblers spend on any given slot machine, the more money they are likely to waste. See Schüll, *Addiction by Design*; For a survey of addictive design methods from a legal perspective, see Bernstein, "Window of Opportunity," 64–83.
54. I will return to the idea of captology in chapter 3. See also Seaver, "Captivating Algorithms," 421–36.
55. Schüll, *Addiction by Design*, 12.
56. Schüll, *Addiction by Design*, 13.
57. Schüll, *Addiction by Design*, 16.
58. Schüll, *Addiction by Design*, 16.
59. Schüll, *Addiction by Design*, 21.
60. Hartogsohn and Vudka, "Technology and Addiction," 1–11.
61. Hartogsohn and Vudka, "Technology and Addiction," 4.
62. Hartogsohn and Vudka, "Technology and Addiction," 4.

63. For a survey of such treatment programs, see Hartogsohn and Vudka, "Technology and Addiction," 5.
64. Hartogsohn and Vudka, "Technology and Addiction," 4.
65. Hartogsohn and Vudka, "Technology and Addiction," 6.
66. Murthy, "Surgeon General."
67. Murthy, "Surgeon General."
68. In 2017, Netflix's founder, Reed Hastings, famously stated that the company's most fierce competitor is sleep: "You get a show or a movie you're really dying to watch, and you end up staying up late at night, so we actually compete with sleep—and we're winning!" See Raphael, "Netflix CEO."
69. Hu, *Digital Lethargy*.
70. Hu, *Digital Lethargy*, 38.
71. For a discussion of "prototypical whiteness," see Browne, *Dark Matters*, 26–27.
72. See, for example, O'Neil, *Weapons of Math Destruction*; see also Eubanks, *Automating Inequality*.
73. The reclaiming of "crip" is attributed to Carrie Sandahl's influential 2003 essay and to Robert McRuer's *Crip Theory* (2006). See Sandahl, QUEERING THE CRIP, 25–56; McRuer, *Crip Theory*.
74. See Lewis, "Crip," 47.
75. Disability scholar Eli Clare, for example, employs "bodymind" as a way to resist common Western assumptions that the body and mind are separate entities, or that the mind is "superior" to the body. See Clare, *Brilliant Imperfection*; see also Lewis, "Crip," 47.
76. Margaret Price, who introduced the term "bodymind" into disability studies, writes that it acknowledges that "mental and physical processes not only affect each other but also give rise to each other—that is, because they tend to act as one, even though they are conventionally understood as two." See Price, "Bodymind Problem," 268–84. For a critique of the health-sickness binary, see Metzl and Kirkland, eds., *Against Health*.
77. For an overview of 1990s techno-utopias of the Internet as a space of empowerment for people with disabilities, see Ellcessor, *Restricted Access*, 78–80.
78. Ellcessor, *Restricted Access*, 74.
79. Galloway, *Interface Effect*, 31.
80. Galloway, *Interface Effect*, 64.
81. For a critique of McLuhan's universalized media consumer, see Sharma and Singh, eds. *Re-Understanding Media*.
82. Critiquing the frequent use of terms like "prosthesis" and "amputation" in media discourse, Elizabeth Petrick warns, "When a marginalized group is treated as merely a metaphor, they become further erased from the history they were a part of." See Petrick, "Computer as Prosthesis?," 401.
83. The artist and writer American Artist theorizes this shift as a denial of Blackness due to its reliance on white-imbued interface design and its emphasis on productivity. See Artist, "Black Gooey Universe," 42.
84. Norman, *Invisible Computer*.

85. See Arnall, "No to No UI."
86. White, *Touch Screen Theory*, 11.
87. White, *Touch Screen Theory*, 14.
88. For an overview of intersectional approaches to disability studies, see Smilges, *Crip Negativity*.
89. Works that offer alternative, queer, and feminist histories of computation include, for example, Pow, "Trans Historiography of Glitches," 197–230; Hicks, "Hacking the Cis-tem," 20–33; Dame-Griff, *Two Revolutions*; and Nooney, "Uncredited," 119–46.
90. Artist, "Black Gooey Universe," 42.
91. Artist, "Black Gooey Universe."
92. Joe Lazzaro, qtd. in Ellcessor, *Restricted Access*, 96.
93. Petrick, "Computer as Prosthesis?," 408.
94. Ellcessor, *Restricted Access*, 96.
95. Hamraie and Fritsch, "Crip Technoscience Manifesto." For a history of disability hacktivism see also Goggin, "Disability and Haptic Mobile Media," 1563–1580.
96. Hamraie and Fritsch, "Crip Technoscience Manifesto."
97. Hamraie and Fritsch, "Crip Technoscience Manifesto."
98. Lucas Hilderbrand uses the term "access entitlement" to connote the rising expectation that video and audio content will be available on demand. See Hilderbrand, *Inherent Vice*, 10. For a disability-informed critique of access as necessarily desired and empowering, see Clark, "Against Access."
99. Goggin, "Disability and Haptic Mobile Media," 1569.
100. Parisi, "Fingerbombing," 323.
101. I will return to the idea of the super-user in chapter 2. See Rezab, "Why I Watch Videos."
102. Little, "Social Media 'Ghosts,'" 1–30.
103. For an exploration of trauma-informed design, see Little, "Social Media 'Ghosts.'"

CHAPTER 1. REPETITION, RELOADED

Epigraph 1. Bill Gates, quoted in Chun, *Updating to Remain the Same*, 71.
1. See, for example, *NBC Boston*, "Massachusetts Vaccination Scheduling Website Crashes."
2. Chen, "Rage Quit."
3. See Applebaum, "Frustration Is Spreading Faster."
4. Dai, "US Government's $44 Million Vaccine."
5. As reported on the local news website *WBUR*, "Olivia Adams, a software developer who created MACovidVaccines.com while on maternity leave, uses one such service from Amazon. That's why her website didn't crash when the state's did, she thinks." See Chen, "Rage Quit."
6. See Dai, "US Government's $44 Million Vaccine."
7. Signed into law in 2016, the BOTS Act takes regulatory action against ticket-buying bots. The bots work by automatically refreshing until new tickets are

released and then buying them before human users have time to access to the sale. Ticketmaster, for example, has long fought off algorithmic refreshers by implementing different identifications methods. See Valdez, "Will the Government Crack Down."

8. For an exploration of refreshing as producing a temporality of "againness," see Coleman, "Refresh," 60.
9. Fogg, *Persuasive Technology*, 1.
10. I return to the idea of "captivating technologies" in chapter 3. See also Seaver, "Captivating Algorithms," 421–36.
11. For an analysis of these utopian ideas in relation to the spread of free, easily available knowledge, see Turner, *From Counterculture to Cyberculture*.
12. Qtd. in White, *Body and the Screen*, 180.
13. See White, *Body and the Screen*, 177–90.
14. I borrow the term "busy idleness" from Tung-Hui Hu. See Hu, *Digital Lethargy*, 70.
15. For a discussion of buffering and other "digital dams," see Alexander, "Rage Against the Machine," 1–24.
16. The need to wait (for new movies, translations, or dubbing) also informs various forms of piracy, as was demonstrated in Brian Larkin's ethnography of the bootleg industry of film distribution in Nigeria. See Larkin, *Signal and Noise*, 217–41.
17. For an analysis of digital latency and waiting, see Alexander, "Rage Against the Machine," 1–24. For a study of "internet rage," see Wald, "Why Your Brain Hates Slowpokes."
18. See Farman, *Delayed Response*.
19. Farman, *Delayed Response*, 14.
20. Farman, *Delayed Response*, 9.
21. Farman, *Delayed Response*, 4.
22. See Alexander, "Rage Against the Machine," 1–24.
23. Petruska and Vanderhoef, "TV That Watches You," 33.
24. I would like to thank Dylan Mulvin for drawing my attention to this commercial. See Mulvin, "Rage Room." To view the commercial, see "BT Broadband Rage," dir. "The Sacred Egg," produced by Riff Raff Films and Saatchi&Saatchi London, YouTube, May 11, 2021, https://www.youtube.com/watch?v=DFSH-zfW4pI.
25. Mulvin, "Rage Room."
26. Mulvin, "Rage Room."
27. In this classic scene-turned-meme, three frustrated office workers take their misbehaving printer out to the middle of a field and beat it to death. See "Printer Scene," *Office Space*, dir. Mike Judge (Los Angeles: 20th Century Studios, 1999). For the full scene, which amassed millions of views, see RP, "Office Space—Printer Scene," YouTube, January 31, 2015, https://www.youtube.com/watch?v=N9wsjroVlu8.
28. For a critique of the utopian discourse and "data fantasies" surrounding the 5G debate, see Mattern, "Networked Dream Worlds."
29. Cubitt, *Practice of Light*, 4.

30. For a useful critique of speed test services offered by streaming companies, see Elkins, "Powered by Netflix," 838–55, emphasis in original.
31. Elkins, "Powered by Netflix," 845.
32. Launching Netflix Canada in 2012, the company's chief content officer, Ted Sarandos, reframed high internet fees in terms of "a human right violation." As Elkins's analysis of Netflix's expansion in Brazil demonstrates, this human right discourse is not accidental, as the company sees itself as "offering necessary VOD [video on demand] aid to those poor, suffering nations who need it." See Elkins, "Powered by Netflix," 840.
33. For an analysis of "false latency," see Farman, *Delayed Response*.
34. Chun, "On 'Sourcery,'" 300.
35. For a critical analysis of the early internet, see Turner, *From Counterculture to Cyberculture*.
36. Geoghegan, "Ecology of Operations," 59.
37. Geoghegan, "Ecology of Operations," 81.
38. Geoghegan, "Ecology of Operations," 87.
39. Shifting from "continuous waves" to "square pulses of fleeting duration," radar technology necessitated a new theory of information and data signaling. This led Friedrich Kittler to theorize the invention of radar as a watershed moment in the shift from analog media like radio or television to media based on "frequency shift." See Kittler and Winthrop-Young, "Real Time Analysis," 16.
40. Hasbroucka and Saar, "Low-Latency Trading," 646–79.
41. Veel, "Latency," 313.
42. Qtd. in Veel, "Latency," 318.
43. Veel, "Latency," 314.
44. I would like to thank one of the anonymous reviewers of the manuscript for alerting me to the importance of spyware in computational latency.
45. Chun, *Updating to Remain the Same*.
46. For an analysis of the programmer body as gendered, broken, and "folded," see White, *Body and the Screen*, 177–97.
47. White, *Body and the Screen*, 186.
48. White, *Body and the Screen*, 186.
49. Ørum, "Throbber," 515.
50. See, for example, Madrigal, "Mechanics and Meaning."
51. Parisi, "Game Interfaces as Disabling Infrastructures."
52. Qtd. in Wikipedia, s.v., "pull-to-refresh," last modified June 2, 2024, https://en.wikipedia.org/wiki/Pull-to-refresh.
53. Initially, Facebook implanted the pull-to-refresh function without attribution, which led to a public apology. See Siegler, "Facebook Apologizes."
54. See Plotnick, *Power Button*.
55. Plotnick, *Power Button*, xiv.
56. For an overview of haptic media studies, see, for example, White, *Touch Screen Theory*.
57. Plotnick, *Power Button*, xxi.
58. Goggin, "Disability and Haptic Mobile Media," 1569.

59. See "Accessible Way of Notifying a Screen Reader about Loading the Dynamic Web Page Update (AJAX)," *UX: User Experience*, May 2020, https://ux.stackexchange.com/questions/131889/accessible-way-of-notifying-a-screen-reader-about-loading-the-dynamic-web-page-u.
60. White, *Touch Screen Theory*, 56.
61. White, *Touch Screen Theory*, 42.
62. White, *Touch Screen Theory*, 42.
63. White, *Touch Screen Theory*, 43.
64. White, *Touch Screen Theory*, 43.
65. Qtd. in White, *Touch Screen Theory*, 64.
66. Parisi, "Game Interfaces as Disabling Infrastructures."
67. Parisi, "Game Interfaces as Disabling Infrastructures."
68. Sicart, "Queering the Controller."
69. Sicart, "Queering the Controller."
70. Postman, *Amusing Ourselves to Death*.
71. Chun goes as far as declaring that "real time" has come to replace the analog indexicality of photography. By pointing to "real time" events, this temporality, whether it is imagined or real, imbues digital systems with an indexicality "that is felt most acutely in moments of crises, which enable connection and demand response." Yet real time is always deferred and mediated as "it relates to the time of computer processing, not to the user's time." See Chun, *Updating to Remain the Same*, 70; for a discussion of digital "liveness" in relation to televisual liveness, see McPherson, "Liveness, Mobility, and the Web," 242.
72. Sontag, *Regarding the Pain of Others*.
73. As Sontag writes, "To photographic corroboration of the atrocities committed by one's own side, the standard response is that the pictures are a fabrication, that no such atrocity ever took place, those were bodies the other side had brought in trucks from the city morgue and placed about the street, or that, yes, it happened and it was the other side who did it, to themselves." See Sontag, *Regarding the Pain of Others*, 12.
74. For the dangers of deepfake images and AI-generated content, see, for example, "Media Literacy in the Age of Deepfakes," Center of Advanced Virtuality, Massachusetts Institute of Technology, https://deepfakes.virtuality.mit.edu/.
75. Sontag, *Regarding the Pain of Others*, 13.
76. Cubitt, "Against Connectivity," 7.
77. Cubitt, "Against Connectivity," 9.
78. For an overview of the content moderation industry, see Pinchevski, "Social Media's Canaries," 9.
79. Pinchevski, "Social Media's Canaries," 9.
80. Pinchevski, "Social Media's Canaries," 9, emphasis added.
81. Nooney, "Have Any Remedies," 420.
82. See Nooney, "Have Any Remedies"; Zuboff, *Age of the Smart Machine*.
83. Nooney, "Have Any Remedies," 420–26.
84. For an overview of the history of Braille and other tactile ways to read, see Clark, "Against Access."

85. Clark, "Against Access."
86. Wikipedia, "pull-to-refresh."
87. Correspondence with the author, December 2022. I wish to thank Mattern for her many thoughtful comments on early drafts of this chapter.
88. For an overview of buffering icons and their cultural significance, see Farman, *Delayed Response*, 65–82.
89. Barron, "Babysitters Club."
90. Barron, "Babysitters Club."
91. De Beule, "Why Does the Yelp iOS App."
92. De Beule, "Why Does the Yelp iOS App."
93. According to Barron, "Yelp wields tremendous power over the owners of small businesses—some of whom have accused the company of gaming the ratings and reviews system to favor those who advertise, pressuring those who don't into doing so—and knows more about consumer habits and travel patterns than we might wish a publicly traded corporation to know." See Barron, "Babysitters Club."
94. Barron, "Babysitters Club."
95. Clark, "Here's How to Turn Off Twitter's Weird New Refresh Sound."
96. Rodriguez, "Playing 'the Game' of Migration."
97. Rodriguez, "Playing 'the Game' of Migration."
98. Heilmann, "'Tap, Tap, Flap, Flap,'" 37.
99. Hu, *Digital Lethargy*, 70.
100. Bouliane, "How to Get an *Ausländerbehörde* Appointment," emphasis added.
101. For an overview of the New Disability Art movement and the use of closed-captions as creative tools, see Mills and Alexander, "Scores," 39-47.
102. For an overview of the manifesto, see introduction. Hamraie and Fritsch, "Crip Technoscience Manifesto."
103. For a critique of "invisible design," see Chalmers, Maccoll, and Bell, "Seamful Design."
104. See Chalmers, Maccoll, and Bell, "Seamful Design."
105. See Chalmers, Maccoll, and Bell, "Seamful Design."
106. Chalmers, Maccoll, and Bell, "Seamful Design."
107. See Arnall, "No to No UI."
108. For a trailer for this project and the full collection of experimentations, see "Digital Well-Being Experiments," Experiments with Google, https://experiments.withgoogle.com/collection/digitalwellbeing.
109. "Anchor" was designed and launched by Brendan Browne-Adams, Lahari Goswami, Miki Chiu, Tayo Kopfer, and Twomuch Studio. See "Anchor," Experiments with Google, https://experiments.withgoogle.com/anchor.
110. I borrow the term "finishability" from David Sax. See Sax, *Revenge of Analog*.
111. In their much-cited conference presentation on the benefits of seamful design, Chalmers, Maccoll, and Bell write, "We can choose a more positive design approach which allows seams to become a resource for users, rather than a system failing. By letting the tool 'be itself' and accepting its characteristics, we can find a more pragmatic design for our systems." See Chalmers, Maccoll, and Bell, "Seamful Design."

112. Marcotte, "Queering the Controller."
113. Marcotte, "Queering the Controller."
114. Marcotte, "Queering the Controller."
115. Hoffman and Novak, "Marketing in Hypermedia," 50–68.
116. Qtd. in Marcotte, "Queering the Controller."
117. Marcotte, "Queering the Controller."
118. For a critique of "Virtuous VR" and its "identity tourism," see Nakamura, "Feeling Good," 47–64.
119. See Nakamura, "Feeling Good."
120. Marcotte, "Queering the Controller."
121. Marcotte, "Queering the Controller."
122. According to Legacy Russell, "Glitch is all about traversing along edges and stepping to the limits, those we occupy and those we push through." For a discussion of "glitch feminism," see Russell, *Glitch Feminism*, 22; for a discussion of early net art and its use of "an aesthetic of failure," see White, *Body and the Screen*, 85–113.
123. Marcotte, "Queering the Controller."
124. I wish to thank Mara Mills for introducing me to this work. For the full video, see the Black Embodiments Studio, "Notes from the Panorama," YouTube, January 11, 2022, www.youtube.com/watch?v=MAbZaMlcqWs.
125. For a theory of Lazard's elaborate use of "scores" in their art practice, see Mills and Alexander, "Scores," 39–47.
126. See, for example, Oppel et al., "Fullest Look Yet"; see also Walker et al., "Pandemic's Racial Disparities."
127. "Amber Rose Johnson + Carolyn Lazard: Notes from the Panorama," *University of Washington School of Art + Art History + Design Recent News*, August 5, 2021, https://art.washington.edu/news/2021/08/05/amber-rose-johnson-carolyn-lazard-notes-panorama.
128. Mills and Alexander, "Scores."
129. This idea is inspired by *Surfacing*, an interactive website designed as a companion to Nicole Starosielski's book *The Undersea Network*. The project, which includes archival photographs along with text and information about various areas and countries that are connected through the Pacific's underwater cable network, was developed by Starosielski, Erik Loyer, and Shane Brennan, with additional writing from Jessica Feldman and Anne Pasek. See www.surfacing.in.

CHAPTER 2. THE RIGHT TO SPEED WATCH

Epigraph 1. Blackmore, "Speed Death of the Eye," 371.
Epigraph 2. Cepeda, "Thrice Unseen," 311.
Excerpts from this chapter were initially published in the anthology *Compact Cinematics*, edited by Pepita Hesselberth and Maria Poulaki (London: Bloomsbury Academic, 2017).

1. Judd Apatow (@JuddApatow), "No @Netflix no. Don't make me have to call every director and show creator on Earth to fight you on this. Save me the time. I will win but it will take a ton of time. Don't fuck with our timing. We give you nice things. Leave them as they were intended to be seen." Twitter, October 28, 2019, 1:18 P.M., https://twitter.com/juddapatow/status/1188867694474350592?lang=en.

2. Quoted in Brownlow, "Silent Films," 167.
3. For an overview of the "edited for content" industry providing entertainment to airline companies, see Stokel-Walker, "In-Flight Movies." On May 29, 2018, Apatow used Twitter to nudge Netflix to acquire and release the longer, "unrated" director's cut of his 2005 comedy, *The 40-Year-Old Virgin*. Judd Apatow (@JuddApatow), "Most people remember the longer director's cut DVD of 40 Year Old Virgin. @netflix shows the theatrical cut. I would love for them to show both!" Twitter, May 29, 2018, 12:01 A.M., https://twitter.com/juddapatow/status/1001312467828473859?lang=en.
4. For a historical overview of "time-shifting" techniques, see Benson-Allott, *Remote Control*.
5. Hilderbrand, *Inherent Vice*, 10.
6. "Player Control Tests," Newsroom, Netflix, last modified July 31, 2020, https://media.netflix.com/en/company-blog/player-control-tests.
7. Fadel, "Advocates for Deaf and Blind."
8. Mills and Sterne, "Aural Speed-Reading," 401–11.
9. Mills and Sterne, "Aural Speed-Reading," 403.
10. Mills and Sterne, "Aural Speed-Reading," 406.
11. A seventy-page dossier in *Cinema Journal*'s Winter 2016 issue, for example, included essays approaching speed "as property of the diegesis; as an element of film style; as an index of specific technologies and modes of production; and as a facet of exhibition and consumption." See Kendall, "Staying on, or Getting off," 116.
12. See Kittler and Winthrop-Young, "Real Time Analysis," 1–18.
13. Kittler and Winthrop-Young, "Real Time Analysis," 7, 11.
14. Writing in 1990, Kittler explains, "Today's television images . . . are composed of 625 lines of 4,000 pixels each that are written onto the screen at a rate of fifty times per second. It is flat-out impossible to see individual pixels. Which is why today's color TV—with the exception of antiquated US standards—can and must use Münsterberg's trick to achieve the reverse effect: it is not a matter of making the audience tremble but of preventing the colors based on US standards from trembling, something the SECAM and PAL systems achieve by resorting to signal time delays." See Kittler and Winthrop-Young, "Real Time Analysis," 9.
15. Kittler and Winthrop-Young, "Real Time Analysis," 8.
16. For a study of "intensified continuity" and the gradual decrease of average shot length in Hollywood, see Bordwell, "Intensified Continuity," 16–28; for an overview of the rise of the slow cinema movement, see De Luca and Jorge, eds., *Slow Cinema*.
17. In a 2015 essay, Perez demonstrates how the conservative Partido Popular government in Spain used the discourse of the Disability Rights Movement to dismantle the Spanish welfare system. Critiquing this trend, Perez compares cripwashing to similar attempts of pinkwashing identified by queer scholars. See Perez, "Cripwashing," 47–56.
18. For a historical analysis of conflating disability with slowness and laziness, see Rose, *No Right to Be Idle*.
19. Quoted in Samuels and Freeman, "Introduction: Crip Temporalities," 251.
20. Samuels and Freeman, "Introduction: Crip Temporalities," 251.

21. Many of these posts are short, technical, and anonymous; focus on recommending the best software for speed watching; and hail it as a time-hacking device. See, for example, a 2010 post on the tech blog *Digital Rune*. https://www.digitalrune.com/Blog/Post/1779/The-Speed watching-Technique.
22. For the full text, see Rezab, "Why I Watch Videos."
23. Reich, "Netflix's Speed-Watching Trial."
24. Fitzpatrick, "Is 'Speed Watching' TV Shows as Stupid."
25. "Too Many Shows? Take Them in a High Speed," *New York Times*, December 12, 2016, https://www.nytimes.com/2016/12/12/technology/favorite-shows-high-speed.html.
26. Sontag, "The Decay of Cinema."
27. Building on empirical studies conducted in libraries and meditation centers, Hanich contends that attention is "contagious," and, in the case of slow cinema, the co-presence of fellow viewers is essential for a complete immersion in the work of art. See Hanich, "Invention with a Future," 590–608.
28. Hanich borrows the term "the pensive spectator" from Raymond Bellour, although it was also discussed and explored by Laura Mulvey in *Death 24× a Second*. See Hanich, "Invention with a Future," 592.
29. Hanich, "Invention with a Future," 599–601.
30. Hanich, "Invention with a Future," 601.
31. Mulvey, *Death 24× a Second*, 171.
32. Hanich, "Invention with a Future," 600. For a discussion of "digital lethargy," a term I borrow from Tung-Hui Hu, see the introduction.
33. For a historical overview of speed-reading, see Dames, *Physiology of the Novel*.
34. Dames, *Physiology of the Novel*, 221.
35. Cmiel and Peters, *Promiscuous Knowledge*, 102.
36. Cmiel and Peters, *Promiscuous Knowledge*, 107.
37. I wish to thank Tasha Oren for alerting me to Wood's method, and for her thoughtful and helpful comments on a draft of this chapter. See Van Gelder, "Evelyn Wood."
38. Van Gelder, "Evelyn Wood."
39. Quoted in Hayles, "How We Read," 66.
40. Quoted in Hayles, "How We Read," 66.
41. Hayles, "How We Read," 67.
42. Hayles, "How We Read," 69–71.
43. Carr, *Shallows*.
44. Jones and Skinner, "Absorbing Text," 26–38.
45. Alex Leff's research at UCL's Aphasia Lab "has observed that it is these eye movements and on-off actions, or rather the struggle to make them and build up a coherent picture from them in relation to a flat plane of text, which can be a substantial cause of reading disorders such as alexia and aphasia." See Jones and Skinner, "Absorbing Text," 6. For further details, see "Prof. Alex Leff," Aphasia Lab, Neurotherapeutics Group @ Institute of Cognitive Neuroscience, University College London, accessed June 27, 2023, http://www.ucl.ac.uk/aphasialab/alex/home.html.
46. Jones and Skinner, "Absorbing Text," 8.

47. Jones and Skinner, "Absorbing Text," 8.
48. According to Jones and Skinner, "At best, studies have shown that readers may still be able to comprehend individual sentences at increased speed, but at worst they can render reading slower than standard rates." See Jones and Skinner, "Absorbing Text," 8.
49. Wasson, "Film, Scale, and the Art Museum," 181.
50. Wasson, "Film, Scale, and the Art Museum," 182.
51. Wasson, "Film, Scale, and the Art Museum," 182.
52. Wasson, "Film, Scale, and the Art Museum," 182.
53. Wasson, "Film, Scale, and the Art Museum," 194, emphasis in original.
54. Moulier-Boutang, *Cognitive Capitalism*, 113.
55. Blackmore, "Speed Death of the Eye," 371.
56. Fitzpatrick, "Is 'Speed Watching' TV Shows as Stupid."
57. See, for example, "How to Save Time by Watching Videos at Higher Playback Speeds," *Contonmat*, January 7, 2009, http://www.catonmat.net/blog/how-to-save-time-by-watching-videos-at-higher-playback-speeds/.
58. Bidasaria, "How to Change."
59. On September 2017, YouTube software engineer Pallavi Powale announced that the company was finally able to overcome some "engineering hurdles" and could now offer playback speed options on mobile devices. According to the tech website *Engadget*, it took YouTube a long time to offer this feature on platform's iOS and Android apps, since the engineers had "to make sure that the app can change the duration of the audio without affecting its quality." See Moon, "YouTube Brings Playback Speed."
60. I borrow the idea of snacking from Ethan Tussey's analysis of media consumption, which—in turn—builds on Nancy Miller's "snackable media." See Tussey, *Procrastination Economy*, 36.
61. An early study of digital video concluded that, when playing digital video files in a 1:64 ratio (i.e., showing only one frame out of every sixty-four), most viewers were able to perform adequately on a range of tasks related to narrative and visual understanding. Wildemuth et al., "How Fast Is Too Fast?," 221–30.
62. In 2021 Zoom released a feature that enables participants to send "non-verbal feedback" from the toolbar, including "yes" and "slow down." This feature once again attests to the importance of speed in the process of learning and the intricate negotiation between content creators and/or public speakers and their audiences.
63. According to its website, Vector Solution offers over 7,000 online courses covering topics such as "emergency response" and "health and safety in the workplace." See https://www.vectorsolutions.com/.
64. Wollen, *Paris Hollywood*, 265.
65. Münsterberg, *Photoplay*, 153.
66. The distinction between technology and assistive technology stands at the center of recent debates within critical disability studies. For an overview of this term and its limitations as based on an abled/disabled binary, see Hendren, "All Technology Is Assistive."

67. Qtd. in Mulvin, *Proxies*, 6.
68. Mulvin, *Proxies*, 6.
69. Mulvin, *Proxies*, 6.
70. For a seminal account of the oppositional gaze of Black women, see hooks, "Oppositional Gaze," 94–105.
71. For an exploration of "television pollution" caused by commercial breaks, see Jacobs, "Television, Interrupted," 255–80.
72. Rangan, "Listening in Crip Time," 27.
73. Rangan, "Listening in Crip Time," 27.
74. Sterne, *Diminished Faculties*, 36.
75. See Clark, "Against Access."
76. See introduction. See also Nooney, "How the Personal Computer."
77. Nooney, "How the Personal Computer."
78. Mills and Sterne, "Aural Speed-Reading," 402.
79. Mills and Sterne, "Aural Speed-Reading," 403.
80. Mills and Sterne, "Aural Speed-Reading," 406.
81. Fields, "Why Can Some Blind People."
82. See Mills and Slater, "Blind Mode," 297.
83. Mills and Slater, "Blind Mode," 297.
84. Burke, "Time, Speedviewing, and Deaf Academics," emphasis added.
85. I wish to thank Jacqueline Ristola for drawing my attention to the use of scaffolding in psychological literature.
86. As someone whose loss of hearing was gradual, Burke prefers speed-reading to speed watching ASL videos: "I don't know whether my born deaf or ASL native friends are able to speedview ASL videos and process these at a rate similar to what skilled speedreaders can do.... I suspect that the features of ASL videotext work against this. Consider: with written English (or any language) one can view a page of text at once. That's a big chunk of information. Now, contrast that with a sped-up video." Burke, "Time, Speedviewing, and Deaf Academics."
87. Cepeda, "Thrice Unseen," 311.
88. Cepeda, "Thrice Unseen," 311.
89. Burke, "Time, Speedviewing, and Deaf Academics."
90. Samuels and Freeman, "Introduction: Crip Temporalities," 247.
91. See Mulvin, "Talking It Out," 58.
92. Ochsner, Spöhrer, and Stock, "Rethinking Assistive Technologies," 65–79.
93. For an analysis of deafness in terms of its intellectual, creative, and cultural benefits, see, for example, Bauman, Dirksen, and Murray, *Deaf Gain*.
94. As I argued elsewhere, this is also the case with the Internet of Medical Things and implanted devices like pacemakers. See Alexander, "My Pacemaker Is Tracking Me."
95. Haagaard, "Notes on Temporal Inaccessibility."
96. Haagaard, "Notes on Temporal Inaccessibility."
97. Haagaard, "Notes on Temporal Inaccessibility."
98. Samuels and Freeman, "Introduction: Crip Temporalities," 245.
99. Grigely and Watlington, "Joseph Grigely and Emily Watlington."

100. While Grigely's works date back to the 1980s, more recently he documented his emails trying to access public events that shifted online due to the COVID-19 pandemic. Out of fifty such events offered by prominent academic and cultural institutions, only two offered ASL or closed captions. Grigely and Watlington, "Joseph Grigely and Emily Watlington."
101. For a critique of the American health insurance system, see Abramson, *Sickening*.
102. Klein, "Netflix Rolls Out Playback Speed Control."
103. Sterne, *Diminished Faculties*, 44.
104. As Gordon writes, "a 2022 internal survey revealed that 58 percent of [Roku's] subscribers use subtitles: 36 percent of them switch the subtitles on because of a diagnosed hearing impairment; 32 percent do it out of force of habit." See Gordon, "Why Is Everyone Watching."
105. National Association of the Deaf, "Landmark Precedent."
106. National Association of the Deaf, "Landmark Precedent."
107. National Association of the Deaf, "Landmark Precedent."
108. Mulvin, "Talking It Out," 58.
109. Costanza-Chock, *Design Justice*, 47. For a critique and historical overview of the idea of the "average user" as a white, able-bodied user, see also Mulvin, *Proxies*.
110. Michael Snow, *WVLNT: Wavelength for Those Who Don't Have the Time*, 2003, video, https://www.youtube.com/watch?v=AQ0row2iTfU&t=332s; Pipilotti Rist, *I'm Not the Girl Who Misses Much*, 1986, video, monitor, color, and sound, Tate, London, https://www.tate.org.uk/art/artworks/rist-im-not-the-girl-who-misses-much-t07972; Rebecca Baron and Douglas Goodwin, dir., *Lossless #5*, 2008, Video Data Bank, https://www.vdb.org/collection/browser-artist-list/lossless-5.
111. For an analysis of Snow's *WVLNT: Wavelength for Those Who Don't Have the Time*, see Alexander, "Speed Watching," 104–12.
112. Baron and Goodwin, *Lossless #5*.
113. Rangan, "Listening in Crip Time," 25–30.
114. In a 2022 interview, Lazard recounted that Canaries made art together for several years, "but it no longer functions as a public-facing art collective." See Bonhomme, "Carolyn Lazard."
115. Bonhomme, "Carolyn Lazard," emphasis added.
116. For an analysis of Lazard's collaboration with writer Amber Rose Johnson, see chapter 1.
117. See Mingus, "Access Intimacy"; Piepzna-Samarasinha, *Care Work*; Rangan, "Listening in Crip Time."
118. Rangan, "Listening in Crip Time," 27.
119. For an overview of the New Disability Arts movement, see Mills and Alexander, "Scores."
120. Damman, "Carolyn Lazard."
121. Carolyn Lazard, *CRIP TIME*, 2018, video, http://www.carolynlazard.com/crip-time.
122. For an analysis of ASMR and how sound effects can be employed for relaxation, see chapter 4.
123. Ben-Moshe, "Dis-Orientation," 3.

124. While Lazard later explained in interviews that *CRIP TIME* documents their own weekly routine, this identification between filmmaker and subject is not made explicit in the film.
125. Damman, "Carolyn Lazard."
126. Damman, "Carolyn Lazard."
127. Clark, "Against Access."
128. Clark, "Against Access."
129. Rangan, "Listening in Crip Time," 28.
130. Bonhomme, "Carolyn Lazard."
131. Münsterberg, *Photoplay*, 154.

CHAPTER 3. AUTOMATING TRAUMA

Epigraph. See Sweeney's LinkedIn profile, https://www.linkedin.com/in/rsweeney21. An excerpt of this chapter initially appeared in "The Unbingeable (or, Saying No to Netflix)," *In Media Res*.

1. Quoted in Alexander, "Netflix Will Now Let You Disable."
2. Bryant, "Stop Netflix Autoplay."
3. Bryant, "Stop Netflix Autoplay."
4. Bryant, "Stop Netflix Autoplay."
5. Jacobs, "Netflix Users Rejoice."
6. Little, "Social Media 'Ghosts,'" 1–30.
7. Little, "Social Media 'Ghosts,'" 18.
8. Little, "Social Media 'Ghosts,'" 18.
9. Little, "Social Media 'Ghosts,'" 1.
10. For a review of the rise, use, and effectiveness of ad-blockers, see Brunton and Nissenbaum, *Obfuscation*.
11. The standards body called WHATWG encourages avoiding the use of automatic playback on HTML5, while the A11Y Project, a community of web developers and users that produces accessibility recommendations, strongly recommends against using autoplay. See McWatters, "Autoplay Blues."
12. See McWatters, "Autoplay Blues."
13. According to McWatters, "Delivering a different, non-autoplay experience to users with screen readers is unrealistic since there is currently no consistent or reliable way to detect when a screen reader is in use." See McWatters, "Autoplay Blues."
14. According to *Fast Company*, "Between 2014 and 2017, the number of viewers pulling off that ambitious feat increased more than twenty times—to 8.4 million Netflix members, pushing the company to hail binge-racing as a 'sport' in a 2017 press release." See Raphael, "Netflix CEO Reed Hastings."
15. In 2017, Netflix's founder, Reed Hastings, famously stated that the company's most fierce competitor is sleep: "You get a show or a movie you're really dying to watch, and you end up staying up late at night, so we actually compete with sleep—and we're winning!" Qtd. in Raphael, "Netflix CEO Reed Hastings."

16. According to disability scholar J. Logan Smilges, experiences in which "the line between 'disability' and 'ability' is uncertain . . . do not circulate frequently in the field of disability studies," as they are "occasioned by violence, by trauma, or by neglect and, as such, can be regarded as loss or as tragedy." Seen in this light, people with invisible disabilities, like PTSD, are less likely to take part in the "collective liberation" and "affirmation" that disability activists call for. See Smilges, *Crip Negativity*, 46–47.
17. I borrow the term "users-survivors" from Little. See Little, "Social Media 'Ghosts,'" 1. See also Smilges, *Crip Negativity*, 47.
18. Fritsch, "Accessible," 25.
19. Fritsch, "Accessible," 26.
20. For a discussion of the etymology of "access" as both "contact" and "attack," see Fritsch, "Accessible," 24. For a discussion of "access thievery," see Smilges, *Crip Negativity*, 39–52.
21. See Smilges, *Crip Negativity*.
22. As I argued elsewhere, binge-watching was recast as a therapeutic device during the early months of the COVID pandemic because it helped millions endure weeks and months of forced isolation during lockdowns. See Alexander, "From Spectatorship to 'Survivorship,'" 52–57. For the potential benefits of media marathoning, see also Perks, "Media Marathoning," 314–29.
23. See Rodman, "Writers Guild Strike."
24. For the rise of "dwell time" and other "captivation metrics" in the 2010s, see Seaver, "Captivating Algorithms," 421–36.
25. Ortega, "'We Pay to Buy Ourselves,'" 138.
26. Unless otherwise stated, Sweeney's citations are based on a Zoom interview I held with him in March 2023. I wish to thank him for his generosity and willingness to share his experience with me. Robert Sweeney, interview with the author, March 1, 2023.
27. See Finn, *What Algorithms Want*, 87–112.
28. Finn, *What Algorithms Want*, 112.
29. Finn, *What Algorithms Want*, 92.
30. See Seaver, "Captivating Algorithms," 428.
31. Seaver, "Captivating Algorithms."
32. The term "the Netflix stretch" was coined by Sam Wollaston in his *Guardian* review of *13 Reasons Why*. As Wollaston explains, the show was originally pitched as a film but, because of Netflix's demand for serialized content, was turned into a multiseason television show. See Wollaston, "*13 Reasons Why*."
33. Keating, *Netflixed*, 256.
34. As of 2023, the US service offers fewer than forty movies released before 1980. Despite the streaming renaissance, many culturally significant films, like *Pink Flamingos* (1972) or *Rebecca* (1940), remain mysteriously unstreamable—a reminder that the digital archive is in fact more limited and unreliable than argued by the streaming giants. See Schonfeld, "I've Rented DVDs."
35. Pallotta, "Netflix Launches 'Basic with Ads.'"

36. See Netflix Technology Blog, "How We Determine Product Success."
37. Seaver, "Captivating Algorithms."
38. Amatriain and Basilico, "Netflix Recommendations."
39. For an analysis of the diminished waiting endurance in the digital age, see Farman, *Delayed Response*, 65–83.
40. Gómez-Uribe and Hunt, "Netflix Recommender System," 2.
41. Qtd. in Ortega, "We Pay to Buy Ourselves," 138.
42. Ortega, "We Pay to Buy Ourselves," 138.
43. Ortega, "We Pay to Buy Ourselves," 138.
44. Ortega, "We Pay to Buy Ourselves," 138.
45. See Alexander, "Catered to Your Future Self," 81–100.
46. Bogost, "Netflix Crossed a Line."
47. Alexander, "Catered to Your Future Self," 81–100.
48. See Seaver, *Computing Taste*.
49. Horeck, "Streaming Sexual Violence," 143–66.
50. Qtd. in Horeck, "Netflix and Heal," 35.
51. Kafka and Molla, "Netflix Effect."
52. When I asked him about a recent bill seeking to outlaw autoplay, Sweeney replied, "Generally speaking, I'm a proponent of less regulation but I think that where there's a need it's really the only option and there's nothing you can do to stop these companies. . . . We can and should implement regulation like this that puts some restraint on these profit-driven organizations for the benefit of society." Robert Sweeney, interview with the author, March 1, 2023.
53. Kelly, "New Bill Would Ban Autoplay."
54. Kelly, "New Bill Would Ban Autoplay."
55. For a survey of the challenges facing regulatory efforts to limit addictive design, see Bernstein, "Window of Opportunity."
56. See Seff, "Netflix Finally Lets Users Disable."
57. For an analysis of YouTube's autoplay and its recommender algorithm, see Alexander, "From 'Elsagate' to the 'Infodemic.'"
58. Roose, "Wonderland."
59. Alexander, "From 'Elsagate' to the 'Infodemic.'"
60. I borrow the concept of insulated flow from Perks, "Media Marathoning," xxii–xxvii. For a critique of programmatic advertising and the attention economy, see Hwang, *Subprime Attention Crisis*.
61. See Alexander, "From 'Elsagate' to the 'Infodemic.'"
62. McWatters, "Autoplay Blues."
63. McWatters, "Autoplay Blues."
64. McWatters, "Autoplay Blues."
65. In March 2020, European Union Commissioner Thierry Breton requested streaming platforms to change their default setting to standard definition in order to trim bit rates. YouTube and Netflix soon agreed to comply. See Bannerman, "Netflix and YouTube Downgrade."
66. See Jancovic and Keilbach, "Streaming Against the Environment," 85–102.

67. As Jancovic and Keilbach argue, "[W]e should not lose sight of computational processes, whose environmental effects cannot be fully captured by tools like carbon footprint calculators." See Jancovic and Keilbach, "Streaming Against the Environment."
68. In a recent example of how tech companies prioritized engagement over mental health, former Facebook employee Frances Haugen revealed that the company knew its algorithm maximizes user time online by exposing kids to harmful content that might increase their risk to develop eating disorders, anxiety, and depression. See Ordonez, "Key Takeaways from Facebook Whistleblower."
69. I borrow the term "edge user" from Lisa Martens. See Martens, "How Autoplay."
70. For a discussion of rape culture in relation to *13 Reasons Why* and other recent television shows depicting sexual assault, see Horeck, "Streaming Sexual Violence," 143–66.
71. For an overview of the controversy around the first season, see Horeck, "Streaming Sexual Violence," 146–49.
72. Sax, *Revenge of Analog*.
73. For an inquiry of analog nostalgia in relation to Sony's Walkman, see Tuhus-Dubrow, *Personal Stereo*.
74. Hale, "Review: 13 Reasons Why."
75. For an overview of the show's production history, see Horeck, "Streaming Sexual Violence," 146–48.
76. Quoted in Horeck, "Streaming Sexual Violence," 145.
77. Horeck, Jenner, and Kendall, "On Binge-Watching," 501.
78. The study was published in the *Journal of the American Academy of Child and Adolescent Psychiatry*. As reported by CBS News, "While the researchers said the study cannot prove that the television show is what caused the rise in suicide, they said the association is troubling." See Brito, "Netflix Deletes."
79. Brito, "Netflix Deletes."
80. The Netflix-designed website also promotes other Netflix titles exploring these dark themes, such as *You* and *Luckiest Girl Alive*. See https://www.wannatalkaboutit.com/.
81. Brito, "Netflix Deletes."
82. See, for example, Limbong, "Netflix Alters Corporate Culture Memo."
83. Horeck, "Streaming Sexual Violence," 146.
84. Horeck, "Streaming Sexual Violence," 146.
85. Horeck, "Streaming Sexual Violence," 152.
86. Horeck, "Streaming Sexual Violence," 153.
87. For a brief overview of the rise of "red-band" trailers, see Cotter, "What a Red-Band Trailer Actually Means."
88. Martens, "How Autoplay."
89. Jones, "*Crime Scene*."
90. Martens, "How Autoplay."
91. Martens, "How Autoplay."
92. Martens, "How Autoplay."
93. Martens, "How Autoplay."

94. Bryant, "Stop Netflix Autoplay."
95. Welch, "Netflix Now."
96. Little, "Social Media 'Ghosts.'"
97. Smilges, *Crip Negativity*.
98. Shobhit, "How to Stop Autoplay."
99. Smilges, *Crip Negativity*, 41.
100. Price, "Precarity of Disability," 196, emphasis in original.
101. Price, "Precarity of Disability," 196.
102. Price, "Precarity of Disability," 196.
103. For an analysis of Netflix's playback speed feature as a case study of "cripwashing," see chapter 2.
104. Fritsch, "Accessible," 26; for an overview of the rise and scope of critical access studies, see Hamraie, *Building Access*.
105. For a close reading of this episode in relation to #MeToo, see Patrick, "Afterward: Destroying the Cycle?," 225–41.
106. McAlone, "Creator of 'Lost.'"
107. In 2017, Damon Lindelof, co-creator of the suspenseful drama *Lost*, sent a letter to television critics begging them not to binge-watch his new show, *The Leftovers*, claiming that bingeing removes "this idea of anticipation" of the next episode. "That Christmas morning feeling," he explained, "doesn't exist in binge culture." Other Hollywood superstars, including *Buffy* and *Firefly* creator Joss Whedon, said that if shows are made for binge-watching, "there is a sense of narrative that is lost." See McAlone, "Creator of 'Lost.'"
108. Jung, "Michaela the Destroyer."
109. As summarized by Stephanie Patrick, "The rape experiences and testimonies of racialized characters in much of popular culture are often sidelined in favor of focusing on the effects of such violence on white, middle-class, thin and able-bodied women and their allies (usually progressive white men)." See Patrick, "Afterward: Destroying the Cycle?," 228.
110. Benson-Allott, "How *I May Destroy You*," 100–105.
111. Coel did not rule out working with the streamer in the future but said that, when it comes to a drama about power and exploitation, "it felt odd that a streaming service would demand 100% of my rights while I was directing, starring and writing the show, so I didn't do it." See Ibekwe, "Michaela Coel."
112. Ibekwe, "Michaela Coel."
113. Ibekwe, "Michaela Coel."
114. Ibekwe, "Michaela Coel."
115. Ibekwe, "Michaela Coel."
116. See *I May Destroy You*, episode 6, "The Alliance," directed by Sam Miller and Michaela Coel, written by Michaela Coel, aired July 13, 2020, on BBC One. For an analysis of how binge culture reshaped the representation of sexual violence, see Havas and Horeck, "Netflix Feminism."
117. Benson-Allott, "How *I May Destroy You*," 105.
118. Patrick, "Afterward: Destroying the Cycle?"
119. Piepzna-Samarasinha, *Care Work*, 33.

120. Smilges, *Crip Negativity*, 60.
121. Disabled trans activist and writer Eli Clare, for example, argues that ideas of cure were invented by colonial Western doctors, settlers, and capitalists and that disabled people should decenter the importance of cure in their lives. "At the centre of cure lies eradication" of what Clare terms "brilliant imperfections." See Clare, *Brilliant Imperfection*, 25.
122. For a historical analysis of disability as a potential threat to productivity, see Rose, *No Right to Be Idle*.
123. See Piepzna-Samarasinha, "What Does It Mean."
124. Piepzna-Samarasinha, "What Does It Mean."
125. Piepzna-Samarasinha, "What Does It Mean."
126. Theroux, "Michaela Coel."
127. Al-Heeti, "Netflix Is Trying No-Binge Release."
128. Pallotta, "Netflix Launches 'Basic with Ads.'"
129. Chaslot was one of the subjects of *Rabbit Hole*, a 2020 *New York Times* podcast unpacking how YouTube became the culprit of political radicalization in the United States through pushing conspiracy theories and videos made by alt-right populists, white supremacists, and QAnon supporters. For the full transcript, see Roose, "Wonderland."
130. The organization's mission is "to shift technology towards a more humane future that supports our well-being, democratic functioning, and shared information environment." See Center for Humane Technology, https://www.humanetech.com/.
131. See Seaver, "Captivating Algorithms," 4.
132. Seaver, "Captivating Algorithms," 431, emphasis in original.
133. Martens, "How Autoplay."

CHAPTER 4. "LOG IN, CHILL OUT"

Epigraph, Joanna Hedva, "Sick Woman Theory," 5.
A shorter version of this chapter was included in *In/Convenience* (ed. Neves and Steinberg).

1. For an overview of spoon theory and "spoonies," see Miserandino, "Spoon Theory"; see also Sterne, *Diminished Faculties*, 163–72.
2. One recent example of the rising popularity of sleep hygiene is Arianna Huffington's 2016 *New York Times* bestseller, *The Sleep Revolution*.
3. For the full statistics, see Heimlich, "Do You Sleep with Your Cell Phone?"
4. For an analysis of "pandemic furniture" and "recumbent labor," see Mattern, "Postures of Pandemic Productivity."
5. I borrow the term "drowsy" in relation to media use from Dan Hassoun and James N. Gilmore. Moving beyond a binary distinction of sleep and wakefulness, they approach drowsiness as "a spectrum of attention and cognition" essential for understanding "how technologies try to routinize the ever-changing qualities of sleep." See Hassoun and Gilmore, "Drowsing," 103–19.
6. Kennedy, "Insomnia Machine."
7. Kennedy, "Insomnia Machine."
8. For an overview of the wellness industry in relation to sleep-inducing products, see Lowrey, "App That Monetized Doing Nothing."

9. For an overview of why tracking is essential for wellness capitalism, see Nopper and Zelickson, *Wellness Capitalism*.
10. See "The Best 7 Sleep Apnea Apps," *CBS19 News*, April 27, 2022, https://www.cbs19news.com/story/43760799/the-best-7-sleep-apnea-apps.
11. Chen, "Sad Truth About Sleep-Tracking Devices and Apps."
12. Kennedy, "Insomnia Machine." See also Pearson, "How to Help."
13. Neves et al., *Technopharmacology*, x.
14. Neves et al., *Technopharmacology*, x.
15. Crary, 24/7, 10.
16. Crary, 24/7, 126.
17. For an overview of the rise of sleep labs in the 1970s and the medicalization of sleep, see Kroker, *Sleep of Others*.
18. See Schüll, "Data for Life," 6.
19. Zeitlin-Wu, "Meditation Apps."
20. Mulvin, "Media Prophylaxis," 181.
21. For a theory of technological nudging, see Schüll, "Data for Life," 1–17.
22. I borrow the term "anti-content" from Amanda Hess's personal account of using Calm. See Hess, "App That Tucks Me In."
23. For a theory of the folded body of avid computer users, see White, *Body and the Screen*.
24. This critique of rest as resistance draws on Jonathan Sterne's analysis of fatigue. See Sterne, *Diminished Faculties*, 157–92.
25. See Piepzna-Samarasinha, *Care Work*.
26. The emphasis on sleep hygiene and strategic napping as crucial for maximizing productivity can be found, for example, in Walker, *Why We Sleep*.
27. Mulvin, "Media Prophylaxis," 181.
28. For an analysis of the rise of solutionism as the prevalent ideology of Silicon Valley, see Morozov, *To Save Everything, Click Here*.
29. For an overview of the history and growing popularity of planned obsolescence, see Appadurai and Alexander, *Failure*.
30. AppleInsider, "How to Use Apple's New Night Shift Mode in iOS 9.3," YouTube, March 24, 2016, https://www.youtube.com/watch?v=qkybUwthZAs.
31. For a critique of Apple's tendency to cast white presenters in its promotional materials, see White, *Touch Screen Theory*.
32. For a discussion of "chrono-diversity" as corporate tool, see Mulvin, "Media Prophylaxis," 182–83. See also Volk et al., "Chronotype Diversity in Teams," 683–702.
33. Terence M. McMenamin, qtd. in Mulvin, "Media Prophylaxis," 183. For the full report, see McMenamin, "A Time to Work." For an overview of the shift to flexible work during the COVID pandemic, see also Mattern, "Postures of Pandemic Productivity."
34. As I discuss in chapter 2, the term "chrononormativity" was coined by Freeman in 2010. See Samuels and Freeman, "Introduction: Crip Temporalities," 245.
35. Crary, 24/7, 2.

36. Crary, 24/7, 2.
37. Mulvin, "Media Prophylaxis," 176.
38. Mulvin, "Media Prophylaxis," 176.
39. Mulvin, "Media Prophylaxis," 176.
40. Mulvin, "Media Prophylaxis," 188.
41. Mulvin, "Media Prophylaxis," 188.
42. Mulvin, "Media Prophylaxis," 191, emphasis in original.
43. Mulvin, "Media Prophylaxis," 191.
44. Mulvin, "Media Prophylaxis," 178.
45. See Sterne, *MP3*.
46. Duraccio et al., "Does iPhone Night Shift," 478–84.
47. Duraccio et al., "Does iPhone Night Shift."
48. Curry, "Calm Revenue."
49. Curry, "Calm Revenue."
50. Lowrey, "App That Monetized Doing Nothing."
51. Curry, "Calm Revenue."
52. Lowrey, "App That Monetized Doing Nothing."
53. Lowrey, "App That Monetized Doing Nothing."
54. Lowrey, "App That Monetized Doing Nothing."
55. Lowrey, "App That Monetized Doing Nothing."
56. Lowrey, "App That Monetized Doing Nothing."
57. Lowrey, "App That Monetized Doing Nothing."
58. Lowrey, "App That Monetized Doing Nothing."
59. The term "orthosomnia" was coined by researchers from Rush University Medical School and Northwestern University's Feinberg School of Medicine, in a 2017 case study published in the *Journal of Clinical Sleep Medicine*. See Zraick and Mervosh, "That Sleep Tracker."
60. Lowrey, "App That Monetized Doing Nothing."
61. Calm's most popular single piece of content is "Dream with Me," a story read by Harry Styles, the former One Direction singer and a Calm investor. When it was released in July 2021, overwhelming traffic crashed the app. See Lowrey, "App That Monetized Doing Nothing."
62. For an analysis of slow TV, see, for example, Puijk, *Slow TV*.
63. See Davies, "Nicole Kidman and Idris Elba."
64. Mulvin, "Media Prophylaxis," 184.
65. Guaraná, "At the Edges of Sleep," 109.
66. Qtd. in Hassoun and Gilmore, "Drowsing," 105.
67. Hassoun and Gilmore, "Drowsing," 106.
68. In his study of Apichatpong Weerasethakul's film *Blissfully Yours*, Leo Goldsmith describes sleep as "an ideal way of appreciating the film's subtle force." See Goldsmith, "Blissfully Yours."
69. Akrami, "Interview with Abbas Kiarostami."
70. See Ma, "Sleeping in the Cinema," 31–52.
71. Ma, *At the Edges of Sleep*, 181.

72. Drive-ins, for example, were patented in the 1930s by an American named Richard Hollingshead, who created them "as a solution for people unable to comfortably fit into smaller movie theater seats." See New York Film Academy, "History of Drive-In Movie Theaters." Wheelchair accommodations in movie theaters were only introduced in the United States as a result of the Americans with Disabilities Act, which was signed into law on July 26, 1990. However, in recent decades, seats for wheelchairs that once numbered five or six per theater have been cut to two or three, to make space for recliner-style seats and other incentives. See Lopez, "How Movie Theaters Are Failing."
73. Hess, "App That Tucks Me In."
74. Hess, "App That Tucks Me In."
75. Hess, "App That Tucks Me In."
76. Hess, "App That Tucks Me In."
77. Qtd. in Kennedy, "Insomnia Machine."
78. Kennedy, "Insomnia Machine."
79. Yates, "Study of Sleep Apps."
80. Yates, "Study of Sleep Apps."
81. A 2019 study, for example, found that "Calm is an effective modality to deliver mindfulness meditation in order to reduce stress and improve mindfulness and self-compassion in stressed college students." See Huberty et al., "Efficacy of the Mindfulness Meditation Mobile App," e14273.
82. See Al Mahmud, Wu, and Mubin, "A Scoping Review of Mobile Apps for Sleep."
83. For a study of ASMR affective economy of "shiveries" and bodily sensations, see Andersen, "Now You've Got the Shiveries," 683–700.
84. Enger, "Without Hope."
85. Enger, "Without Hope."
86. Enger, "Without Hope."
87. Enger, "Without Hope."
88. Enger, "Without Hope."
89. According to Reed Enger, "Striking suffragettes were violently force fed in UK jails until the Prisoners Act of 1913, and in the U.S., activist Ethel Byrne was force-fed while jailed for campaigning to legalize birth control in 1917." See Enger, "Without Hope."
90. Qtd. in Hess, "App That Tucks Me In."
91. Hess, "App That Tucks Me In."
92. Kafer, *Feminist, Queer, Crip*, 27.
93. Mitter, "Behind Basquiat's 'Defacement.'"
94. Mitter, "Behind Basquiat's 'Defacement.'"
95. Stone, "Designing Self-Care," 424.
96. Stone, "Designing Self-Care," 424.
97. Qtd. in Stone, "Designing Self-Care," 417.
98. Stone, "Designing Self-Care," 425.
99. For an exploration of long COVID and fatigue, see Hebert and Juhasz, "You're Still Sick."

100. Hebert and Juhasz, "You're Still Sick," emphasis added.
101. *2020-09-16 at 11:19:28 AM*, directed by Hannah Bullock (2020), video, https://vimeo.com/463909993.
102. Hedva, "Sick Woman Theory."
103. Hedva, "Sick Woman Theory."
104. Hedva, "Sick Woman Theory."
105. Hillenbrand, "A Sudden Illness."
106. Samuels, "Six Ways."
107. Samuels, "Six Ways."
108. *Covid Sleep*, directed by Dayna Mcleod, April 20 2020, video, https://www.youtube.com/playlist?list=PLCxxIPfj-5HRU933P6lOSoSQZJPASoBzJ.
109. See Joseph, "The Play of Repetition," 29–33.
110. Qtd. in Mezzapelle, "Parallel Lines."
111. Mattern, "Postures of Pandemic Productivity."
112. In their analysis of Twitch gamers, Bo Ruberg, Daniel Lark, and Jordan Youngblood write that "these bedrooms often featured a crafted mise-en-scène [that] performed their spaces as inviting, intriguing, cozy, personal, and personalized," which in turn "communicated a tone of emotional accessibility and personal connection." Quoted in Mattern, "Postures of Pandemic Productivity."
113. Chen, "Sad Truth About Sleep-Tracking Devices and Apps."

CODA. DIGITAL DEBILITY AND THE NORMALIZATION OF FATIGUE

1. Marilene Oliver, *Whoever Screams the Loudest*, Vimeo video, 5:38, https://vimeo.com/493139902.
2. Sterne, *Diminished Faculties*, 123.
3. Hu, *Digital Lethargy*, 178.
4. For a discussion of these tech forums, see White, *Body and the Screen*, 177–90.
5. See Kelly, "Zoom's Massive 'Overnight Success.'"
6. See, for example, Fosslien and Duffy, "How to Combat Zoom Fatigue."
7. Barbaro, "Hybrid Worker Malaise."
8. Barbaro, "Hybrid Worker Malaise."
9. Coklyat and Fleet, "Blind New Yorkers," 214.
10. Coklyat and Fleet, "Blind New Yorkers.," 218.
11. For a theory of access *as* friction, see Hamraie and Fritsch, "Crip Technoscience Manifesto," 1–33.
12. For a critique of the expectation of speech fluency as an ableist social norm, see, for example, Ellis, "Liturgy of the Name."
13. As demonstrated by Halcyon M. Lawrence, speakers with a "non-standard accent" such as African American vernacular or cockney often find virtual assistants like Siri and Alexa to be "unresponsive and frustrating," leading to the rise of endless YouTube parodies. See Lawrence, "Siri Disciplines," 179–97.
14. Mills et al., *How to Be Disabled in a Pandemic*.
15. See Kornstein and Rogers, "When Postviral Goes Viral," 191–213.
16. Kornstein and Rogers, "When Postviral Goes Viral," 192.

17. Smilges, *Crip Negativity*, 40.
18. Smilges, *Crip Negativity*, 40, emphasis in original.
19. Smilges, *Crip Negativity*, 41.
20. Disability activist and painter Riva Lehrer, for example, praised videoconferencing for helping her maintain a connection to her community and friends during the pandemic: "I live alone, and video calls are the only time now where I get to look at someone and they get to look at me without any masks or any distance. I'm grateful for this." See Wong, "Q&A with Riva Lehrer."
21. Gianpiero Petriglieri, quoted in Jiang, "Reason Zoom Calls Drain Your Energy."
22. In March 2020, for example, journalists Kara Swisher and Jessica Lessin hosted a Zoom event focused on the challenges women tech founders face. The event did not go as expected. Within fifteen minutes, the hosts were forced to end the encounter abruptly because a participant began broadcasting a pornographic video. This is only one example of Zoombombing, that is, using Zoom's screen-sharing feature to project graphic or racist content to unwitting participants. See Paul, "'Zoom Is the Malware.'" See also Stiverson, Lindsey, and Nakamura, *Racist Zoombombing*.
23. See Fung, "Execs Ignored the Damage."
24. For a rich theoretical analysis of the close-up and its relationship to the digital screen, see Casetti, *Screening Fears*, 126–28.
25. For an analysis of "pandemic furniture" and "recumbent labor," see Mattern, "Postures of Pandemic Productivity."
26. The Remote Access Archive is created with support from the Social Science Research Council, National Science Foundation, and Vanderbilt University. For the project description, see https://www.mapping-access.com/the-remote-access-archive.
27. See https://www.mapping-access.com/the-remote-access-archive.
28. I wish to thank Lehrer for giving me permission to include Alice Wong's portrait in this book. For an overview of this series, see Lehrer, "Virus Has Stolen Your Face."
29. Lehrer, "Virus Has Stolen Your Face."
30. Lehrer, "Virus Has Stolen Your Face."
31. The recent launch of the Remote Access Archive, for example, documents a plethora of stories and examples of tech-based accessibility. For the complete archive, researched and established by the Critical Design Lab and its director, Aimi Hamraie, see https://www.mapping-access.com/the-remote-access-archive.
32. See Rogers, "Recursive Debility," 412–28.
33. Rogers, "Recursive Debility."
34. For a critique of techno-utopian narratives of innovation, see Gil, "Fablab at the Periphery," 721–33.
35. Gil, "Fablab at the Periphery," 725.
36. For a critique of the tech industry's lack of diversity, see, for example, Lawrence, "Siri Disciplines."
37. Hagood, *Hush*, 225.
38. Hagood, *Hush*, 225.

39. See Sorkin, "Sunday Special."
40. Sorkin, "Sunday Special."
41. Sorkin, "Sunday Special."
42. Sorkin, "Sunday Special."
43. For an exploration and critique of the "curative imaginary" as limiting disability discourse to either medical intervention and eventual elimination, see Kafer, *Feminist, Queer, Crip*.

BIBLIOGRAPHY

Abramson, Ben. *Sickening: How Big Pharma Broke American Health Care and How We Can Repair It*. New York: HarperCollins, 2022.

Akrami, Jamsheed. "Interview with Abbas Kiarostami." *A Taste of Cherry*, directed by Abbas Kiarostami, special ed. DVD. New York: Criterion Collection, 1999.

Alexander, Julia. "Netflix Will Now Let You Disable Its Awful Autoplaying Feature." *Verge*, February 6, 2020. https://www.theverge.com/2020/2/6/21126867/netflix-autoplay-feature-disable-homepage-episodes-series.

Alexander, Neta. "Catered to Your Future Self: Netflix's Predictive Personalization and the Mathematization of Taste." In *The Netflix Effect*, edited by Daniel Smith-Rowsey and Kevin McDonald, 81–100. New York: Bloomsbury Academic, 2016.

Alexander, Neta. "From Spectatorship to 'Survivorship' in Five Critical Propositions." *Film Quarterly* 75(1) (Fall 2021): 52–57.

Alexander, Neta. "From 'Elsagate' to the 'Infodemic:' On the Weaponization of YouTube's Autoplay." (forthcoming).

Alexander, Neta. "My Pacemaker Is Tracking Me from Inside My Body." *Atlantic*, January 27, 2018. https://www.theatlantic.com/technology/archive/2018/01/my-pacemaker-is-tracking-me-from-inside-my-body/551681/.

Alexander, Neta. "Rage Against the Machine: Buffering, Noise, and Perpetual Anxiety in the Age of Connected Viewing." *Cinema Journal* 56(2) (Winter 2017): 1–24.

Alexander, Neta. "Speed Watching, Efficiency, and the New Temporalities of Digital Spectatorship." In *Compact Cinematics: The Moving Image in the Age of Bit-Sized Media*, edited by Pepita Hesselberth and Maria Poulaki, 104–12. New York: Bloomsbury Academic, 2017.

Alexander, Neta. "The Unbingeable (or, Saying no to Netflix)." *In Media Res* (May 2023), 1–6.

Al-Heeti, Abrar. "Netflix Is Trying No-Binge Release Schedules for Shows. It's About Time." *CNET*, February 23, 2022. https://www.cnet.com/culture/entertainment/netflix-is-trying-no-binge-release-schedules-for-shows-its-about-time/.

Al Mahmud, Abdullah, Jiahuan Wu, and Omar Mubin. "A Scoping Review of Mobile Apps for Sleep Management: User Needs and Design Considerations." *Frontiers in Psychiatry* 13 (October 18, 2022). https://doi.org/10.3389/fpsyt.2022.1037927.

Amatriain, Xavier, and Justin Basilico. "Netflix Recommendations: Beyond the Five Stars (Part Two)." *Netflix Tech Blog*, June 20, 2012. https://medium.com/netflix-techblog/netflix-recommendations-beyond-the-5-stars-part-2-d9b96aa399f5.

Andersen, Joceline. "Now You've Got the Shiveries: Affect, Intimacy, and the ASMR Whisper Community." *Television and New Media* 16(8) (December 1, 2015): 683–700.

Appadurai, Arjun, and Neta Alexander. *Failure*. Cambridge: Polity, 2020.

Applebaum, Anne. "Frustration Is Spreading Faster than the Vaccine Is." *Atlantic*, February 5, 2021. https://www.theatlantic.com/ideas/archive/2021/02/americas-soviet-style-vaccine-rollout/617942/.

Arnall, Timo. "No to No UI." *Elastic Space*, blog, March 2013. https://www.elasticspace.com/2013/03/no-to-no-ui.

Artist, American. "Black Gooey Universe." Accessed on June 1, 2024. https://static1.squarespace.com/static/59238d36d2b8575d127794a4/t/5a60bdecf9619a7f881b02a0/1516289526013/UNBAG_2_AmericanArtist.pdf.

Bannerman, Natalie. "Netflix and YouTube Downgrade due to COVID-19." *Capacity*, March 20, 2020. https://www.capacitymedia.com/article/29otc4cbu6due4mxkcidc/news/netflix-and-youtube-downgrade-due-to-covid-19.

Barbaro, Michael. "The Hybrid Worker Malaise." *Daily* podcast, produced by the *New York Times*, 30:46, January 25, 2024. https://www.nytimes.com/2024/01/25/podcasts/the-daily/hybrid-work.html.

Barron, Jesse. "The Babysitters Club." *Real Life Magazine*, July 27, 2016. https://reallifemag.com/the-babysitters-club/.

Basel Action Network and Silicon Valley Toxics Coalition. *Exporting Harm: The High-Tech Trashing of Asia*. Reston, VA: Healthcare Without Harm, 2002. https://noharm-uscanada.org/documents/exporting-harm-high-tech-trashing-asia.

Bauman, H., L. Dirksen, and Joseph J. Murray. *Deaf Gain: Raising the Stakes for Human Diversity*. Minneapolis: University of Minnesota Press, 2014.

Ben-Moshe, Liat. "Dis-Orientation, Dis-Epistemology, and Abolition." *Feminist Philosophy Quarterly* 4(2) (2018): 1–9.

Ben-Moshe, Liat, A. J. Withers, Lydia X. Z. Brown, Loree Erickson, Rachel da Silva Gorman, Talila A. Lewis, Lateef McLeod, and Mia Mingus. "Disability Politics." In *Routledge Handbook of Radical Politics*, edited by Ruth Kinna and Uri Gordon, 178–93. Philadelphia: Routledge, 2019.

Benson-Allott, Caetlin. "How *I May Destroy You* Reinvents Rape Television." *Film Quarterly* 74(2) (Winter 2020): 100–105.

Benson-Allott, Caetlin. *Remote Control*. London: Bloomsbury Academic, 2015.

Bernstein, Gaia. *Unwired: Gaining Control over Addictive Technologies*. Cambridge,: Cambridge University Press, 2023.

Bernstein, Gaia. "A Window of Opportunity to Regulate Addictive Technologies." *Wisconsin Law Review* 64 (2022): 64–83.

Berthold, Jess. "Adolescents' Recreational Screen Time Doubled During Pandemic, Affecting Mental Health," UCSF, November 1, 2021. https://www.ucsf.edu/news/2021/11/421701/adolescents-recreational-screentime-doubled-during-pandemic-affecting-mental.

Bidasaria, Gaurav. "How to Change Netflix's Playback Speed: Top 5 Chrome Extensions." *Guiding Tech*, September 18, 2018. https://www.guidingtech.com/netflix-playback-speed-chrome/.

Blackmore, Tim. "The Speed Death of the Eye: The Ideology of Hollywood Film Special Effects." *Bulletin of Science, Technology & Society* 27(5) (October 1, 2007): 367–72.

Bogost, Ian. "Netflix Crossed a Line." *Atlantic*, February 21, 2023. https://www.theatlantic.com/technology/archive/2023/02/netflix-account-password-sharing-family-intimacy/673145/.

Bonhomme, Edna. "Carolyn Lazard on Illness, Intimacy and the Aesthetics of Access." *Frieze*, February 28, 2022. https://www.frieze.com/article/carolyn-lazard-edna-bonhomme-interview-2022.

Bordwell, David. "Intensified Continuity: Visual Style in Contemporary American Film." *Film Quarterly* 55(3) (Spring 2002): 16–28.

Bouliane, Nicolas. "How to Get an *Ausländerbehörde* Appointment." *All About Berlin*, July 4, 2022. https://allaboutberlin.com/guides/berlin-auslanderbehorde-same-day-appointment.

Brito, Christopher. "Netflix Deletes Graphic Suicide Scene from First Season of *13 Reasons Why*." *CBS News*, July 16, 2019. https://www.cbsnews.com/news/13-reasons-why-suicide-scene-hannah-baker-season-finale-death-katherine-langford-season-1-episode-13/.

Broussard, Meredith. *Artificial Unintelligence*. Cambridge, MA: MIT Press, 2018.

Browne, Simone. *Dark Matters*. Durham, NC: Duke University Press, 2015.

Brownlow, Kevin. "Silent Films: What Was the Right Speed?" *Sight and Sound* 49(3) (Summer 1980): 164–67.

Brunton, Finn, and Helen Nissenbaum. *Obfuscation: A User's Guide for Privacy and Protest*. Cambridge, MA: MIT Press, 2016.

Bryant, Melissa. "Stop Netflix Autoplay Advertisements." Change.org, petition, December 21, 2019. https://www.change.org/p/stop-netflix-autoplay-advertisements?redirect=false.

Burke, Teresa Blankmeyer. "Time, Speedviewing, and Deaf Academics." *Possibilities and Finger Snaps*, March 20, 2016. https://possibilitiesandfingersnaps.wordpress.com/2016/03/20/time-speedviewing-and-deaf-academics/.

Carr, Nicholas. *The Shallows: What the Internet Is Doing to Our Brains*. London: W. W. Norton, 2010.

Casetti, Francesco. *Screening Fears: On Protective Media*. New York: Zone Books, 2023.

Cepeda, María. "Thrice Unseen, Forever on Borrowed Time." *South Atlantic Quarterly* 120 (April 2021): 301–20.

Chalmers, Matthew, Ian Maccoll, and Marek Bell. "Seamful Design: Showing the Seams in Wearable Computing." Paper presented at IEE Eurowearable, Birmingham, UK, 2003. https://doi.org/10.1049/ic:20030140.

Chen, Angus. "Rage Quit: Mass. Residents Furious over State's Faulty Vaccine Websites." *WBUR*, February 19, 2021. https://www.wbur.org/news/2021/02/18/hours-and-hours-of-frustration-mass-residents-emote-about-states-faulty-vaccine-websites.

Chen, Brian X. "Everything You Need to Know About Slow Internet Speeds." *New York Times*, May 20, 2020. https://www.nytimes.com/2020/05/20/technology/personaltech/slow-internet-speeds.html.

Chen, Brian X. "The Sad Truth About Sleep-Tracking Devices and Apps." *New York Times*, July 17, 2019. https://www.nytimes.com/2019/07/17/technology/personaltech/sleep-tracking-devices-apps.html.

Chun, Wendy Hui Kyong. "On 'Sourcery,' or Code as Fetish." *Configurations* 16(3) (Fall 2008): 299–324.

Chun, Wendy Hui Kyong. *Updating to Remain the Same: Habitual New Media*. Cambridge, MA: MIT Press, 2016.

Clare, Eli, *Brilliant Imperfection: Grappling with Cure*. Durham, NC: Duke University Press, 2017.

Clark, John Lee. "Against Access." *McSweeney's*, August 2021. https://audio.mcsweeneys.net/transcripts/against_access.html.

Clark, Mitchell. "Here's How to Turn Off Twitter's Weird New Refresh Sound." *Verge*, July 21, 2022. https://www.theverge.com/2022/7/21/23273010/twitter-refresh-sound-turn-off-how-to.

Cmiel, Kenneth, and John Durham Peters. *Promiscuous Knowledge: Information, Image, and Other Truth Games in History*. Chicago: University of Chicago Press, 2020.

Coklyat, Bojana, and Chancey Fleet. "Blind New Yorkers, Online and Offline, During the Pandemic." In *How to Be Disabled in a Pandemic*, edited by Mara Mills, Harris Kornstein, Faye Ginsburg, and Rayna Rapp, 214–27. New York: NYU Press, 2025.

Coleman, Rebecca. "Refresh: On the Temporalities of Digital Media 'Re's." *Media Theory* 4(2) (December 2020): 55–84.

Costanza-Chock, Sasha. *Design Justice*. Cambridge, MA: MIT Press, 2020.

Cotter, Padraig. "What a Red-Band Trailer Actually Means (and Where It Comes From)." *ScreenRant*, September 8, 2019. https://screenrant.com/red-band-trailer-meaning-history/.

Crary, Jonathan. *24/7: Late Capitalism and the Ends of Sleep*. New York: Verso Books, 2013.

Cubitt, Sean. "Against Connectivity." Paper presented at In/Between: Cultures of Connectivity, the NECS European Network for Cinema and Media Studies Conference, Potsdam, Germany, July 28–30, 2016.

Cubitt, Sean. *The Practice of Light: A Genealogy of Visual Technologies from Prints to Pixels*. Cambridge, MA: MIT Press, 2014.

Curry, David. "Calm Revenue and Usage Statistics (2022)." *Business of Apps*, July 1, 2022. https://www.businessofapps.com/data/calm-statistics/.

Dai, Tinglong. "The US Government's $44 Million Vaccine Rollout Website Was a Predictable Mess—Here's How to Fix the Broken Process Behind It." *Conversation*, February 3, 2021. https://theconversation.com/the-us-governments-44-million-vaccine-rollout-website-was-a-predictable-mess-heres-how-to-fix-the-broken-process-behind-it-154463.

Dame-Griff, Avery. *The Two Revolutions: A History of the Transgender Internet*. New York: NYU Press, 2023.

Dames, Nicholas. *The Physiology of the Novel: Reading, Neural Science, and the Form of Victorian Fiction*. Oxford: Oxford University Press, 2007.

Damman, Catherine. "Carolyn Lazard by Catherine Damman." *BOMB Magazine*, September 10, 2020. https://bombmagazine.org/articles/carolyn-lazard/.

Davies, Hannah J. "Nicole Kidman and Idris Elba Lead HBO Series to Help People Sleep." *Guardian*, July 17, 2020. https://www.theguardian.com/media/2020/jul/17/nicole-kidman-idris-elba-lead-hbo-series-sleep-a-world-of-calm.

De Beule, Yoni. "Why Does the Yelp iOS App Use Hamsters in Their Loading Animations and Error Screens?" *Forbes*, January 14, 2014. https://www.forbes.com/sites/quora/2014/01/14/why-does-the-yelp-ios-app-use-hamsters-in-their-loading-animations-and-error-screens/?sh=3ef6d81c462c.

De Luca, Tiago, and Nuno Barradas Jorge, eds. *Slow Cinema*. Edinburgh: Edinburgh University Press, 2016.

Duraccio, Kara M., Kelsey K. Zaugg, Robyn C. Blackburn, and Chad D. Jensen. "Does iPhone Night Shift Mitigate Negative Effects of Smartphone Use on Sleep Outcomes in Emerging Adults?" *Sleep Health* 7(4) (August 2021): 478–84.

Elkins, Evan. "Powered by Netflix: Speed Test Services and Video-on-Demand's Global Development Projects." *Media, Culture and Society* 40(6) (September 2018): 838–55.

Ellcessor, Elizabeth. *Restricted Access: Media, Disability, and the Politics of Participation*. New York: NYU Press, 2016.

Ellis, JJJJJerome. "Liturgy of the Name." *BOMB Magazine*, October 10, 2023. https://bombmagazine.org/articles/2023/10/10/liturgy-of-the-name/.

Enger, Reed. "Without Hope." *Obelisk Art History*, July 30, 2017. http://arthistoryproject.com/artists/frida-kahlo/without-hope/.

Eubanks, Virginia. *Automating Inequality: How High-Tech Tools Profile, Police, and Punish the Poor*. New York: St. Martin's, 2018.

Fadel, Leila. "Advocates for Deaf and Blind Laud Netflix's New Playback Features." *NPR*, August 8, 2020. https://www.npr.org/2020/08/08/900536509/advocates-for-deaf-and-blind-laud-netflixs-new-playback-features.

Farman, Jason. *Delayed Response: The Art of Waiting from the Ancient to the Instant World*. New Haven, CT: Yale University Press, 2018.

Fields, R. Douglas. "Why Can Some Blind People Process Speech Far Faster than Sighted Persons?" *Scientific American*, December 13, 2010. https://www.scientificamerican.com/article/why-can-some-blind-people-process/.

Finn, Ed. *What Algorithms Want*. Cambridge, MA: MIT Press, 2017.

Fitzpatrick, Molly. "Is 'Speed Watching' TV Shows as Stupid as It Sounds?" *New York Times*, December 13, 2016. https://nymag.com/speed/2016/12/is-speed-watching-tv-shows-as-stupid-as-it-sounds.html.

Fogg, B. J. *Persuasive Technology: Using Computers to Change What We Think and Do*. San Francisco: Morgan Kaufman, 2003.

Forlano, Laura. "Crip Futurity, Cyborg Disability and Designing the World Otherwise." Paper presented at Anticipation 2022, Arizona State University, December 23, 2022.

Fosslien, Liz, and Mollie West Duffy. "How to Combat Zoom Fatigue." *Harvard Business Review*, April 29, 2020. https://hbr.org/2020/04/how-to-combat-zoom-fatigue.

Fritsch, Kelly. "Accessible." In *Keywords for Radicals: The Contested Vocabulary of Late-Capitalist Struggle*, edited by Kelly Fritsch, Clare O'Connor, and A. K. Thompson, 23–28. Chico, CA: AK Press, 2016.

Fung, Brian. "Execs Ignored the Damage Instagram Does to Teens, Meta Whistleblower Tells Congress." *CNN*, November 7, 2023. https://www.cnn.com/2023/11/07/tech/meta-ignored-warnings-instagrams-harm/index.html.

Galloway, Alexander. *The Interface Effect*. Hoboken, NJ: Wiley, 2012.

Geoghegan, Bernard. "An Ecology of Operations: Vigilance, Radar, and the Birth of the Computer Screen." *Representations* 147(1) (Summer 2019): 59–96.

Gil, Liliana. "A Fablab at the Periphery: Decentering Innovation from São Paulo." *American Anthropologist* 124(4) (December 2022): 721–33.

Goggin, Gerard. "Disability and Haptic Mobile Media." *New Media & Society* 19(10) (2017): 1563–80.

Goldsmith, Leo. "Blissfully Yours." *Not Coming to a Theater Near You*, June 14, 2006. http://www.notcoming.com/reviews/blissfullyyours/.

Gómez-Uribe, Carlos, and Neil Hunt. "The Netflix Recommender System: Algorithms, Business Value and Innovation." *ACM Transactions on Management Information Systems* 6(4) (January 2016): 1–19.

Gordon, Devin. "Why Is Everyone Watching TV with the Subtitles On?" *Atlantic*, June 6, 2023. https://www.theatlantic.com/ideas/archive/2023/06/watching-movies-tv-with-subtitles/674301/.

Grigely, Joseph, and Emily Watlington. "Joseph Grigely and Emily Watlington in Conversation." Event at New York University's Center for Disability Studies, New York, NY, April 9, 2021.

Guaraná, Bruno. "At the Edges of Sleep." *Film Quarterly* 76(2) (Winter 2022): 109–12.

Haagaard, Alex. "Notes on Temporal Inaccessibility." *Medium*, March 12, 2021. https://alexhaagaard.medium.com/notes-on-temporal-inaccessibility-28ebcdf1b6d6.

Hagood, Mack. *Hush: Media and Sonic Self-Control*. Durham, NC: Duke University Press, 2019.

Hale, Mike. "Review: 13 Reasons Why She Killed Herself, Drawn Out on Netflix." *New York Times*, March 30, 2017. https://www.nytimes.com/2017/03/30/arts/television/netflix-13-reasons-why-tv-review.html.

Hamraie, Aimi. *Building Access: Universal Design and the Politics of Disability*. Minneapolis: University of Minnesota Press, 2017.

Hamraie, Aimi. "Universal Design and the Problem of 'Post-Disability' Ideology." *Design and Culture* 8(3) (2016): 1–22.

Hamraie, Aimi, and Kelly Fritsch. "Crip Technoscience Manifesto." *Catalyst* 5(1) (2019). https://catalystjournal.org/index.php/catalyst/article/view/29607.

Hanich, Julian. "An Invention with a Future: Collective Viewing, Joint Deep Attention and the Ongoing Value of the Cinema." In *Oxford Handbook of Film Theory*, edited by Kyle Stevens, 590–608. Oxford: Oxford University Press, 2022.

Hartogsohn, Ido, and Amir Vudka. "Technology and Addiction: What Drugs Can Teach Us About Digital Media." *Transcultural Psychiatry* 6(4) (2022): 1–11.

Hasbroucka, Joel, and Gideon Saar. "Low-Latency Trading." *Journal of Financial Markets* 16 (2013): 646–79.

Hassoun, Dan, and James N. Gilmore. "Drowsing: Toward a Concept of Sleepy Screen Engagement." *Communication and Critical/Cultural Studies* 14(2) (2017): 103–19.

Havas, Julia, and Tanya Horeck. "Netflix Feminism: Binge Watching Rape Culture in *Unbreakable Kimmy Schmidt* and *Unbelievable*." In *Binge-Watching and Contemporary Television Studies*, edited by Marieke Jenner, 250–73. Edinburgh: Edinburgh University Press, 2021.

Hayles, N. Katherine. "How We Read: Close, Hyper, Machine." *ADE Bulletin* 150 (2010): 62–79.

Hebert, Pato, and Alexandra Juhasz. "You're Still Sick." *BOMB Magazine*, July 28, 2020. https://bombmagazine.org/articles/youre-still-sick/.

Hedva, Johanna. "Sick Woman Theory." Johannahedva.com, accessed on June 1, 2024. https://tobyspgcertblog.myblog.arts.ac.uk/files/2022/05/SickWomanTheory_Hedva_2020.pdf.

Heilmann, Till A. "'Tap, Tap, Flap, Flap': Ludic Seriality, Digitality, and the Finger." *Eludamos: Journal for Computer Game Culture* 8(1) (2014): 33–46.

Heimlich, Russell. "Do You Sleep with Your Cell Phone?" Pew Research, September 13, 2010. https://www.pewresearch.org/fact-tank/2010/09/13/do-you-sleep-with-your-cell-phone/.

Hendren, Sara. "All Technology Is Assistive." *Wired*, October 16, 2014. https://www.wired.com/2014/10/all-technology-is-assistive/.

Hess, Amanda. "The App That Tucks Me in at Night." *New York Times*, July 17, 2019. https://www.nytimes.com/interactive/2019/07/17/arts/calm-app-sleep-meditation.html.

Hesselbert, Pepita, and Maria Poulaki, eds. *Compact Cinematics: The Moving Image in the Age of Bit-Sized Media*. London: Blomsbury Academic, 2017.

Hicks, Mar. "Hacking the Cis-tem." *IEEE Annals of the History of Computing* 41(1) (January–March 2019): 20–33.

Hilderbrand, Lucas. *Inherent Vice: Bootleg Histories of Videotape and Copyright*. Durham, NC: Duke University Press, 2009.

Hillenbrand, Laura. "A Sudden Illness." *New Yorker*, July 7, 2003. http://www.newyorker.com/magazine/2003/07/07/a-sudden-illness.

Hoffman, Donna L., and Thomas P. Novak. "Marketing in Hypermedia Computer-Mediated Environments: Conceptual Foundations." *Journal of Marketing* 60(3) (July 1996): 50–68.

hooks, bell. "The Oppositional Gaze: Black Female Spectators." In *The Feminism and Visual Cultural Reader*, edited by Amelia Jones, 94–105. New York: Routledge, 1992.

Horeck, Tanya. "Netflix and Heal: The Shifting Meanings of Binge-Watching During the Covid-19 Crisis." *Film Quarterly* 75(1) (Fall 2021): 35–40.

Horeck, Tanya. "Streaming Sexual Violence: Binge-Watching Netflix's *13 Reasons Why*." *Journal of Audience and Reception Studies* 16(2) (November 2019): 143–66.

Horeck, Tanya, Mareike Jenner, and Tina Kendall. "On Binge-Watching: Nine Critical Propositions." *Critical Studies in Television: The International Journal of Television Studies* 13(4) (December 2018): 499–504.

Hu, Tung-Hui. *Digital Lethargy: Dispatches from an Age of Disconnection*. Cambridge, MA: MIT Press, 2022.

Huberty, Jennifer, Jeni Green, Christine Glissmann, Linda Larkey, Megan Puzia, and Chong Lee. "Efficacy of the Mindfulness Meditation Mobile App 'Calm' to Reduce

Stress Among College Students: Randomized Controlled Trial." *JMIR mHealth uHealth* 7(6) (June 25, 2019): e14273.

Huffington, Arianna. *The Sleep Revolution: Transforming Your Life, One Night at a Time.* New York: Harmony Books, 2016.

Hwang, Tim. *Subprime Attention Crisis: Advertising and the Time Bomb at the Heart of the Internet.* New York: FSG Originals x Logic, 2020.

Ibekwe, Desiree. "Michaela Coel: 'TV Is Unforgiving—But I'm Built for This.'" *Broadcast Now*, June 8, 2020. https://www.broadcastnow.co.uk/drama/michaela-coel-tv-is-unforgiving-but-im-built-for-this/5150183.article.

Jacobs, Jason. "Television, Interrupted: Pollution or Aesthetic?" In *Television as Digital Media*, edited by James Bennett and Niki Strange, 255–80. Durham, NC: Duke University Press, 2011.

Jacobs, Julia. "Netflix Users Rejoice: Goodbye, Autoplay." *New York Times*, February 6, 2020. https://www.nytimes.com/2020/02/06/arts/television/netflix-makes-autoplay-optional.html.

Jain, Lochlann S. "Inscription Fantasies and Interface Erotics: Keyboards, Law, Repetitive Strain Injuries." *Hastings Journal of Women and Law* 9(2) (Spring 1998): 219–53.

Jain, Lochlann S. "The Prosthetic Imagination: Enabling and Disabling the Prosthesis Trope." *Science, Technology, and Human Values* 24(1) (1999): 31–54.

Jancovic, Marek, and Judith Keilbach. "Streaming Against the Environment: Digital Infrastructures, Video Compression, and the Environmental Footprint of Video Streaming." In *Situating Data: Inquiries in Algorithmic Culture*, edited by Karin van Es and Nanna Verhoff, 85–102. Amsterdam: Amsterdam University Press, 2023.

Jiang, Manyu. "The Reason Zoom Calls Drain Your Energy." *BBC*, April 22, 2020. https://www.bbc.com/worklife/article/20200421-why-zoom-video-chats-are-so-exhausting.

Jones, Ellen E. "*Crime Scene: The Vanishing at the Cecil Hotel* Review—Not Spooky, Just Desperately Sad." *Guardian*, February 10, 2021. https://www.theguardian.com/tv-and-radio/2021/feb/10/scene-the-vanishing-at-the-cecil-hotel-review-not-spooky-just-desperately-sad.

Jones, Nathan, and Sam Skinner. "Absorbing Text: Rereading Speed Reading." *APRJA* 6(1) (2017): 26–38.

Joseph, Branden W. "The Play of Repetition: Andy Warhol's *Sleep*." *Grey Room* 19 (Spring 2005): 29–33.

Jung, Alex E. "Michaela the Destroyer." *Vulture*, July 6, 2020. https://www.vulture.com/article/michaela-coel-i-may-destroy-you.html.

Kafer, Alison. *Feminist, Queer, Crip*. Bloomington: Indiana University Press, 2013.

Kafka, Peter, and Rani Molla. "The Netflix Effect." *Land of the Giants*, podcast, season 2, June 23–August 4, 2020. https://www.vox.com/land-of-the-giants-podcast.

Keating, Gina. *Netflixed: The Epic Battle for America's Eyeballs*. New York: Penguin, 2012.

Kelly, Makena. "New Bill Would Ban Autoplay Videos and Endless Scrolling." *Verge*, July 30, 2019. https://www.theverge.com/2019/7/30/20746878/.

Kelly, Samantha Murphy. "Zoom's Massive 'Overnight Success' Actually Took Nine Years." *CNN Business*, March 27, 2020. https://www.cnn.com/2020/03/27/tech/zoom-app-coronavirus/index.html.

Kendall, Tina. "Staying on, or Getting off (the Bus): Approaching Speed in Cinema and Media Studies." *Cinema Journal* 55(2) (Winter 2016): 112–18.

Kennedy, Pagan. "The Insomnia Machine." *New York Times*, September 18, 2016. https://www.nytimes.com/2016/09/18/opinion/sunday/the-insomnia-machine.html.

Kitchin, Rob, and Alistair Fraser. *Slow Computing: Why We Need Balanced Digital Lives*. Bristol, UK: Policy Press, 2020.

Kittler, Friedrich, and Geoffrey Winthrop-Young. "Real Time Analysis, Time Axis Manipulation." *Cultural Politics* 1(1) (2017): 1–18.

Klein, Matt. "Netflix Rolls Out Playback Speed Control—So Who's the Real Director During Our Ambient TV Era?" *Forbes*, December 7, 2020. https://www.forbes.com/sites/mattklein/2020/12/07/netflix-rolls-out-playback-speed-control-so-whos-the-real-director-during-our-ambient-tv-era/?sh=7041129518d2.

Kornstein, Harris, and Emily Lim Rogers. "When Postviral Goes Viral: Myalgic Encephalomyelitis, Long COVID, and Pandemic Déjà Vu." In *How to Be Disabled in a Pandemic*, edited by Mara Mills, Harris Kornstein, Faye Ginsburg, and Rayna Rapp, 191–213. New York: NYU Press, 2025.

Kroker, Kenton. *The Sleep of Others*. Toronto: University of Toronto Press, 2007.

Larkin, Brian. *Signal and Noise: Media, Infrastructure, and Urban Culture in Nigeria*. Durham, NC: Duke University Press, 2008.

Lawrence, Halcyon M. "Siri Disciplines." In *Your Computer Is on Fire*, edited by Thomas Mullaney, Benjamin Peters, Mar Hicks, and Kavita Philip, 179–97. Cambridge, MA: MIT Press, 2021.

Lehrer, Riva. "The Virus Has Stolen Your Face from Me." *New York Times*, December 10, 2020. https://www.nytimes.com/2020/12/10/opinion/coronavirus-mask-faces-art.html.

Lewis, Victoria Ann. "Crip." In *Keywords for Disability Studies*, edited by Rachel Adams, Benjamin Reiss, and David Serlin, 46–47. New York: NYU Press, 2015.

Limbong, Andrew. "Netflix Alters Corporate Culture Memo to Stress the Importance of Artistic Freedom." *NPR*, May 13, 2022. https://www.npr.org/2022/05/13/1098753056/netflix-corporate-culture-memo.

Little, Nicolette. "Social Media 'Ghosts': How Facebook Meta Memories Complicates Healing for Survivors of Intimate Partner Violence." *Feminist Media Studies* 23(8) (November 30, 2022): 3901–23. https://doi.org/10.1080/14680777.2022.2149593.

Livingston, Julie. *Debility and the Moral Imagination in Botswana*. Bloomington: Indiana University Press, 2005.

Lopez, Kristen. "How Movie Theaters Are Failing Viewers with Disabilities." *IGN*, June 3, 2018. https://www.ign.com/articles/2018/06/03/how-movie-theaters-are-failing-viewers-with-disabilities.

Lowrey, Annie. "The App That Monetized Doing Nothing." *Atlantic*, June 4, 2021. https://www.theatlantic.com/technology/archive/2021/06/do-meditation-apps-work/619046/.

Ma, Jean. *At the Edges of Sleep: Moving Images and Somnolent Spectators*. Berkeley: University of California Press, 2022.

Ma, Jean. "Sleeping in the Cinema." *October* 176 (2021): 31–52.

Madrigal, Alexis C. "The Mechanics and Meaning of That Ol' Dial-Up Modem Sound." *Atlantic*, June 1, 2012. https://www.theatlantic.com/technology/archive/2012/06/the-mechanics-and-meaning-of-that-ol-dial-up-modem-sound/257816/.

Magnet, Shoshana. *When Biometrics Fail*. Durham, NC: Duke University Press, 2015.

Marcotte, Jess Rowan. "Queering the Controller." *Jeka Games*, blog, 2017. https://tag.hexagram.ca/jekagames/cgsa-2017-queering-game-controls-slides-and-talk/.

Martens, Lisa. "How Autoplay F**** with My PTSD." Medium.com, February 20, 2021. https://medium.com/you-seem-fine/how-autoplay-f-with-my-ptsd-e7dff6fbb391.

Mattern, Shannon. "Networked Dream Worlds." *Real Life Magazine*, July 8, 2019. https://reallifemag.com/networked-dream-worlds/#!.

Mattern, Shannon. "Postures of Pandemic Productivity: Work-from-Home Furniture and Information Labor." Paper presented at the Society of Cinema and Media Studies Conference, Denver, CO, April 18, 2023.

McAlone, Nathan. "The Creator of 'Lost' Explains Why He Doesn't Like Netflix-Style Binge-Watching." *Business Insider*, April 2017. https://www.businessinsider.com/lost-creator-damon-lindelof-doesnt-like-netflix-style-binge-watching-2017-4.

McMenamin, Terence M. "A Time to Work: Recent Trends in Shift Work and Flexible Schedules." *Monthly Labor Review*, December 2007. https://www.bls.gov/opub/mlr/2007/article/time-to-work-recent-trends-in-shift-work-and-flexible-schedules.htm.

McPherson, Tara. "Liveness, Mobility, and the Web." In *New Media, Old Media: A History and Theory Reader*, edited by Wendy Hui Kyong Chun, Anna Watkins Fisher, and Thomas Keenan, 240–49. London: Routledge, 2005.

McRuer, Robert. *Crip Theory: Cultural Signs of Queerness and Disability*. New York: NYU Press, 2006.

McWatters, Michael. "Autoplay Blues." Medium.com, January 23, 2017. https://medium.com/@mmcwatters/autoplay-blues-9f41564fe030.

Metzl, Jonathan M., and Anna Kirkland, eds. *Against Health: How Health Became the New Morality*. New York: NYU Press, 2010.

Mezzapelle, Lorenza. "Parallel Lines Considers What It Means to Be Alone, Together." *Concordian*, May 12, 2020. https://theconcordian.com/2020/05/parallel-lines/.

Mills, Mara, and Neta Alexander. "Scores: Carolyn Lazard's Crip Minimalism." *Film Quarterly* 76(2) (December 1, 2022): 39–47.

Mills, Mara, Harris Kornstein, Faye Ginsburg, and Rayna Rapp, eds. *How to Be Disabled in a Pandemic*. New York: NYU Press, 2025.

Mills, Mara, and Andy Slater. "Blind Mode/Blind Listening Techniques." *English Studies in Canada* 46(2) (May 2023): 297–302.

Mills, Mara, and Jonathan Sterne. "Aural Speed-Reading: Some Historical Bookmarks." *PMLA* 135(2) (2020): 401–11.

Mills, Mara, and Jonathan Sterne. "Dismediation: Three Propositions and Six Tactics Afterword." In *Disability Media Studies*, edited by Elizabeth Ellcessor and Bill Kirkpatrick, 365–78. New York: NYU Press, 2017.

Mingus, Mia. "Access Intimacy, Interdependence, and Disability Justice." *Leaving Evidence*, blog, April 12, 2017. https://leavingevidence.wordpress.com/2017/04/12/access-intimacy-interdependence-and-disability-justice/.

Miserandino, Christine. "The Spoon Theory Written by Christine Miserandino." *But You Don't Look Sick*, blog, April 25, 2013. https://butyoudontlooksick.com/articles/written-by-christine/the-spoon-theory/.

Mitter, Siddhartha. "Behind Basquiat's 'Defacement': Reframing a Tragedy." *New York Times*, July 30, 2019. https://www.nytimes.com/2019/07/30/arts/design/behind-basquiats-defacement-reframing-a-tragedy.html.

Moon, Mariella. "YouTube Brings Playback Speed Choices to Mobile." *Engadget*, September 9, 2017. https://www.engadget.com/2017/09/09/youtube-playback-speed-mobile-ios-android/.

Morozov, Evgeny. *To Save Everything, Click Here*. New York: PublicAffairs, 2014.

Moulier-Boutang, Yann. *Cognitive Capitalism*. Cambridge: Polity, 2011.

Mulvey, Laura. *Death 24× a Second: Stillness and the Moving Image*. London: Reaktion, 2006.

Mulvin, Dylan, "Media Prophylaxis: Night Modes and the Politics of Preventing Harm." *Information and Culture* 53(2) (2018): 175–202.

Mulvin, Dylan. *Proxies: The Cultural Work of Standing In*. Cambridge, MA: MIT Press, 2021.

Mulvin, Dylan. "The Rage Room." Paper presented at the Society for Cinema and Media Studies Conference, online, March 18, 2022.

Mulvin, Dylan. "Talking It Out: An Interview with Mara Mills." *Seachange* 1(3) (2012): 52–64.

Münsterberg, Hugo. *The Photoplay: A Psychological Study and Other Writings*, edited by Allan Langdale. New York: Routledge, 2001.

Murthy, Vivek H. "Surgeon General: Why I'm Calling for a Warning Label on Social Media Platforms." *New York Times*, June 17, 2024. https://www.nytimes.com/2024/06/17/opinion/social-media-health-warning.html.

Nakamura, Lisa. "Feeling Good About Feeling Bad: Virtuous Virtual Reality and the Automation of Racial Empathy." *Journal of Visual Culture* 19(1) (April 2020): 47–64.

National Association of the Deaf. "Landmark Precedent in NAD vs. Netflix." Last modified on June 19, 2012. https://www.nad.org/2012/06/19/landmark-precedent-in-nad-vs-netflix/.

NBC Boston. "Massachusetts Vaccination Scheduling Website Crashes as Appointments Open for 65+." February 18, 2021. https://www.nbcboston.com/news/local/nearly-1-million-people-now-eligible-for-covid-vaccine-in-mass/2305907/.

Netflix Technology Blog. "How We Determine Product Success." Last modified on January 19, 2011. https://netflixtechblog.com/how-we-determine-product-success-980f81f0047e.

Neves, Joshua, Aleena Chia, Susanna Paasonen, and Ravi Sundaram. *Technopharmacology*. Minneapolis: University of Minnesota Press, 2022.

Neves, Joshua, and Marc Steinberg, eds. *In/Convenience: Inhabiting the Logistical Soundeditors*. Theory on Demand 54. Institute of Network Cultures. November 26, 2024. https://networkcultures.org/blog/2024/11/26/out-now-tod54-in-convenience-inhabiting-the-logistical-surround-edited-by-joshua-neves-and-marc-sternberg/.

New York Film Academy. "The History of Drive-In Movie Theaters." Last modified June 7, 2017. https://www.nyfa.edu/student-resources/the-history-of-drive-in-movie-theaters-and-where-they-are-now/.

New York Times. "Too Many Shows? Take Them In a High Speed." Last modified on December 12, 2016. https://www.nytimes.com/2016/12/12/technology/favorite-shows-high-speed.html.

Nooney, Laine. "Have Any Remedies for Tired Eyes? Computer Pain as Computer History." In *Abstractions and Embodiments*, edited by Janet Abbate and Stephanie Dick, 416–34. Baltimore: Johns Hopkins University Press, 2022.

Nooney, Laine. "How the Personal Computer Broke the Human Body." *Motherboard*, May 12, 2021. https://www.vice.com/en/article/y3dda7/how-the-personal-computer-broke-the-human-body.

Nooney, Laine. "The Uncredited: Work, Women and the Making of the American Computer Game Industry." *Feminist Media Histories* 6(1) (2020): 119–46.

Nopper, Tamara K., and Eve Zelickson. *Wellness Capitalism: Employee Health, the Benefits Maze and Worker Control*. New York: Data and Society Research Institute, June 21, 2023. https://datasociety.net/library/wellness-capitalism-employee-health-the-benefits-maze-and-worker-control/.

Norman, Don. *Invisible Computer*. Cambridge, MA: MIT Press, 1998.

Ochsner, Beate, Markus Spöhrer, and Robert Stock. "Rethinking Assistive Technologies: Users, Environments, Digital Media, and App-Practices of Hearing." *NanoEthics* 16 (2022): 65–79.

O'Neil, Cathy. *Weapons of Math Destruction*. New York: Penguin Random House, 2016.

Oppel, Richard A., Jr., Robert Gebeloff, K. K. Rebecca Lai, Will Wright, and Mitch Smith. "The Fullest Look Yet at the Racial Inequity of Coronavirus." *New York Times*, July 5, 2020. https://www.nytimes.com/interactive/2020/07/05/us/coronavirus-latinos-african-americans-cdc-data.html.

Ordonez, Victor. "Key Takeaways from Facebook Whistleblower Frances Haugen's Senate Testimony." *ABC News*, October 5, 2021. https://abcnews.go.com/Politics/keytakeaways-facebook-whistleblower-frances-haugens-senatetestimony/story?id=80419357.

Ortega, Vicente Rodríguez. "'We Pay to Buy Ourselves': Netflix, Spectators and Streaming." *Journal of Communication Inquiry* 47(2) (July 1, 2023): 126–44.

Ørum, Kristoffer. "Throbber." In *Uncertain Archives: Critical Keywords for Big Data*, edited by Nanna Bonde Thylstrup, Daniela Agostinho, Annie Ring, Catherine D'Ignazio, and Kristin Veel, 513–21. Cambridge, MA: MIT Press, 2021.

Pallotta, Frank. "Netflix Launches 'Basic with Ads'—Its Much Anticipated Commercial-Supported Plan." *CNN*, November 3, 2022. https://www.cnn.com/2022/11/03/media/netflix-with-ads-launch/index.html.

Parisi, David. "Fingerbombing, or 'Touching Is Good': The Cultural Construction of Technologized Touch." *Senses and Society* 3(3) (2008): 307–28.

Parisi, David. "Game Interfaces as Disabling Infrastructures." *Analog Game Studies*, May 30, 2017. https://analoggamestudies.org/2017/05/compatibility-test-videogames-as-disabling-infrastructures/.

Patrick, Stephanie. "Afterward: Destroying the Cycle?" In *The Forgotten Victims of Sexual Violence in Film, Television and New Media: Turning to the Margins*, edited by Stephanie Patrick and Mythili Rajiva, 225–41. New York: Springer International, 2022.

Paul, Kari. "'Zoom Is the Malware': Why Experts Worry About the Video Conferencing Platform." *Guardian*, April 2, 2020. https://www.theguardian.com/technology/2020/apr/02/zoom-technology-security-coronavirus-video-conferencing.

Pearson, Catherine. "How to Help a Teen Who Can't Sleep." *New York Times*, May 8, 2023. https://www.nytimes.com/2023/05/08/well/family/teens-sleep-insomnia.html.

Perez, Melania Moscoso. "Cripwashing: Undermining the Civil Liberties in the Name of Disability Rights in Contemporary Spain." *Actas I Congreso internacional de la Red española de Filosofía* 8 (2015): 47–56.

Perks, Lisa G. "Media Marathoning Through Health Struggles: Filling a Social Reservoir." *Journal of Communication Inquiry* 43(3) (July 1, 2019): 314–29.

Petrick, Elizabeth. "The Computer as Prosthesis? Embodiment, Augmentation, and Disability." In *Abstractions and Embodiments*, edited by Janet Abbate and Stephanie Dick, 399–415. Baltimore: Johns Hopkins University Press, 2022.

Petruska, Karen, and John Vanderhoef. "TV That Watches You: Data Collection and the Connected Living Room." *Spectator* 34(2) (2014): 33–42.

Piepzna-Samarasinha, Leah Lakshmi. *Care Work: Dreaming Disability Justice*. Vancouver: Arsenal Pulp Press, 2018.

Piepzna-Samarasinha, Leah Lakshmi. "What Does It Mean to 'Crip' Healing?" *Tyee*, December 28, 2021. https://thetyee.ca/Culture/2021/12/28/What-Does-Crip-Healing-Mean/.

Pinchevski, Amit. "Social Media's Canaries: Content Moderators Between Digital Labor and Mediated Trauma." *Media, Culture and Society* 45(1) (January 2023): 212–21.

Plotnick, Rachel. *Power Button: A History of Pleasure, Panic, and the Politics of Pushing*. Cambridge, MA: MIT Press, 2018.

Polglase, Katie, Gianluca Mezzofiore, Eliza Mackintosh, Livvy Doherty, Henrik Pettersson, Byron Manley, and Lou Robinson. "How Gaza's Hospitals Became Battlegrounds." *CNN*, January 12, 2024. https://www.cnn.com/interactive/2024/01/middleeast/gaza-hospitals-destruction-investigation-intl-cmd/.

Postman, Neil. *Amusing Ourselves to Death: Public Discourse in the Age of Show Business*. New York: Viking, 1985.

Pow, Whit. "A Trans Historiography of Glitches and Errors." *Feminist Media Histories* 7(1) (2021): 197–230.

Price, Margaret. "The Bodymind Problem and the Possibilities of Pain." *Hypatia* 30(1) (2014): 268–84.

Price, Margaret. "The Precarity of Disability/Studies in Academe." In *Precarious Rhetorics*, edited by Wendy S. Hesford, Adela C. Licona, and Christa Teston, 191–211. Columbus: Ohio State University Press, 2018.

Puar, Jasbir. *The Right to Maim*. Durham, NC: Duke University Press, 2017.

Puijk, Roel. *Slow TV: An Analysis of Minute-by-Minute Television in Norway*. Bristol: Intellect Books, 2021.

Rangan, Pooja. "Listening in Crip Time: Toward a Countertheory of Documentary Access." *Film Quarterly* 76(2) (December 1, 2022): 25–30.

Raphael, Rina. "Netflix CEO Reed Hastings: Sleep Is Our Competition." *Fast Company*, November 6, 2017. https://www.fastcompany.com/40491939/netflix-ceo-reed-hastings-sleep-is-our-competition.

Reich, Hannah. "Netflix's Speed-Watching Trial Joins a Long History of Content Cramming, but May Be Bad for Artists and Viewers." *ABC Arts*, December 6, 2019. https://www.abc.net.au/news/2019-12-07/netflix-playback-speed-filmmaker-neuroscience-speedwatching/11773756.

Rezab, Jan. "Why I Watch Videos and TV Shows at Twice the Speed." *Forbes*, April 25, 2015. http://www.forbes.com/sites/janrezab/2015/04/29/why-i-watch-tv-shows-and-movies-at-twice-the-speed/.

Rodman, Howard. "Writers Guild Strike with Howard Rodman." *Jacobin Radio*, podcast, 38:00, May 9, 2023. https://shows.acast.com/jacobin-radio/episodes/jacobin-radio-writers-guild-strike-howard-rodman.

Rodriguez, Juan Llamas. "Playing 'the Game' of Migration." Seminar from the Center for Latinx Digital Media's Virtual Seminar Series, Northwestern University, Evanston, IL, February 27, 2023.

Rogers, Emily. "Recursive Debility: Symptoms, Patient Activism, and the Incomplete Medicalization of ME/CFS." *Medical Anthropology Quarterly* 36 (2022): 412–28.

Roose, Kevin. "Wonderland." *Rabbit Hole* podcast, produced by the *New York Times*, 26:48, April 16, 2020. https://www.nytimes.com/2020/04/16/podcasts/rabbit-hole-internet-youtube-virus.html.

Rose, Sarah F. *No Right to Be Idle: The Invention of Disability, 1850–1930*. New York: NYU Press, 2017.

Russell, Legacy. *Glitch Feminism*. New York: Penguin Random House, 2020.

Samuels, Ellen. "Six Ways of Looking at Crip Time." *Disability Studies Quarterly* 37(3) (Summer 2017). https://doi.org/10.18061/dsq.v37i3.5824.

Samuels, Ellen, and Elizabeth Freeman. "Introduction: Crip Temporalities." *South Atlantic Quarterly* 120 (April 2021): 245–55.

Sandahl, Carrie. "QUEERING THE CRIP OR CRIPPING THE QUEER? Intersections of Queer and Crip Identities in Solo Autobiographical Performance." *GLQ* 9(1–2) (April 1, 2003): 25–56.

Sax, David. *The Revenge of Analog: Real Things and Why They Matter*. New York: PublicAffairs, 2016.

Schneier, Bruce. *Beyond Fear: Thinking Sensibly About Security in an Uncertain World*. New York: Copernicus Books, 2003.

Schonfeld, Zach. "I've Rented DVDs from Netflix for Half My Life—Streaming Is a Poor Substitute." *Guardian*, April 27, 2023. https://www.theguardian.com/commentisfree/2023/apr/27/rented-dvds-netflix-streaming-movie-fans-cinema-history.

Schüll, Natasha Dow. *Addiction by Design: Machine Gambling in Las Vegas*. Princeton, NJ: Princeton University Press, 2012.

Schüll, Natasha Dow. "Data for Life: Wearable Technology and the Design of Self-Care." *BioSocieties* 11(3) (March 2016): 1–17.

Seaver, Nick. "Captivating Algorithms: Recommender Systems as Traps." *Journal of Material Culture* 24(4) (2019): 421–36.

Seaver, Nick. *Computing Taste: Algorithms and the Makers of Music Recommendation*. Chicago: University of Chicago Press, 2022.

Seff, Jon. "Netflix Finally Lets Users Disable Post Play." *Hive*, January 24, 2014. https://www.techhive.com/article/602264/netflix-finally-lets-users-disable-post-play-feature.html.

Sharma, Sarah, and Rianka Singh, eds. *Re-Understanding Media: Feminist Extensions of Marshall McLuhan*. Durham, NC: Duke University Press, 2022.

Shobhit. "How to Stop Autoplay Previews on Netflix on Mouse Hover?" *I Love Free Software*, blog, November 30, 2019. https://www.ilovefreesoftware.com/30/windows/internet/plugins/how-to-stop-autoplay-previews-on-netflix-on-mouse-hover.html.

Sicart, Miguel. "Queering the Controller." *Analog Game Studies*, July 31, 2017. https://analoggamestudies.org/2017/07/queering-the-controller/.

Siegler, M. G. "Facebook Apologizes over Pull to Refresh Lift." *TechCrunch*, August 20, 2010. https://techcrunch.com/2010/08/19/facebook-pull-to-refresh/.

Smilges, J. Logan. *Crip Negativity*. Minneapolis: University of Minnesota Press, 2023.

Sontag, Susan. "The Decay of Cinema." *New York Times*, February 25, 1996. https://www.nytimes.com/1996/02/25/magazine/the-decay-of-cinema.html.

Sontag, Susan. *Regarding the Pain of Others*. New York: Picador/Farrar, Straus and Giroux, 2003.

Sorkin, Andrew Ross. "Sunday Special: Elon Musk at 'DealBook.'" *Daily* podcast, produced by the *New York Times*, 1:34:00, December 3, 2023.

Starosielski, Nicole. *The Undersea Network*. Durham, NC: Duke University Press, 2015.

Sterne, Jonathan. *Diminished Faculties: A Political Phenomenology of Impairment*. Durham, NC: Duke University Press, 2022.

Sterne, Jonathan. *MP3: The Meaning of a Format*. Durham, NC: Duke University Press, 2012.

Stiverson, Hanah, Kyle Lindsey, and Lisa Nakamura. *Racist Zoombombing*. New York: Routledge, 2021.

Stokel-Walker, Chris. "In-Flight Movies Are Censored for the Most Bizarre Reasons." *Medium.com*, November 7, 2019. https://gen.medium.com/in-flight-movies-are-censored-for-the-most-bizarre-reasons-66686aff5cda.

Stone, Kara. "Designing Self-Care Affect and Debility in #SelfCare." In *Krankheit in Digitalen Spielen*, edited by Arno Görgen and Stefan Heinrich Simond, 417–32. Bielefeld: Interdisziplinäre Betrachtungen, 2020.

Theroux, Louis. "Michaela Coel." *Grounded with Louis Theroux* podcast, produced by BBC, 57:00, November 30, 2020. https://www.bbc.co.uk/programmes/p08ybstk.

Tuhus-Dubrow, Rebecca. *Personal Stereo*. London: Bloomsbury Academic, 2017.

Turner, Fred. *From Counterculture to Cyberculture*. Chicago: University of Chicago Press, 2006.

Tussey, Ethan. *The Procrastination Economy*. New York: NYU Press, 2018.

Valdez, Jonah. "Will the Government Crack Down on Bots After Ticketmaster's Taylor Swift Meltdown?" *Los Angeles Times*, November 29, 2022. https://www.latimes.com/entertainment-arts/music/story/2022-11-29/ticketmaster-ftc-bots-crackdown-taylor-swift.

Van Gelder, Lawrence. "Evelyn Wood, Who Promoted Speed Reading, Is Dead at 86." *New York Times*, August 30, 1995. https://www.nytimes.com/1995/08/30/obituaries/evelyn-wood-who-promoted-speed-reading-is-dead-at-86.html.

Veel, Kristin. "Latency." In *Uncertain Archives: Critical Keywords for Big Data*, edited by Nanna Bonde Thylstrup, Daniela Agostinho, Annie Ring, Catherine D'Ignazio, and Kristin Veel, 313–20. Cambridge, MA: MIT Press, 2021.

Volk, Stefan, Matthew J. Pearsall, Michael S. Christian, and William J. Becker. "Chronotype Diversity in Teams: Toward a Theory of Team Energetic Asynchrony." *Academy of Management Review* 42(4) (October 2017): 683–702.

Wald, Chelsea. "Why Your Brain Hates Slowpokes." *Nautilus*, March 5, 2015. http://nautil.us/issue/22/slow/why-your-brain-hates-slowpokes.

Walker, Amy Schoenfeld, Anjali Singhvi, Josh Holder, Robert Gebeloff, and Yuriria Avila. "Pandemic's Racial Disparities Persist in Vaccine Rollout." *New York Times*, March 5, 2021. https://www.nytimes.com/interactive/2021/03/05/us/vaccine-racial-disparities.html.

Walker, Matthew. *Why We Sleep: Unlocking the Power of Sleep and Dreams*. New York: Scribner, 2017.

Wasson, Haidee. "Film, Scale, and the Art Museum." In *Useful Cinema*, edited by Charles R. Acland and Haidee Wasson, 178–204. Durham, NC: Duke University Press, 2011.

Welch, Chris. "Netflix Now Lets You Disable Post-Play to Avoid Binge Watching Entire TV Seasons." *Verge*, January 27, 2014. https://www.theverge.com/2014/1/27/5351268/netflix-now-lets-you-disable-post-play-avoid-binge-watching-tv.

White, Michele. *The Body and the Screen: Theories of Internet Spectatorship*. Cambridge, MA: MIT Press, 2006.

White, Michele. *Touch Screen Theory: Digital Devices and Feelings*. Cambridge, MA: MIT Press, 2022.

Wildemuth, B. M., Gary Marchionini, Meng Yang, G. Geisler, T. Wilkens, A. Hughes, and Richard Gruss. "How Fast Is Too Fast? Evaluating Fast Forward Surrogates for Digital Video." In *Proceedings of the 2003 Joint Conference on Digital Libraries, 2003*. Houston, TX, 2003, pp. 221–30. doi: 10.1109/JCDL.2003.1204866.

Wollaston, Sam. "*13 Reasons Why*: Season Two Review—Netflix's Teen Saga Struggles to Find Purpose Second Time Out." *Guardian*, May 18, 2018. https://www.theguardian.com/tv-and-radio/2018/may/18/13-reasons-why-season-2-review-and-just-too-many-reasons-why-not.

Wollen, Peter. *Paris Hollywood: Writings on Film*. London: Verso, 2002.

Wong, Alice. "Q&A with Riva Lehrer." *Disability Visibility Project*, December 9, 2020. https://disabilityvisibilityproject.com/2020/12/09/qa-with-riva-lehrer/.

Yates, Diana. "Study of Sleep Apps Finds Room for Improvement." University of Illinois Urbana-Champaign News Bureau, April 12, 2017. https://news.illinois.edu/view/6367/486860.

Zeitlin-Wu, Lida. "Meditation Apps and the Unbearable Whiteness of Wellness." *Just Tech*, November 1, 2023. https://just-tech.ssrc.org/field-reviews/meditation-apps-and-the-unbearable-whiteness-of-wellness/.

Zraick, Karen, and Sarah Mervosh. "That Sleep Tracker Could Make Your Insomnia Worse." *New York Times*, June 13, 2019. https://www.nytimes.com/2019/06/13/health/sleep-tracker-insomnia-orthosomnia.html.

Zuboff, Shoshana. *In the Age of the Smart Machine: The Future of Work and Power*. New York: Basic Books, 1988.

INDEX

Page locators in italics indicate figures and tables

able-bodiedness: assumed of users, 3–4, 18, 37–38, 59, 69; decentering, 161–62; gaming industry assumption of, 37–38
abled/disabled binary, 59, 181n66, 185n16
ableism, 4–6, 70–74, 82; algorithmic bias, 16, 169n7; cripwashing, 22, 59, 76, 109, 161, 163, 179n17; cure, notions of, 114, 138–39, 163, 189n21, 195n43; "loss-of-wholeness" thesis, 69; in platform design and tech industry, 26, 37–38, 109–10, 154, 161; productivity, notions of, 73, 114, 124; and racism, 19–20, 49, 52, 66; super-user myth, 22, 59–60, 83, 124, 129; test subjects, disabled people as, 70–72, 76, 126, 162–63
acceleration, 64, 72, 76, 134; as business model, 7, 9, 32. *See also* playback speed; refresh; speed watching
access, 2–3; access entitlement, 21, 56, 173n98; access friction, 153–54; access intimacy, 79; access math, 74; access thievery, 88, 108–9, 116, 154–55; as attack, 108–9, 116; collective approach to, 77; monetizing, 55–82; rebranding of playback speed as, 57, 59, 74–76; wholeness of film used to contest, 69–70, 83
adaptation, 109
ad blockers, 87, 108
addiction, 23, 28, 35; autoplay as a cause of, 98; gambling, 13–14, 171n53; streaming platforms that reject, 88; technology as, 13–15. *See also* autoplay; buffering
addictive design, 12, 25, 38–39, 88, 95–96, 104. *See also* autoplay; sleep apps; soporific products
Affordable Care Act, 26
"Against Access" (Clark), 81–82
ageism, 22, 25–26, 46
agency, 39–41, 44, 46
algorithms: algorithmic bias, 16, 169n7; algorithmic trading, 33; predictive personalization, 94–95; prototypical whiteness used in design, 16, 170n15; recommendation, 22–23; ticket-buying bots, 174n7; trained on white male models, 5
Amazon, 29
American Council of the Blind, 59
American Sign Language (ASL), 182n66, 183n100
Americans with Disabilities Act (ADA), 75–76, 192n72
amputation metaphor, 18, 172n82
analog media, 29; in *13 Reasons Why*, 98–99; fast-forward effect, 65; finishability, 48, 99; nostalgia for, 99, *100*; as physical object, 99; and time manipulation, 58, 65
Anchor, 40, *48*, 177n109
anxiety: perpetual, 23, 30, 34, 46; sleep-related, 145, 148; and videoconferencing, 155. *See also* buffering

Apatow, Judd, 56, 178n1, 179n3
apparatus theory, 133
Apple, 19, 37-38. *See also* Night Shift (Apple)
Applebaum, Anne, 25-26
apps: health-related, 11; #SelfCare, 122, 139-42, *140*, *141*, 148; speed-reading, 62-63. *See also* browser add-ons; sleep apps
archives, digital, 156-57
ascetic technologies, 7, 120
assimilation, 6, 170n19
assistive technology, technology distinguished from, 181n66
attention economy, 29, 34, 97
audiences: access entitlement, 21, 56, 173n98; invited to activate works, 79-80; somnolent spectator, 133-34; and movie theater experience, 60-61, 69, 133-34, 192n72
audile scarification, 11
audiobooks, 54, 57, 59, 60, 119, 126
aural speed-reading, 57-59
Autonomous Sensory Meridian Response (ASMR), 81, 119, 148
autoplay, 2, 3, 84; ability to disable feature, 87, 96, 106-7, *107*; captology features, 13; countdown clock, 92-93, *93*; as default option, 96; digital debility produced by, 88, 116; drop-release model, 95, 97, 107, 110-12, 115; embedded or default, 86-87; inline playback, 85-86, *87*; legislative initiatives, 14-15, 186n52; opting out of, 4, 87-88, 96, 108, 116; postplay, 86-87, 90-97, *92*, *93*, *94*, 96, 102, 104, 107, 115; PTSD triggered by, 87-88; and recommendation algorithms, 22-23; Skip Intro, 83, 93; subscribers exposed to potentially triggering content by, 86, 87; unhealthy dependency on, 116-17. *See also* binge-watching; streaming
"Autoplay Blues" (McWatters), 97
avatars, 31, 51
"average" user, 3-4, 17, 30, 169n6, 183n104

Bacon, Everette, 57
Balint, Michael, 66
bandwidth, 1-2, 97-98, 169n1, 187n67
Baron, Rebecca, 77-78, *78*
Barron, Jesse, 43-44, 177n93
Basquiat, Jean-Michel, 121, 138-39

BBC One, 112
bedridden/homebound people, 17, 154, 155; media made by and for, 21, 24, 122, 137. *See also* COVID *Sleep* (McLeod); Kahlo, Frida; 2020-09-16 at 11:19:28 a.m. (Bullock)
The Behavior of the Museum Visitor (Wasson), 63
Ben-Moshe, Liat, 81, 170n19
Benson-Allott, Caetlin, 112
Berkeley, Busby, 77
Biden, Joseph, 14
binary distinctions: abled/disabled, 59, 181n66, 185n16; rejection of, 17; slow/fast, 32, 59
binge-watching, 3, 18, 22, 95, 188n107; *13 Reasons Why*, 99-101, 104; binge-racing, 87, 90, 184n14; Coel's attacks on, 111-12; during COVID, 185n22; dead white girl trope, 101; unbingeable, 112-15. *See also* autoplay; speed watching
biometric technologies, 5-6, 170n15
Black and Brown viewers, video art for, 51-53, *53*, 79
Black disability politics, 51-52
Black Embodiments Studio, 51-52
Blackmore, Tim, 55, 64
blind users, 4; audio books, 57; aural speed-reading, 57-59; auto-refreshing software, 22; Braille, use of, 42; hacking of talking books via phonographs, 22, 57, 70, 126; Lisa GUI incompatible with screen readers or voice synthesizers, 20; and Netflix playback speed feature, 18, 57; pull-to-refresh incompatible with screen readers, 29, 37; as test subjects, 70-72, 76, 126
bodyminds, 7, 17, 72, 172n75, 172n76
boredom, 28, 50-51, 81
BOTS Act, 174n7
Braille, 42, 160
brain: and micro-delays between audio and video signals, 155; rewiring or hacking, 59, 62, 64, 129; scaffolding, 58, 71-74
Brichter, Loren, 35-36, 43, 44, 54
Browne, Simone, 170n15
browser add-ons, 57, 65, 88, 108. *See also* apps; hacking
Bryant, Melissa, 85-86, 106, 109
BT commercial, 30-32, *31*, 35

214 INDEX

buffering, 1–2, *23*, 29; loading symbols, 30, 43, 53. *See also* addiction; latency; refresh
Bullock, Hannah, 24, 122, 143–46. *See also* 2020-09-16 at 11:19:28 a.m. (Bullock)
Bürgeramt system (Germany), 45–46
Burke, Teresa Blankmeyer, 71–72, 74, 182n86
"busy idleness," 29, 45, 174n14
button, 33–36, 87; gesture versus, 36, 38, 43, 54. *See also* refresh

calibration, 32, 54, 58, 74, 82; of light spectrum, 2, 21, 119, 121–26; recalibration, 72
Calm, 119; "Basquiat in New York" sleep story, 138–39; "Dream with Me" story, 191n61; origin stories, 128–29; sleep stories, 24, 121, 127. *See also* "Dreaming with Frida" (Calm sleep story)
Canaries collective, 79, 80, 122
canaries in the coal mine, 7, 41, 79
capitalism, 59; 24/7, 124, 148; cognitive, 64, 72, 76, 83–84; digital lethargy, 15–16; friction-less, 21, 25; surveillance, 49, 73, 116, 120–21, 148, 161
captioning: AI-generated, 154; closed, 69, 72, 74–76, 183n100; Netflix lawsuit, 75–76; and videoconferencing, 153
captivation/captology, 13, 88–89, 108, 174n10; dark patterns, 15; resistance to, 115–16
care: anticapitalist potential of, 144; care webs, 114, 116, 161; communal, 24, 144, 146–48, *147*; self-care and work schedule, 112–13; #SelfCare app, 122, 139–42, *140*, *141*, 148
carpal tunnel syndrome, 28, 42, 171n50
Carr, Nicholas, 62
causality, 15–16, 74, 104
Center for Humane Technology, 115, 189n130
Cepeda, Maria Elena, 55, 72
Chaslot, Guillaume, 115, 189n129
Chewing Gum (Coel), 112
Chrome, 65, 108
chronic fatigue syndrome (myalgic encephalomyelitis), 122, 145, 154
chronic illness, 51, 73, 79, 82, 142–43
chrono-diversity, corporate co-optation of, 124, 145, 148
chrononormativity, 73–74, 80, 124
Chun, Wendy Hui Kyong, 38, 42, 176n71
circadian rhythms, 4, 120, 123, 125–26

Clare, Eli, 172n75, 189n121
Clark, John Lee, 21, 42, 81–82
Coel, Michaela, 110–15, 188n111; *Chewing Gum*, 112; "Rest, reflect, rejuvenate" (three R's), 111–13; self-care and shooting schedule, 112–13. *See also I May Destroy You*
Coklyat, Bojana, 153
cold start problem, 91
Cold War, 33
Cole, Allison, 50
command-line interface, 19–20
commercials, 37–38; Apple Night Shift, 123–24; BT premium service, 30–32, *31*, 35; digital debility depicted in, 31; white, able-bodied men in, 124
compression, 4, 16, 24, 33, 58–59, 61; audio formats, 126; and computer pain, 64; crip alternatives to, 80, 113; gainfulness, 77; Varispeech, 70. *See also* crip time; temporality
computer pain, 7–9; biological and emotional, 7, 12–13; and clerical/administrative workers, 42; and compression, 64; as consensual impairment, 10–13, 34–35, 151; in fingers and thumbs, 34, 53–54; physical, 3, 28; psychological, 3; and rage rooms, 30; repetitive strain injury (RSI), 10, 12
consensual impairment, 10–13, 34–35, 151
content-agnostic products, 18, 121–22, 127, 132–33
content moderators, 9–10, 11, 41
control, illusion of, 36, 45
co-optation of crip creativity and innovation, 121, 124, 145, 148, 161; disabled people used as test subjects, 70–73, 76, 126, 163
countdown clocks, 22, 92–93, *93*, 101, 107
COVID-19 pandemic, 1–3, 119, 169n1; "being alone together," 146; denial and dismissal of long COVID, 143; elderly/senior users' failed attempts at refreshing, 22, 25–26, 46; "essential workers" and remote workers, 1–2, 10–11, 152–53; infodemic of fake news and denial, 97; lockdowns, 1, 97, 135, 146, 148, 150, 153–54, 159, 171n40, 185n22; Netflix memes, 99; "pandemic déjà vu," 154; screen time increase during, 171n40; vaccine distribution websites, 22, 25–26, 34, 45–46

INDEX 215

COVID Sleep (McLeod), 146–48, *147*
Crary, Jonathan, 120, 124, 147
Crime Scene: The Vanishing at the Cecil Hotel (Netflix), 105–6
"crip," as term, 16–17, 172n73
crip interfaces, 16, 21–22, 24
Crip Negativity (Smilges), 88
cripping, 16–21; cripping the interface, 16–21; crip technoscience, 20–21; innovation from below, 161; of production industry standards, 112–13; refresh, 51–54
"Crip Technoscience Manifesto" (Hamraie and Fritsch), 20–21, 47, 51, 173n95, 173n96
crip time, 49, 59, 68, 138; long shots, 80; temporal debt of living in, 73, 154; as uncertain time, 72; as vampire time, 156. *See also* compression; temporality
CRIP TIME (video art work), 21, 76, 78–82, *80*
cripwashing, 22, 59, 76, 109, 161, 163, 179n17
critical access studies, 109, 170n20, 188n104
Critical Lab Design, 157–58
Cubitt, Sean, 31–32, 39
curb cuts, 5, 170n14
cure, ableist notions of, 114, 189n21; "curative imaginary," 163, 195n43

dark patterns, 15, 96, 115
data centers, 7, 92, 97
"dead white girl" trope, 101
DeafBlind people, 42–43
Deaf users, 4, 75; wearables pushed on, 73
debility: digital economy based on, 9–10; disability distinguished from, 8–10, 35; folded body of computer users, 28, 35, 122; as gendered and class-based, 12; wearing down of populations, 8–9. *See also* digital debility
decision fatigue, 61, 91, 93
Defacement (The Death of Michael Stewart) (Basquiat), 138–39
Deren, Maya, 77
digital dams, 29, 174n15
digital debility, 7–8; autoplay's production of, 88, 116; desynchronization of body, 67; and refresh, 28; and soporific products, 121, 128; theory of, 8–16; and Zoom fatigue, 151–52, 155, 160. *See also* debility
digital detox workshops, 11, 49

digital economy/ecosystem, 9–10, 27, 92, 116
digital epidermalization, 170n15
digital interface: as effect, 17; graphic user interface (GUI), 17, 19–20, 125; ideal user position, 7; interdisciplinary theory of, 24; multisensorial, 38, 53. *See also* human-machine interaction; interface design
digital lethargy, 15–16, 24, 29, 53, 61
Digital Well-being Experiments (Google), 47
disability: debility distinguished from, 8–10, 35; definitions, 5–7; dis-/ability as a spectrum, 70, 76; as legally binding category, 11–12; loss-of-wholeness thesis, 69–70; media production of, 4; as spectrum, 6–7
disability activism, 49, 54, 170n19; activist fatigue, 161; and aural speed-reading, 57, 59; disability justice, 6, 51–52; Netflix lawsuit, 75–76. *See also* frictional aesthetics
disability capital, 76
disability minimalism, 79
Disability Rights Education and Defense Fund, 75
disability studies, 4, 5, 32, 42, 58, 77, 122, 181n66; critical access studies, 109; slow/fast binary challenged by, 32, 59
disconnection, digital, 13, 31, 38, 49, 116, 142
disembodiment, 11, 12, 17, 171n50
dismediation, 1, 4, 169n10
District Court of Massachusetts, 75–76
domestic abuse survivors, 86, 108
"Do Nothing for 2 Minutes," 127, *128*. *See also* Calm
dopamine-seeking behavior, 13, 38–42, 48, 82
"Dreaming with Frida" (Calm sleep story), 121, *130*, *131*, 131–33, 136; disability glossed over, 132, 137, *137*, 192n89
drowsiness, 19, 119, 133, 189n5
DSM-5, 14
dwell time, 88–90, 98

edge users, 98, 107–8, 113
Edison, Thomas, 58
educational gaming industry, 50
efficiency, 64, 83
elderly/senior users, 22, 25–26, 46
Elkins, Evan, 32

Ellcessor, Elizabeth, 6–7, 17
embodiment, 8, 49, 51–52; folded body of computer users, 28, 35, 122
emotion: buttonization of, 36; and edge users, 98, 107–8, 113; in educational games, 51; refresh as sublimation of difficult feelings, 27. *See also* trauma
endurance, 16, 32, 38, 59, 80, 150–51; for waiting, 43, 92
Engelbart, Douglas, 33
Enger, Reed, 137, 192n89
enjoyability, 50
e-sports industry, 37
Expedia, *28*
Eyal, Nir, 115
eye movements, 62–64, 180n45
eye strain, 2, *23*, 127. *See also* speed watching

Facebook, 32, 36, 41, 187n68; Facebook Memories, 86
facial recognition, as security method, 5–6
Farman, Jason, 29
fatigue, *23*, 119; activist fatigue, 161; chronic fatigue syndrome, 122, 145, 154; and communal care, 144; decision fatigue, 61, 91, 93; digitally induced, 24; dismissal of, 145–46; and hypersensitivity to light, 146; and spoons, 7, 118; technology as a source of, 15–16; Zoom fatigue, 151–52, 155, 160. *See also* insomnia; soporific media
feedback loops, 51, 90–91
film: captioning, 69, 72, 74–76, 80, 183n100; disabled filmmakers and video artists, 76–82, *80*; durational techniques, 78–79; early days of projection, 56; fair use, 56; made by disabled artists, 70; Metropolitan Museum of Art education program, 63–64; movie trailer industry, 105; silent films, 58; slow cinema, 58, 134; movie theater experience, 60–61, 69, 133
fingers: ableist assumptions about, 37; golden hands/hardcore gamers, 37–38; pre-Braille training, 42; thumb-based gestures/thumbification, 4, 13, 22, 36–38, 41–43. *See also* pull-to-refresh gesture
finishability, 48, 99
Fitbit, 121
five-star rating system (Netflix), 89, 91
flow, 49–50, 138
Fogg, B. J., 27–28, 115
Freeman, Elizabeth, 72, 73
frictional aesthetics, 21–22, 25, 46, 47–51, 109–10, 153–54, 163; access as attack, 108–9, 116; alternative design solutions, 22; developed by disability scholars and activists, 49; and embodiment, 49; and gaming, 49
Fritsch, Kelly, 20–21, 25, 47, 88

Galloway, Alexander, 17–18
gambling, 13–14, 28–29, 52, 171n53
game controllers, 37–38
gamification: arcade games, 44–45; infantilization, 43–45; of loading icon, 43–45; of refresh features, 27, 28; of sexual violence, 103
Gates, Bill, 21, 25
gender and women, 21, 50; pink-collar workers, 12, 41–42, 171n50
Geoghegan, Bernard Dionysius, 33
Gil, Liliana, 161
GitHub, 49, 108
glitch, 27, 33; "glitch feminism," 51, 178n122
Global South, workers in, 9
Gómez-Uribe, Carlos, 93
Goodwin, Douglas, 77–78, *78*
Google, 29; Digital Well-being Experiments, 47
Google Hangouts, 150–51, *158*, 158–59
graphic user interface (GUI), 17, 19–20, 125
grid failure, 29
Grigely, Joseph, 74, 183n100

Haagard, Alex, 73
hacking: by blind users, 22, 57, 70, 126; Kahlo's easel, *136*, 137; of refresh and latency, 26–27, 45–46; time hacking, 22, 58, 59–60, 67–68, 72, 76, 180n21; waiting as, 47. *See also* browser add-ons
hacktivism, 20
Hagood, Mack, 162
Hammy (Yelp loading symbol), 30, 43–44, 50
Hamraie, Aimi, 10, 20–21, 25, 47, 157
hand pointer, 19
Hanich, Julian, 60–61, 69, 180n27, 180n28
haptic affordances, 33, 36
Harris, Tristan, 115

INDEX 217

Hartogsohn, Ido, 14
Hastings, Reed, 95, 172n68, 184n15
Haugen, Frances, 187n68
Hawley, Josh, 96
Hayles, N. Katherine, 62
HBO, 5, 84, 95, 110, 112, 128; HBO Max, 87, 97
HealthCare.gov website, 26
Hedva, Johanna, 118, 144
Hess, Amanda, 134–35
high-speed internet, 31
Hilderbrand, Lucas, 56, 173n98
Hillenbrand, Laura, 145
HIV patients, latency in, 34
Hoffman, Donna L., 49–50
Hollowell, Sarah, 107
Hooked (Eyal), 115
Horeck, Tanya, 101, 103, 104
horizontal media, 122–23, 139, 143–48; *COVID Sleep*, 146–48; night-vision surveillance footage, 146, 147; *2020-09-16 at 11:19:28 a.m.*, 143–46, *144*
House of Cards (Netflix), 95
Hu, Tung-Hui, 15–16, 152
Huey, Edmund, 61
human-machine interaction, 8, 12, 21; disabled users and thumbification, 36–37; machine zone, 13; and military technology, 33–34, 54; multisensorial, 18, 43; seamful design, 22, 47–49, 177n111; stuckness, 27, 42, 51. *See also* digital interface
Hunt, Neil, 93
hybrid broadband service, 30–31
"hydraulic system of labor," 79, 122
hyperactivity, versus paralysis, 15, 29
hypervisibility, 49

I May Destroy You (dir. Miller and Coel), 84, 110–15, *111*, 188n116; as unbingeable, 112–15
immunocompromised people, 12, 154
impairment: consensual, 10–13, 34–35, 151; depoliticization of, 5; normal, 9–10. *See also specific disabilities*
infantilization, 43–45, 137, 145
information overload, twentieth century, 61
injectables, 34
insomnia, 4, 119, 122
Instagram, 14, 36, 156
intensified continuity, 58, 67, 179n16

interaction design, 19
interface design, 3–7, 18–20, 26; addictive, 12, 25, 38–39, 88, 95–96, 104; as negotiation, 76; opting out, 4, 11, 14–15, 73, 87–88, 96, 108, 116, 156, 162; reshaped by user complaints, 23, 87, 104–7, *107*; seamful, 22, 47–49, 177n111; "speed tests" websites, 32; as visual metaphor, 42. *See also specific design types*
internet rage, 29–31, *31*
internet service providers (ISPs), 30–32, 90, 96; and forced bandwidth consumption, 97; switching as cure for internet rage, 30–31, *31*
invisibility, 19, 54; hypervisibility as alternative to, 49; of sexual assault survivors, 113
Invisible Computer (Norman), 19
invisible demands, 73–74
invisible disabilities, 4, 185n16; disbelief as response to, 145–46. *See also* post-traumatic stress disorder (PTSD); sleep disorders

Jain, Lochlann, 1, 12
Jancovic, Marek, 187n67
Jenner, Mareike, 101
Jobs, Steve, 19, 20, 37
Johnson, Amber Rose, 51–53, *53*
joint deep attention, 60, 69
Jones, Nathan, 63, 181n48
Juhasz, Alex, 142–43

Kafer, Alison, 5, 13, 59, 138
Kahlo, Frida, 24; sleep stories about, 121, *130*, *131*, 131–33; *Works: Roots*, 132, 136; *Without Hope*, 136, 136–37. *See also* bedridden people
Kanopy, 108
Kare, Susan, 19
Keating, Gina, 90
Kendal, Tina, 101
Kennedy, Pagan, 119
Kiarostami, Abbas, 133
Kittler, Friedrich, 58, 175n39, 179n14
Klein, Matt, 75
Kornstein, Harris, 154

labor inequalities, normalization of, 152–53
Lanier, Jaron, 28

218 INDEX

latency, 1, 16, 26; effects on brain, 155; moment, 33–34; and premium service, 31–32; in radar technology, 33; as undetectability, 34–35; as villain, 30, 32–33. *See also* buffering
Lauer, Harvey, 70–72, 76
lawsuits: against Netflix, 75–76; over work-related PTSD, 41; product liability suits, 12
Lazard, Carolyn, 51–53, *53*, 78–82, *80*, 122
learning disabilities, 20
legislative initiatives, 14–15, 96, 186n52
Lehrer, Riva, *158*, 158–60, 194n20
Levitt, Tamara, 134, 137–38
light spectrum, calibration of, 2, 21, 119, 121–26
Lisa (GUI), 20
Little, Nicolette, 23, 86, 88, 107
Livingston, Julie, 8–9
loading symbols, 30, 43–44, 50, 53
longevity industry, 17
Lord, Jordan, 78
Lossless series (Baron and Goodwin), 77, *78*
Lowrey, Annie, 128–29

Ma, Jean, 134
Macintosh, 19
manipulation, temporal, 58
Marcotte, Jess Rowan, 49–51
marginalized communities: computing technology pushed on, 41–42; mass debilitation of, 8–9; treated as metaphors, 172n83; unintended consequences of assimilation on, 6; virtuous VR and educational gaming, 50
Martens, Lisa, 105–6, 116
Mattern, Shannon, 43, 148
Matvy, Mike, 20
Mayerson, Arlene, 75–76
McLeod, Dayna, 24, 122, 146–48
McPherson, Tara, 38
McRuer, Robert, 172n73
McWatters, Michael, 87, 97
media literacy, 22
media prophylactics, 125–26, 132–33
mediation-as-negotiation, 4
medical-industrial complex, 73, 114
medical model of disability, 5, 6, 34, 146

Méliès, George, 58
mental health conditions, 14; post-traumatic stress disorder (PTSD), 23, 41, 87–88; resources websites, 101–2; stigmatized in previews, 106
Meshes of the Afternoon (Deren), 77
micro-movements, 4, 8, 9, 34. *See also* pull-to-refresh gesture; refresh
Microsoft, 37, 38, 89
military-industrial complex, 54; radar technology, 22, 33–34, 175n39; "sleepless soldier," 124
Mills, Mara, 1, 4–5, 22, 52, 57, 70, 71, 76; on disability capital, 76
Mingus, Mia, 79
misinformation, 96–97, 115, 189n129
modem connections, 35
monetization: of accessibility, 55–82; of dexterity and endurance, 38; of disability activism, 59; of refresh, 27, *28*; of sleep, 120–21; and speed reading, 61–62; of waiting, 31–32
movie theater experience, 60–61, 69, 133–34; accessibility issues, 134, 192n72
multisensorial approaches, 18, 38, 43, 53, 153, 161
Mulvey, Laura, 61
Mulvin, Dylan, 30, 68, 125, 126, 132–33
Munch, Edvard, 151
Münsterberg, Hugo, 66–67, 83, 179n14
muscle memory, 22, 45, 80–81, 159
museums, 61, 63–64
Musk, Elon, 162–63

Nakamura, Lisa, 50
National Association of the Blind, 76
National Association of the Deaf (NAD), 75
National Federation of the Blind, 57, 70
nature films, 130–31
neoliberalism, 9, 17
Netflix, 4, 172n68, 175n32, 185n34; *13 Reasons Why* (2017–20), 98–104, *100*, *102*, *103*; A/B testing, 91; ad-free insulated flow, 97; "Are You Still Watching?" feature, 92; backlash from filmmakers and actors, 55–56, 59; countdown clocks, 22, 92–93, *93*, 107; *Crime Scene: The Vanishing at the Cecil Hotel*, 105–6; dark content and true

Netflix (continued)
   crime, 102, 105; drop-release model, 95, 97, 107, 110–12, 115; hours watched and retention, 89, 115; inline playback, 85–86; "Netflix stretch," 90, 100, 185n32; password sharing, 94–95; petition for ability to disable autoplay, 105–10, *107*; playback speed feature, 7, 18, 22, 54, 55–57, 66–68, 96; rebranding of playback speed as accessibility feature, 57, 59, 74–76
Neuralink, 162–63
neurodiverse people, 154–55, 157
Neves, Joshua, 120
New Disability Arts movement, 79, 177n101
news media, 38–39
New York Public Library online programs, 153
Night Shift (Apple), 3, *23*, 24, 117; advertising for, 123–24; device location required, 121, 123; no significant differences in sleep outcome, 126–27
noise and audile techniques, 11
non-average users, 3–4, 37, 86–88, 160–61; edge users, 98, 107–8, 113
Nooney, Laine, 3, 10, 42, 70
Norman, Don, 19
Notes from the Panorama (Johnson and Lazard), 51–53, *53*, 79
Novak, Thomas P., 49–50

Office Space (film), 30, 174n27
Oliver, Marilene, 150
online forums, 34–35
on/off binary, 36
opting out, 11, 14–15, 73, 156, 162; of autoplay, 4, 87–88, 96, 108, 116
Orlando, Philip, 25–26, 45
Ortega, Vicente Rodríguez, 93–94
orthosomnia, 129
Orum, Kristoffer, 35

pacing, 56, 58; in *13 Reasons Why*, 99–101; as communal, 79
paralysis: facial, 2, 6, 118; hyperactivity versus, 15, 29; in Kahlo's self-portraits, 136; and remission, 72
Parisi, David, 37
password sharing (Netflix), 94–95

Patrick, Stephanie, 114, 188n109
Paul, Aaron, 56
Perez, Melania Moscoso, 59, 179n17
perpetual anxiety, 23, 30, 34, 46
persuasive technology, 27–28
Persuasive Technology Lab (Stanford University), 115
Peters, John Durham, 61
Petrick, Elizabeth, 172n82
Petriglieri, Gianpiero, 155
pharmakon, 34, 159
philobats, 66
phonographs, used to hack talking books, 22, 57, 70, 126
photography, 39, 176n71, 176n273
Piepzna-Samarasinha, Leah Lakshmi, 79, 114
Pinchevski, Amit, 41
pink-collar workers, 12, 41–42, 171n50
planned obsolescence business model, 72, 123
platform violence, 23, 86–88; crip solutions to, 88; Netflix's previews autoplay as, 105–10. *See also* trauma
playback speed, 3, 4, 18, 22, 54; backlash from filmmakers and actors, 55–56; browser add-ons, 57, 65; "chipmunk effect," 57; compressed history of, 65–68; in experimental and avant-garde film, 77; lack of standardization, 64–68, *67*; options, 66, 67, 68; scaffolding, 58, 69–76; tested on smartphones and tablets, 56–57. *See also* speed listening; speed watching
Plotnick, Rachel, 36
pneumograph, *144*, 145–46
PocketCasts, 67, 68
political/relational model, 6, 13
Pornhub, 66
post-disability ideology, 10
Postman, Neil, 38
postplay, 86–87, 90–97, *92*, *93*, *94*, 96, 102, 104, 107, 115
post-traumatic stress disorder (PTSD), 23, 41, 87–88. *See also* trauma
postural limitations, 15, 45, 160, 163
postural media, 8, 18–19, 24, 121–22, 127, 134, 139
premium service, 31–32
Price, Margaret, 109, 172n76

productivity, 59, 73, 124; healing confused with, 114; and playback speed, 155–56
prosthesis metaphor, 18, 172n82
Protactile language, 42–43, 160
Puar, Jasbir, 8–9
public health, 26–27, 34, 125–26
pull-to-refresh gesture, 13, 22, 27, 33–38, 54; disabled people excluded by, 29, 36–37; as stretching the screen, 36, 42; thumbification, 4, 36–38, 43. *See also* refresh

queering, 16–17; of game design, 38, 49
queer intimacy, 147

racism, 49, 52, 66, 114, 121; ableism, slip with, 19–20
radar technology, 22, 33–34, 175n39
randomness and unpredictably, 13, 14, 28–29, 46, 51
Rangan, Pooja, 69, 78
rape culture, 98–104, 112, 114, 187n70, 188n109
reading techniques, 61–63
"Real Time Analysis, Real Axis Manipulation" (Kittler), 58
recommendation systems, 22–23, 89–90
redundancy, aesthetic of, 82
Reed, Peyton, 56
ReelAbilites Film Festival, 1–3
refresh, 1–2, 3, 23; auto-refresh, 41, 43; auto-refreshing, 41, 43; commands, 27; cripping, 51–54; elderly/senior users' failed attempts at, 22, 25–26, 46; gamification and monetization of, 27, 28; as hacking technique, 26–27, 45–46; haptic affordances, 33; history of, 33–43; liveness and realtime-ness, 38–39, 42; loading symbols, 30, 43, 53; migration of to mind, 41; of others' pain, 38–39; sense of emergency and agency reinforced by, 39–41, 40; stuckness, 27, 42, 51; as sublimation of difficult feelings, 27; tension between activity and passivity, 29; weaponization of button, 33. *See also* buffering; pull-to-refresh gesture
Regarding the Pain of Others (Sontag), 39
reinforcement and conditioning, 13, 89
remission, 72
Remote Access Archive, 153, 157–58, 194n31

repetition: as means of renewed embodiment, 51–52; muscle memory as, 80–81; tapping, 52; of traumatic visual images, 41
repetitive strain injury (RSI), 10, 12
responsibility, shifted to users, 32, 48, 103, 146
rest: need for, 51–52; as resistance, 122, 144; "Rest, reflect, rejuvenate (three R's)," 111–13
Restricted Access (Ellcessor), 6–7
retention, 23, 89, 115
Rezab, Jan, 59–60, 66, 68, 72, 83
Rios, Emily, 131–33
Rist, Pipilotti, 77
Rivera, Diego, 131
Rodriguez, Juan Llamas, 44–45
Rogers, Emily Lim, 154, 161
Roots (Kahlo), 132, 136
Russell, Legacy, 178n122

saccades, 62–63
Samuels, Ellen, 72–73, 145
Sandahl, Carrie, 172n73
Sarandos, Ted, 175n32
Sax, David, 99
scaffolding, 58, 71–74
scanning and skimming, 62
Schrank, Brian, 50
Schüll, Natasha Dow, 13, 171n53
scores, 52
The Scream (Munch), 151
screenless future, 162
screen readers: autoplay incompatible with, 87; auto-refresh incompatible with, 22, 29; Lisa GUI incompatible with, 20; pull-to-refresh incompatible with, 29, 37; and time-limited posts, 73
seamful design, 22, 47–49, 177n111
Seamless, 43
seamlessness, 3, 19, 22; myth of, 29–51; rejection of, 112; responsibility for shifted to users, 32, 48
Seaver, Nick, 89, 115–16
security, 5–6, 32, 54; "security theater," 6, 170n22
#SelfCare app, 122, 139–42, *140*, *141*, 148; call to stay home today, 142; depression, fatigue, and burnout normalized by, 141

sensory hangover, 154–55
Seventy-Eight (video game/platform), 21, 50–51
The Shallows: What the Internet Is Doing to Our Brain (Carr), 62
Shared Resources (Lord), 78
Sicart, Miguel, 38
"Sick Woman Theory" (Hedva), 144
side effects, 81
Skinner, B. F., 89
Skinner, Sam, 63, 181n48
Slater, Andy, 71
sleep: circadian rhythms, 4, 120, 123, 125–26; collective and communal care, 24, 144, 146–48, *147*; as means for value production, 148–49; media prophylactics, 125–26, 132–33; and melatonin production, 123; monetization of, 120–21; pathologization of, 148; personal electronics associated with, 121, 123; repoliticization of, 122; as site of value production, 120; as social issue, 147–48; technological solutionism, 121, 123; war on, 84
Sleep (Warhol), 147
sleep apps: as anti-content, 134–35, 139; crib alternative to, 122, 139–42, 148; horizontal posture encouraged by, 127, 132, 134, 135–36; as postural media, 18–19, 24, 121–22, 127, 134, 138; sleep disorders exacerbated by, 119, 125, 127, 148; studies, 123, 126–27, 135–36; unhealthy dependency on, 116–17
SLEEPCINEMAHOTEL (Weerasethkul), 133
sleep disorders: autoplay as a cause of sleep loss, 95; exacerbated by sleep apps and wearables, 119, 125, 127; orthosomnia, 129; and soporific media industry, 15, 178n68, 184n15. *See also* insomnia
Sleep Health, 126–27
sleep hygiene, 24, 118, 122–23
sleep labs, 120
sleep stories, 18–19, 24, 121, 127; about famous artists, 130–31; about Frida Kahlo, 121, *130*, 131, *131*; childhood bedtime ritual, 129–30
Sleep with Me (podcast, Ackerman), 135
slow computing movement, 11
slow/fast binary, 32, 59
slowness, 51–52
small businesses, 177n93

smartphones, 10; inaccessible to non-average users, 37; playback speed, 56–57. *See also* pull-to-refresh gesture; sleep apps
Smilges, J. Logan, 88, 108–10, 154–55, 185n16
Smith, Michael Acton, 127, 129
Snow, Michael, 77, 80
The Social Dilemma (Netflix), 115
social media, 10, 14, 86
Social Media Addiction Reduction Technology Act (SMART Act), 96
social model of disability, 5, 6
Sontag, Susan, 38–39, 60, 176n73
Sony Betamax, 56
Sony Walkman, 99
soporific products, 15, 23, 24, 119; as content-agnostic, 18, 121–22, 127, 132–33; and digital debility, 121, 148; synchronizing oneself with others, 145. *See also* Night Shift (Apple); sleep apps
Sosnoski, James, 62
speech impairments, 154, 180n45
speed, 179n11, 181n59; deliberate slowing of services, 32; and reading comprehension, 181n48; users habituated to, 32
speed listening, 4, 54, 63, 71. *See also* playback speed
speed-reading, 61–62, 71–72
speed watching, 3, 4, 18, 54, 181n61; ASL videos, 182n86; dis-/ability as a spectrum in context of, 70; disability-oriented theory of, 82; moral panic over, 56, 58, 60; at museums, 63–64; speed watchers, 59–65; subversive potential of, 76–77; as survival mode, 22. *See also* binge-watching; cognitive overload; eye strain; playback speed
spoons, 7, 118
Spotify, 67, 68
spyware, 34
standardization, 64–68, 156–57
Starosielski, Nicole, 178n129
stasis, 15–16
Sterne, Jonathan, 1, 4–5, 11, 22, 57, 70, 151
Stewart, Michael, 138–39
Stone, Kara, 142
streaming, 1–2, 22, 188n111; changed by autoplay, 89–98; forced bandwidth consumption, 97; standard definition, 186n65. *See also* autoplay; Netflix

222 INDEX

stuckness, 27, 42, 51
subjugation, 50
Sundaram, Ravi, 120
super-crip stereotype, 71
super-user myth, 22, 59–60, 83, 124, 129
Surfacing, 178n129
surveillance capitalism, 49, 73, 116, 120–21, 148, 161
survival techniques: access thievery as, 88, 108–9, 116, 154–55; lying down as, 144–45; speed watching as, 22
Sweeney, Robert, 23, 85, 89–92, 95–96, 115, 186n52

tactile language, 42–43
Tarr, Béla, 133
technical stack, 18, 26, 47–48, 51
techno-chauvinism, 3, 169n7
technology: as addiction, 13–15, 171n53; distinguished from assistive technology, 181n66; as source of exhaustion and fatigue, 15–16
technopharmacology, 120
techno-social system, 7, 9, 18, 49, 162–63
techno-solutionism, 24, 121, 123
techno-utopian discourses, 7, 29, 129, 162–63
television, 38, 90, 128, 179n14, 187n78; slow TV shows, 130
temporality: chrono-diversity, 124, 145, 148; chrononormativity, 73–74, 80, 124; manipulation of, 58, negotiations imposed on people with disabilities, 74; perpetual temporal debt, 73, 154; "real time," 176n71; temporal poverty, 73; time axis manipulation, 58; time-on-device, 13, 171n53. *See also* compression; crip time; speed listening; speed watching
test subjects, disabled people as, 70–72, 76, 126; risky testing, 162–63
Tew, Alex, 127, 129
Theroux, Louis, 114–15
13 Reasons Why (Netflix, 2017–20), 98–104, *100*, *102*, *103*; *Behind the Reasons* (aftershow special), 102; binge-watching promoted, 99–104; empirical studies of, 101–2; warning videos, 101, *102*, *103*
"throbbers," 43

thumb-based gestures/thumbification, 4, 13, 22, 36–38, 41–43, 53–54
time hacking, 22, 58, 59–60, 67–68, 72, 76, 138, 180n21
time management, 59, 61–63
Titanic (Cameron), 55
trauma: automatization of, 23; and autoplay, 86; and content moderation industry, 9–10, 41; nonlinear process of healing from, 113–14; suicides, 101, 103–4; trauma-informed design, 23, 87, 108. *See also* emotion; platform violence; post-traumatic stress disorder (PTSD)
trauma-informed design, 23, 87, 108, 161
trigger warnings, 106
TRU LUV studio, 139
Turkey and Syria earthquake, 39, 40
twelve-step programs, 14
2020-09-16 at 11:19:28 a.m. (Bullock), 143–46, *144*
Twitch gamers, 148, 193n112
Twitter, 44, 73, 107; Tweetie app, 35–36

Undersea Network (Starosielski), 178n129
universal design, 75
upgrades, 32, 72, 123
user experience (UX), 14
user interface (UI), 14
users, 18–19, 151, 161; "average," 3–4, 17, 30, 169n6, 183n104; black box/magic experiences of internet and software, 32–33, 45; complaints and reshaping of interface design, 23, 87, 104–7, *107*; as de facto employees, 91; desynchronized, 20, 45, 67; disabled as canaries in the coal mine, 7, 41, 79; habituated to ignore biological and emotional needs, 7, 87; habituated to speed, 32; as historical construct, 19; impatience of, 29; as inclusive term, 18; recast as medical subjects, 120; responsibility shifted to, 32, 48, 103, 146; super-user myth, 22, 59–60, 83, 124, 129; user/programmer dichotomy, 19
US National Association of School Psychologists, 101

vaccine distribution websites, 22, 25–26, 34; US online appointment system, 25–26

"vampire time," 156
Varispeech, 70
Vector Solutions, 66, 181n63
Veel, Kristin, 34
The Verge, 96
video art, 51–52, 122; for Black and Brown viewers, 51–53, *53*, 79; and horizontal media, 143
videoconferencing platforms, 151; as crip interfaces and crippling interfaces, 24; as pharmakon, 159. *See also* Google Hangouts; Zoom
video games, 49; *13 Reasons Why* comparison, 102–3; *Seventy-Eight*, 21
Vimeo, 150
virtuous VR, 50
visuality: ableist focus on, 18, 79; unintended results of war photography, 39
voice-based technologies, 38
voice-recognition industry, 154
voice synthesizers: Lisa GUI incompatible with, 20
Vudka, Amir, 14

waiting, 29; endurance for, 43, 92; as hacking, 47; monetization of, 31–32
Warhol, Andy, 147
Wasson, Haidee, 63
waste, electronic, 9
Wavelength (Snow), 77
wearables, 73, 119, 121, 162
Weerasethkul, Apichatpong, 133
White, Michele, 19, 28, 34–35, 37
whiteness, 19–20; assumed of "average user," 3–4, 169n6; assumed of "power user," 126, 129; in commercials, 37; of hand pointer, 19; prototypical, 16, 170n15
Whoever Screams the Loudest (Oliver), 150–51, *151*
Withers, A. J., 170n19
Without Hope (Kahlo), *136*, 136–37
Wollen, Peter, 66
Wong, Alice, *158*, 158–60
Wood, Evelyn, 61–62
Woolf, Virginia, 39
WVLNT: Wavelength for those who don't have the time (Snow), 77, 80

Xbox, 37–38, 89

Yelp, 177n93; Hammy loading symbol, 30, 43–44, 50
YouTube, 181n59; misinformation spread on, 96–97, 115, 189n129; MySpeed, 65; playback speed options, 66, 67, 68; and work-related PTSD, 41; YouTube Kids app, 97

Zeitlin-Wu, Lida, 121
Zoom, 24, 148, 150–57; non-verbal feedback feature, 181n62; normalization of fatigue, 160; playback speed, 66, 67, 155–56; self-view, 156; Zoombombing, 155, 194n22; Zoom fatigue, 151–52, 155, 160. *See also* videoconferencing platforms
Zoom Portrait: Alice Wong (Lehrer), *158*, 158–59
Zoom Portraits series (Lehrer), 158
Zuboff, Shoshana, 42

www.ingramcontent.com/pod-product-compliance
Lightning Source LLC
Chambersburg PA
CBHW020813230426
43666CB00007B/993